Juicy Tales from the Big Apple

New York City

WEST SIDE PUBLISHING

Contributing Writers: Jeff Bahr, Richard Buskin, Mary Fons-Misetic, Dave Gerardi, Amanda Green, Bruce Herman, Laura Hill, J. K. Kelley, Rhonda Markowitz, Winter D. Prosapio, Suzanne Reisman, Donald Vaughan

Factual Verification: Hollie Deese

Front Cover Illustrations: iStockphoto, Shutterstock

Back Cover Illustrations: Robert Schoolcraft

Interior Illustrations: Bettmann/Corbis, Erin Burke, Dynamic Graphics, Jupiterimages, PIL Collection, Robert Schoolcraft, Shutterstock

Louis Weber, CEO
Publications International, Ltd.
7373 North Cicero Avenue
Lincolnwood, Illinois 60712

Permission is never granted for commercial purposes.

ISBN-13: 978-1-60553-915-7
ISBN-10: 1-60553-915-5

Manufactured in USA.

8 7 6 5 4 3 2 1

Contents

♥ ♥ ♥ ♥

The City That Never Sleeps

♥ ♥ ♥ ♥

Was the phrase *world-class city* coined just to describe New York City? We may never know for sure, but it might as well have been. Few metropolises around the world even begin to compete with the size and influence of the Big Apple. It is the world's financial center, its cultural mecca, and its communications hub.

Armchair Reader™: New York City celebrates the city in all its vastness. But New York is also made up of a number of small things, an accumulation of detail. And those are present in this book, as well. All five boroughs are represented, from the tip of Manhattan Island to the outer reaches of Queens. Visit the Bronx and Brooklyn, and even take a ferry ride to Staten Island, all within these pages.

Some of the juicy tales of the Big Apple found inside include:

• The building of the Brooklyn Bridge

• Marilyn Monroe's iconic pose over a subway grate and how it led to the downfall of her marriage to Joe DiMaggio

• A trip to Coney Island's annual Mermaid Parade

• Fresh Kills Landfill, depository of more than half a century's worth of the city's trash

• The plane that crashed smack-dab into the Empire State Building

• Nellie Bly's adventure to Blackwell's Island and how it turned the mental health industry upside down

• Ex-Beatle John Lennon's encounter with a UFO

Never sleeps? This is a city that never even gets tired! Once you begin your journey of discovery, whether as a New Yorker or someone visiting the city for the first time, you'll find it hard to stop to catch your breath. So sit back in your big, comfy armchair, and start reading.

PS—We are always trying to make our books the best that we can, so please, if you have any comments—whether good or bad—contact us at armchairreader.com.

On the Streets with a Gypsy Cab Driver

♥ ♥ ♥ ♥

Johnny slowed his car in front of a crumbling residential building in the South Bronx. "This is it," said his passenger, a heavyset man in his 20s. He reached deep into his pocket as Johnny watched from the rearview mirror, his foot on the brake and his shoulders tensed; just another stressful moment in the life of a gypsy cab driver.

The New York City of the movies is a sea of yellow cabs, landmark buildings, and pedestrians on the go. The New York City of real life is like that, too—in a few parts. But above 125th Street in Harlem, a yellow cab can't always be found.

When Yellow Is Hard to Come By

Like their namesake, gypsy cabs are nomads that will pick up and drive passengers anywhere for a fare. These un-marked cars—often black sedans owned by their drivers—don't have the meters, credit card readers, or often even the protec-tive partitions between the front and back seats one would see in  yellow cabs. In rougher, less-traveled neighborhoods, such as Washington Heights uptown, or in the outer boroughs of Queens and Brooklyn, they're often the only alternative to taking the bus or subway or to walking. In bad weather and peak travel times, gypsy cabs effectively compete for business even in areas dominated by yellow cabs.

Licensed gypsy cab drivers are supposed to work only through a car service that riders call to reserve a ride. Flat-rate fares are negotiated on the phone or at pick-up, where some riders haggle before the driver hits the gas. Fares tend to be less expensive than those in metered cabs, because time stuck in traffic isn't calculated.

The standard minimum fare is six dollars. Many drivers work ten hours straight, or more. It's a grind, and so tiring that a driver can easily become careless about potential danger.

Picking up passengers who haven't called for a ride is technically illegal, and gypsy cab drivers can be ticketed for doing so, but many pick up fares right off the street when they can. Work can be slow; someone always needs a ride, and hey, you've got to make a living. They hardly have to be hailed by passengers, as drivers tend to slow down and honk to gauge interest in their services. Police usually turn a blind eye.

From grittier times in the 1970s to now, gypsy cabs and their operators have had a bad rap. (Martin Scorsese's classic film *Taxi Driver* couldn't have helped; however, it should be noted that the homicidal Travis Bickle drove a yellow cab.) Though urban legends of killer cabbies have made the rounds, the drivers themselves face the most danger. All transportation workers have to worry about customers who run out without paying their fare, as well as violent passengers. But gypsy cab drivers risk their safety even more by picking up passengers in some of the most dangerous areas of the city. Each year, some gypsy cab drivers are robbed, assaulted, or even killed on the job.

The Brotherhood

Luckily, there's a kind of gypsy cab brotherhood. When drivers report an emergency via radio, help comes in the form of fellow cabbies ready to defend or comfort their comrade. Off duty, many drivers socialize as friends, often referring to each other by their drivers' numbers.

What should you keep in mind if you decide to travel by gypsy cab? Start by checking for a Taxi Limousine Commission (TLC) medallion on the back window of the car. This shows that the cab is licensed. Before you settle in for the ride, find out the flat-rate fee to your destination, or negotiate if you want. Make sure you have small bills to cover it, as many drivers don't have much change. If you're happy when you get to your destination, consider asking for a card with the car service's phone number so you can call ahead for a ride in the future.

Little Fugitive

♥ ♥ ♥ ♥

A small boy runs away and has an eventful time at Coney Island.

It's just another summer day in Brooklyn in the early 1950s—until seven-year-old Joey is tricked into believing he's killed his older brother, Lennie. Rather than face the music when Mom gets home, Joey travels alone to Coney Island. When Joey doesn't return, Lennie has to find him before Mom learns he's missing. That, in a nutshell, is the plot of the 1953 movie, *Little Fugitive.*

Joey's two-day excursion at Coney is the film's charming centerpiece. The busy midway and beach turn Joey (played by a freckle-faced nonprofessional named Richie Andrusco) wide-eyed with wonder. He doesn't exactly forget about his brother, but he's young enough to become absorbed in the moment. Unable to knock down the bottles at a midway game, he practices with paper cups before returning to win a prize. He takes some swings in a batting cage, eats a gigantic slice of watermelon, and rides the merry-go-round. By the time he finds the pony ride, he's out of money. Riding a horse like a real cowboy is all Joey dreams about, so when he sees a boy on the beach returning deposit bottles for money, Joey does the same until he has enough money to ride a pony for the rest of the day.

Independent Spirit

Little Fugitive is an indie film from a time when nobody said "indie film." Morris Engel and his future wife, Ruth Orkin, put it together outside the studio system with very little money and no crew. Engel designed a special 35mm camera that he could carry and use without a tripod. His footage is spontaneous and documentarylike.

At its core, *Little Fugitive* is a love letter to New York. Joey's Brooklyn neighborhood and Coney are no less vivid as characters than Joey himself. There are the kids who play on the street outside Joey's apartment house; the bustling crowds that jam the subway; Coney's snack bars and other gaudy delights. In addition to its intimate charm (everything works out fine for Joey and his brother), *Little Fugitive* is a priceless record of post–World War II Brooklyn and Coney.

Terror on the 79th Floor!

♥ ♥ ♥ ♥

*Although this disaster may have become just a footnote in history,
those who lived through it will never forget the day an Army
bomber rammed headlong into the Empire State Building.*

For many years, the Empire State Building was the tallest structure
in the world. That heralded attribute cost the skyscraper dearly on
the morning of July 28, 1945, when an Army B-25 training bomber
crashed into the 79th floor, resulting in 14 deaths and severe damage
to the building's interior.

The Unimaginable

Lt. Col. William Smith Jr., a veteran pilot with 100 combat missions
to his credit, intended to land the plane at La Guardia Airport. New
York City, however, was enveloped in thick fog. Disoriented, Smith
apparently didn't see the Empire State Building until it was too late.

The plane punched an 18-by-20-foot hole in the building and
rained glass and debris on pedestrians below. The fuel tanks exploded,
shooting thick flames in all directions, and an engine plowed completely through the building and plunged through a nearby rooftop.

The number of fatalities was limited because the crash occurred
on a Saturday, when an estimated 1,500 people were in the building.
(On a weekday, the number swelled to more than 10,000.) Worst hit
was the Catholic War Relief Office directly in the path of the wayward aircraft. Of the 14 people who were killed that day, 11 were
office employees and 3 were in the plane—Smith and two passengers.

"Going Down?"

Elevator operator Betty Lou Oliver had a particularly traumatic day.
Because she was badly burned in the accident, rescue workers
placed her in an elevator car on the 75th floor for a quick ride down
to a waiting ambulance. Almost immediately, the stressed elevator
cables snapped, dropping Oliver more than 1,000 feet to the sub-
basement. Cables tangled beneath the car helped cushion the fall,
and Oliver, though severely injured, survived—again.

Life (and Death) at the Hotel Chelsea

♥ ♥ ♥ ♥

While many celebs have stayed there, some who have left in body bags may still be hanging around.

It is the place where poet Dylan Thomas was staying when he died, where author Charles R. Jackson committed suicide, where Sex Pistol Sid Vicious may have murdered his girlfriend, and where singer-songwriter Bob Dylan composed part of *Blonde on Blonde.* "Beat" icon Jack Kerouac penned *On the Road* there, novelist Arthur C. Clarke wrote *2001: A Space Odyssey* within the Chelsea's walls, and avant-garde filmmaker Andy Warhol shot much of *Chelsea Girls* there (before he himself was shot nearby).

Many other famous people have stayed at the Chelsea over the years: Mark Twain, Eugene O'Neill, Thomas Wolfe, and Tennessee Williams; William Burroughs, Willem de Kooning, Madonna, and Arthur Miller; Edith Piaf, Jane Fonda, Jimi Hendrix, and Janis Joplin; Leonard Cohen, Allen Ginsberg, and the Grateful Dead.

Today, the Hotel Chelsea, once the creative hub and long-term residence of so many artists, has a policy that limits the short-term visitors who occupy 40 percent of its 240 apartments (the other suites are residential) to stays of no longer than three weeks.

Glory and Ruin

The Chelsea, which proclaims itself the first New York City structure to be listed as a historic building and cultural preservation site, started life in 1883 as a luxury apartment cooperative designed in the Queen Anne style. An impressive 12 stories high, it was Manhattan's tallest structure until the completion of the 20-story World Building in 1890.

Back then, the building's address, 222 West 23rd Street, was in the heart of the city's thriving theater district, yet by 1903 the apartment was bankrupt due to high overhead and the relocation of many theaters. The place was closed, and when it reopened a couple of years later, it was as a hotel.

18 Straight Whiskies

Over the years, many people residing behind the red-brick walls and wrought-iron balconies have elected not to observe house rules requiring them to behave with decorum and to clean up before they leave. The poet Dylan Thomas, for example, returned to his room at the Chelsea on the night of November 3, 1953, following a boozy session at the White Horse Tavern in Greenwich Village. He purportedly exclaimed, "I've had 18 straight whiskies, I think that is a record." Whether or not he was exaggerating, the noted Welsh imbiber had a monster hangover the next morning, but he managed to put himself back together and return to the White Horse for more hooch. Shortly after midnight on November 5, Thomas (by now back at the hotel again) slipped into a coma caused by pneumonia complicated by acute alcoholism. He was transported from the Chelsea to St. Vincent's Hospital, where he died four days later.

Writer Charles R. Jackson, whose semiautobiographical novel *The Lost Weekend* helped Ray Milland snag a Best Actor Oscar after the book was filmed in 1945, was another tormented soul given to binge drinking. Although heavily involved with Alcoholics Anonymous, Jackson continued to struggle with alcohol before committing suicide in his room at the Chelsea on September 21, 1968.

Punk Mayhem

Ten years later, Nancy Spungen apparently had little say in her death, which came in Room 100 after months of drug abuse and domestic violence at the hands of her boyfriend, punk rocker Sid Vicious. Their clashes seemed to climax with Nancy's death from a stab wound to the abdomen on October 12, 1978. The injury was linked to a knife owned by Vicious, who confessed (later retracted) to the murder. Vicious, of course, was no more serene emotionally than his deceased gal pal, and he died from a heroin overdose just three months later.

The fact that Vicious never stood trial encouraged speculation that Spungen was killed by a burglar or drug dealer who entered the room while Sid was in a junk-induced stupor. *Well,* New Yorkers seemed to say, *anything is possible at the Chelsea.*

Not every Chelsea tale is a sad one. Before the artist Alphaeus Cole passed away at the hotel on November 25, 1988, he was, at 112 years and 136 days, verified as the world's oldest living man. Since Cole had resided at the hotel for the last 35 years of his life, the place evidently had an invigorating effect on him, and the same can be said for many others who have passed through the Chelsea's doors.

The Chelsea on Film

Still, the who's who of Chelsea guests and a what's what of their colorful indiscretions have given rise to much speculation along the lines of "If only these walls could talk!" Andy Warhol's 1966 movie *Chelsea Girls* firmly established the hotel in pop culture legend. Yet, even though that rambling, three-hour-plus, underground film (codirected by Paul Morrissey) focused on the "alternative" lives of several of its residents—including Warhol "superstars" Nico, Ondine, legit actress Mary Woronov, Ingrid Superstar, International Velvet, and Brigid Berlin—the only cast member who actually lived there was poet René Ricard. Banned upon its release in Chicago and Boston, *Chelsea Girls* was a hit in New York and stands as the only Warhol cinematic effort to have achieved any kind of mainstream acceptance.

The Dead Don't Sleep Easily

These days, the hotel lobby is decorated with the artwork of former residents, yet the Chelsea rarely accepts paintings as a form of payment. And maybe that's why this onetime mecca of bohemians, oddballs, and assorted fringe characters is reputedly haunted by many of their ghosts. The phantom of Sid Vicious has allegedly been spotted in the elevator, while a stop with Sid on the eighth floor may lead to an encounter with the ectoplasmic presence of novelist Thomas Wolfe, who wrote *Look Homeward, Angel* and *The Web and the Rock* while residing at the Chelsea. According to some of the hotel's residents, it is artistic spirits such as these that inspire creativity in the living.

Women of the Beat

♥ ♥ ♥ ♥

*We hear mostly about the men of the city's Beat movement, but
what about the women? Hey, it wasn't a boys' club after all!*

Dig it: The Beats were a group of countercultural writers and poets
that coalesced during the 1940s and 1950s in Greenwich Village, San
Francisco, and Los Angeles. Rebelling against the postwar ranch-
house-with-basement model of social conformity, they glorified
rootlessness, creativity, and travel for travel's sake. But the male
Beats were products of their generation, and many held frankly
sexist views of women. Still, that didn't discourage numerous women
from gravitating to the Beat scene and developing modes of self-
expression inspired by Beat thought. Here are some of them.

Joan Vollmer Adams Burroughs

Joan Adams, daughter of an affluent upstate family, roomed with
Jack Kerouac's future wife Edie Parker at Barnard College during
World War II. She left an early stamp upon the Beat movement
partly by providing a hangout. Joan and Edie's Upper West Side
apartment became an early Beat gathering point, hosting discussion-
and-substance-abuse sessions that included Parker, Adams, Kerouac,
Allen Ginsberg, William Burroughs, and other seminal Beat think-
ers. Adams and Burroughs became a couple in 1946. Both had drug
problems so serious that the couple eventually moved to Mexico City
to avoid charges in Louisiana. In 1951, William accidentally killed
Joan at a gin-soaked party, when he tried to shoot a plastic cup off
her head. His family evidently bribed Mexican officials so that he
avoided a probable jail sentence. He later became a world-famous
writer and arts guru who often cited Joan as his greatest inspiration.

Diane Di Prima

This important Beat poet was born in 1934, making her one of the
younger Beats of real importance. Di Prima dropped out of
Swarthmore in 1953 and headed for Manhattan. As founder of the
Poets Press and a cofounder of the New York Poets Theatre, she

nurtured many young poets' creativity while making her own mark in the field. Di Prima's first poetry collection, *This Kind of Bird Flies Backward,* was published in 1958. Her early interest in alternative spirituality has long invested her poetry with overtones of the paranormal and the feminine divine. Some call this Brooklyn Italian "the Poet Priestess of the Beat movement." Di Prima has formally written about her Beat experiences twice, first in a fact-based but fanciful 1969 book, *Memoirs of a Beatnik,* and more literally in 2001, with *Recollections of My Life as a Woman: The New York Years.* She moved to California in the 1970s and was named Poet Laureate of San Francisco in 2009.

Janine Pommy Vega

Inspired at 16 by Jack Kerouac's *On the Road,* this New Jersey native began to make weekend pilgrimages to Greenwich Village in 1958, while a high school junior. She mingled with Kerouac, Gregory Corso, and other Beat luminaries and was quickly accepted as part of the scene. Pommy married Peruvian painter Fernando Vega in the early 1960s and then began a globetrot that would outlast her husband (who died in 1965) and culminate with her first collection of poetry, *Poems to Fernando,* in 1968. A subsequent hermitlike period spent along Lake Titicaca in Peru brought forth two more volumes of verse. Others would follow, and Pommy Vega found additional callings as an activist, environmentalist, and prison poetry teacher.

Elise Cowen

This sensitive fixture of the NYC Beat scene was a native of suburban Long Island, the daughter of a successful but neurotic couple that insisted Elise achieve—in all the proper, conformist ways. But the young woman was drawn more to poetry than to her studies; she had a special fondness for Ezra Pound and other poets who expressed a dark, even cynical view of life. While attending Barnard College, Cowen dated Beat god Allen Ginsberg. Like Ginsberg, Cowen was emotionally fragile—and although she expressed herself in melancholy, highly imagistic poetry that is simultaneously "free" and disciplined, she couldn't escape her own demons. After she was released from Bellevue's psychiatric ward early in 1962, Elise Cowen hurled herself through her parents' living room window. She wasn't quite 30 years old.

Jane Bowles

A generation older than Cowen and some other Beat women, Bowles was born Jane Auer in 1917 and spent her earliest years on Long Island before moving with her mother to Manhattan when Jane was 13. Inactivity that was forced by tuberculosis encouraged the youngster's love of reading and creative expression. Her marriage to noted writer Paul Bowles was based on mutual intellectual respect but fell apart when Jane began to freely explore her lesbianism. In her life, Jane Bowles published one novel, one play, and half a dozen short stories. The play, *In the Summer House,* was produced on Broadway in 1953, and one of her short stories, "Camp Cataract," is an uncomfortably funny piece that explores blurred identity and a woman's obsessive attraction to her own sister. Bowles was vivacious and extraordinarily witty, and she easily won the attention of friends and new acquaintances. Tennessee Williams was convinced she was one of the most underrated writers of her generation. She died in 1973 of complications from a stroke suffered 16 years earlier.

Hettie Jones

By the time Hettie Jones published her first book of poetry, *Drive,* in 1997, she'd been writing for more than 30 years. Born Hettie Cohen in 1934, by the mid-1950s she was living in New York, active in the literary and civil rights scenes with her husband, the African American writer and activist LeRoi Jones (later known as Amiri Baraka). Kerouac, Frank O'Hara, and many other seminal Beats were published by Hettie and LeRoi's Totem Press and in *Yugen,* the couple's literary magazine. Hettie was managing editor of *The Partisan Review* from 1957 to 1961 and worked at her own poetry and other writing late at night, after putting her children to bed. Her 1990 memoir, *How I Became Hettie Jones,* is a frank look at the personal blows she absorbed because of her work, her association with the Beat scene, and her marriage. For example, she was dis-owned by her Jewish parents after marrying Jones and was later divorced by Jones because she was white. In the 1990s, Jones became deeply involved with the literary aspirations of female prisoners in New York State and assembled a collection of inmate writing in 1997.

🧁 Taste of New York

Some say it's better than an ice cream soda. Some say it's the ultimate New York City treat. (And some say it's better in Brooklyn.) But nobody says an egg cream has either egg or cream in it.

So what is an egg cream, then? Traditionally, it's a careful mixture of milk, seltzer water, and chocolate syrup. As if anything about New York food was actually that simple.

First, it must be served in a small, curvy Coke glass. Second, the only chocolate syrup, purists insist, must be Fox's U-bet syrup. A proper egg cream must contain seltzer, not soda water or mineral water, since those contain salt. The order in which the ingredients are added and the method by

 which they are then mixed is precise—though not everyone agrees on exactly how.

Egg creams are such a part of life in New York that Lou Reed even wrote a tune about them called, well, "Egg Cream." He recalled that drinking the concoction made it easier to deal with the knife fights in his neighborhood, but most people find egg creams simply a refreshing, not-too-rich fountain treat.

The origins of the egg cream are shrouded in mystery, but the most popular story has it that the egg cream was the early 20th-century creation of Louis Auster, who ran a neighborhood candy store on the corner of Second Avenue and Seventh Street in Manhattan. Why call it an "egg cream" if no eggs are involved? One theory is that "egg" in the name derives from the Yiddish word *echt,* which means "true."

Want to make one of your own? Here's the recipe: Pour an inch or so of chocolate syrup in the glass, then add an inch or so of milk (but not skim). Put in six to eight ounces of seltzer, allowing a head to form. Alternatively, add seltzer to the milk first, stir vigorously, and then gently pour the chocolate syrup down the side of the glass.

However you decide to make it, all agree you must drink your egg cream quickly before the foamy top dissipates.

Wanna Buy a Bridge?

♥ ♥ ♥ ♥

The Brooklyn Bridge is one of the most famous suspension bridges in the world. And it costs nothing to cross.

You don't have to live in New York City to love the architecturally stunning Brooklyn Bridge. Completed in 1883, it's one of the Big Apple's best-known landmarks and is currently crossed by an estimated 131,500 commuters each day to traverse the East River between Manhattan and Brooklyn.

Over the years, a number of myths have sprung up regarding the Brooklyn Bridge. Among them:

- **Several bodies were entombed in the structure during construction.** This myth is also commonly said of Nevada's Hoover Dam and is untrue on both counts. It is true that between 20 and 50 workers perished during the construction of the bridge, but none were entombed there.

- **Gullible rubes have actually tried to purchase the Brooklyn Bridge.** This hoary tale has been around almost as long as the bridge itself, but there is no proven account of anyone actually being tricked into purchasing the bridge, which is public property.

Here are a few fascinating tidbits regarding the Brooklyn Bridge's construction and history:

- **The bridge was designed by John Augustus Roebling and Wilhelm Hildenbrand.** Roebling died before construction began; his son, Washington, took over the project.

- **Construction of the bridge spanned 13 years and cost $15.1 million. It has a total length of 5,989 feet.**

- **President Chester Arthur and New York Governor Grover Cleveland attended the bridge's dedication on May 23, 1883.** Washington Roebling's wife, Emily, took the first ride across the bridge with a rooster in her lap, a symbol of victory.

- **On its dedication day, the Brooklyn Bridge charged a toll of one penny, and three cents thereafter. Today, it's free.**

The 1863 "Draft Riots": African American Pogrom

♥ ♥ ♥ ♥

*New York City played a heralded role in the Union's
Civil War victory. How then did the city explode
into riot over conscription in July 1863?*

When war broke out between United and Confederate states in
spring 1861, New Yorkers rushed to the colors. Dozens of New York
volunteer infantry and cavalry regiments formed in the city. Like
their Southern counterparts who donned gray, dashing young New
Yorkers put on blue in high spirits, sure of victory. Such a grand
adventure it seemed, with ladies moved to tears by the gallant,
manly sight of the Army of the Republic marching to war!

Reality soon set in. War wasn't a gallant spectacle, nor was
victory sure. War meant inept, politically appointed generals ordering inexperienced, politically connected colonels to send their men
forth to die. Many would perish moaning for water, and for mothers
they would never see again. For most of the first two years of war in
the East, Union forces got spanked. "Johnny Reb" had proved
himself a tough, obstinate foe.

Manpower Crisis

By 1862, Union staff officers ran short of volunteers to replace the
dead and the AWOL, the amputated and the captured. Late that
year, New York elected as governor Democrat Horatio Seymour, a
staunch Lincoln opponent. Seymour's election warned of growing
discontent with the "rich man's war, poor man's fight."

While the Union's manpower dilemma was tame compared to
the Confederacy's, in March 1863 Congress enacted the long-
discussed conscription solution. Able-bodied males from ages 20 to
45 became liable for three years' involuntary military service. The
most divisive proviso in Congress's legislation was the means to *avoid*
service. A conscript who could scrape up $300 (about $5,300 in 21st-
century purchasing power) could buy his way out. Failing that, he

could hire a substitute. New York City was full of destitute immigrants, mostly Irish and German, ready to risk their lives for a stake that could elevate them from dire poverty.

Racial Overtones

The issue, though, wasn't simply about money. On New Year's Day 1863, President Lincoln signed the Emancipation Proclamation, freeing slaves in the core Confederate states. This raised a question in the mind of the average soldier: *What am I fighting for?* To risk his life for his country was one thing. Risking it for African Americans (for whom the typical Union soldier would use a racial slur) was quite another. If the Union won, slavery would almost surely end nationwide. Our typical soldier envisioned himself returning home only to find that he had helped liberate a whole lot of new competition for employment. Some regiments became mutinous. The racial factor, then, would play a very sordid part in the city's antidraft explosion.

IN LEXINGTON AVENUE

On July 11, 1863, the NYC provost marshal held the first draft lottery. African Americans were not included in the draft—not that they needed to be; free and freedman alike, they would soon volunteer in great numbers. Recent war news may have contributed to draftee dissent, namely the pivotal Union victories at Gettysburg and Vicksburg. *If we've turned the tide, why do we need a draft?* At the time, of course, no one knew exactly how long the Confederacy might fight on.

July 13, 1863

A sultry day began with a protest in Manhattan. Germans, Irish, men, women, workers, and firefighters gathered numbers as they marched toward the offices of the provost marshal at 47th Street and

Third Avenue. Hopes of a peaceful protest ended when the mob torched the marshal's building. The arson had a professional touch: A rioting fire engine company took the lead in torching the place.

Monday dissolved into pandemonium as rioting and arson spread throughout lower Manhattan. Many firefighters were unavailable for service, having joined the rioting. The state militia was away in Pennsylvania, leaving the NYPD ill-equipped to contend with angry mobs. Overwhelmed police resorted to nightsticks and pistols. Undeterred, a gang beat and slashed NYPD Superintendent John Kennedy.

The violence fell most heavily upon African Americans. Many were beaten, sometimes to death. Residents of homes that dared shelter African Americans received similar treatment. Rioters even burned an African American orphanage. Other primary targets were the homes and businesses of major Republican supporters, such as Horace Greeley's *New York Daily Tribune*.

July 14

A night of rain didn't quench the desire to riot. Mobs barricaded the streets of lower Manhattan. What began as a draft protest had become open warfare on vocal Republicans, African Americans of any station, and war-profiting businesses.

The only Federal troops close enough to play a part on Tuesday were fortress garrison troops from the harbor and West Point. As always, Federal troops played rougher, but the rioters matched them. The 11th New York Volunteers opened fire on rioters at 34th Street and Second Avenue with a six-pounder howitzer. Noting the identity of the colonel in command, a mob hunted him down and beat him to death near his home. The state militia and other nearby regiments hastened to the city.

July 15

The violence focused still more intensely on African Americans, who were now unsafe in any part of lower Manhattan. By Wednesday, authorities had identified all areas under mob control. Calling them "infected areas," military and police units moved to contain the rioters inside them. The strategy wasn't entirely successful, however,

as the rioting spread to Staten Island and Brooklyn—never mind newspaper reports that the draft had been suspended.

July 16

The arrival of more Federal troops quashed the remaining rioters, with the final fight taking place on 22nd Street between Second and Third avenues.

Cleaning Up and Taking Stock

The official death toll was 119; the true toll may have been higher. Thousands were injured, and thousands of African Americans chose not to stay in Manhattan. Estimates of property damage ranged as high as $5 million (today, that would be about $88.5 million).

The lasting damage was to the city's diversity and the justice of the Union cause. While the Union did not go to war to end slavery, surely the Confederacy went to war to preserve it. The riots wrote the message in letters of blood underlined in fire: The average white Northerner was uninterested in a war to free slaves and had no inclination to regard African Americans as equals.

As for the draft, it resumed in August—this time with the equivalent of a division of Federal troops in town. Manhattan's African American community wouldn't recover for years.

- *On July 14, seeing prime political opportunity, Tammany Hall's infamous Democratic machine started drafting a bond issue to cover the $300 fee for any New Yorker drafted.*

- *By 1863, the Five Points area had become an important center of African American social life in Manhattan. The area experienced little violence, with white and black New Yorkers joining forces to drive mobs away.*

- *One of the burnt businesses was Brooks Brothers, which made uniforms for the military then (and now).*

- *The real winners in the riots were Tammany politicos, whose power increased when antidraft immigrants saw in the Tammany machine a way to assert their position in the city's political life.*

Fast Facts

- *Before the baseball team was the Giants, it was called the New York Gothams (1883–84). Name-wise, the Polo Grounds boys were one of baseball's most stable franchises: They played as the New York Giants for 73 seasons.*

- *The Dutch briefly got New York back after handing it to Britain. In 1673, with the two at war, a Dutch fleet reoccupied Manhattan. Everything was re-Dutchified until the Netherlands traded Manhattan for Suriname.* Suriname?

- *The worst tenements in early 1900s Manhattan were "back lots"—those in a block's center reached by narrow alleys. Invisible from the street, back lots harbored medieval levels of lice, rats, and squalor.*

- *Winston Churchill's mother, Jennie Jerome (later Lady Randolph Churchill, 1854–1921), grew up in Brooklyn. Oddly enough, though she helped young Winston's career, she opposed women's suffrage (as did Winston). She didn't live to see full suffrage for British women, which didn't come until 1928.*

- *Boxer Gene Tunney, who grew up on 52nd Street in Manhattan, was the beneficiary of the 1927 "long count" fight with Jack Dempsey. Tunney retired in 1928 with a 65–1–1 record.*

- *It would be erroneous to think of Harlem's original African American influx (1905–25) as poor. Many were actually making better-than-ever wages thanks to World War I. Many also invested it in real estate and grew wealthy.*

- *Central Park is a great place to see evidence of the glaciers that once scraped across the boroughs. Rocks embedded in the moving glaciers scored deep grooves in exposed rock, easily seen in several spots.*

- *The first U.S.-born saint, Elizabeth Ann Seton (1774–1821), was a native New Yorker. Of course, time marches slowly. The tireless benefactress of Maryland's poor wasn't canonized until 1975.*

Hizzoner!

♥ ♥ ♥ ♥

New York City has had its share of colorful mayors over the years.
Many worked hard to make the Big Apple a better place to live,
while others spent their careers embroiled in controversy.

The governor may reign over the state of New York, but it's the
mayor—or "hizzoner," as the tabloids usually refer to him—who
controls New York City.

The municipality's first mayor was Thomas Willett, who was
appointed to the post in 1665 by Governor Richard Nicolls. For
more than a century and a half, the position of mayor would remain
an appointment that came with limited authority. Today, however,
the mayor heads the executive branch of the city government and
oversees an annual budget of $50 billion—the largest municipal
budget in the country. Here are some of the most memorable
characters to hold the job of mayor:

Robert Van Wyck (1898–1901). A graduate of Columbia University
Law School and former chief judge of the city court, Van Wyck was a
product of the Tammany Hall machine. His race against political
reformer Seth Low was a bloody battle that Van Wyck managed to
win despite refusing to give a single public speech. A man of few
words, Van Wyck's acceptance speech consisted of just two sentences.

Van Wyck's single term as mayor was rife with political scandal,
including allegations that he was part of a scam to artificially inflate
the price of milk. An investigation by the state legislature concluded
that he was a "dictator" who remained under the influence of
Tammany Hall bosses. Following the inauguration of his successor, it
was reported that Van Wyck left City Hall via a back entrance and
walked unrecognized into the crowd outside.

George Binton McClellan (1904–9). The son of renowned Civil
War general George McClellan, George Binton McClellan was a bit
of a political prodigy, winning a congressional seat at age 27 and
becoming president of the New York City Board of Aldermen at 30.
Although he ran and won on the Tammany Hall ticket, McClellan

quickly proved that he wasn't beholden to his political bosses. He won his second term as mayor by defeating newspaper mogul William Randolph Hearst but spent the remainder of his tenure suffering almost daily attacks from Hearst's muckraking newspapers. Much to the chagrin of his political patrons, McClellan also spent much of his second term attempting to dismantle the Tammany Hall machine.

William Jay Gaynor (1910–13). Gaynor holds the distinction of being the only New York City mayor to have an attempt made on his life: Early in his first year, he was shot in the throat by a disgruntled city employee. Gaynor survived the shooting, but the bullet could not be removed; he died three years later from residual effects of the attack.

James "Jimmy" Walker (1926–32). One of the city's more flamboyant mayors, Walker was an accomplished actor and musician as well as a state politician. (Among his most famous works was the ballad "Will You Love Me in December as You Do in May?") Another product of the Tammany Hall machine, Walker paid off his political benefactors with cushy jobs and lucrative city contracts. Citizens of New York City were willing to overlook this until the Depression revealed just how neglected many city services had become. In 1932, accused of accepting bribes from business leaders with ties to the city, Walker was called before the governor. He resigned as mayor in the middle of the hearings and moved to Europe with his mistress.

Fiorello La Guardia (1934–45).

Considered by most historians to be one of the most effective mayors in the city's history, La Guardia worked extremely hard to better the lives of his constituents. He strived to eliminate the corruption that infested city government, strengthened the city's infrastructure, and quickly gained renown for putting the city before political gain. He often used the radio to reach out to the citizens of New York, and in 1945 turned to that device to read the Sunday funnies during a newspaper delivery strike, an act that endeared him to many.

John Lindsay (1966–73). Lindsay served during one of the most turbulent times in modern American history and hoped to make city government more accessible to the poor and disenfranchised through efforts such as the Urban Action Taskforce and Neighborhood City Halls. However, things didn't start smoothly for Lindsay—on his first day in office, a transit strike threatened to bring the city to its knees. It was just the first of many such emergencies Lindsay would face. While still mayor, Lindsay mounted a short-lived bid for the 1972 Democratic presidential nomination. Two decades later, his finances a wreck, he accepted honorary city posts from Mayor Rudy Giuliani, in order to have health insurance and a pension.

Abraham Beame (1974–77). New York's first Jewish mayor, Beame came into office with the city on the verge of bankruptcy, a situation that forced him to make drastic cuts to the city's budget and eliminate numerous jobs. It was during Beame's tenure that President Gerald Ford refused to help bail out the city, resulting in the infamous *New York Daily News* headline "Ford to New York: Drop Dead." However, in 1976, Beame managed to land annual federal loans that helped keep the city financially solvent.

Edward Koch (1978–89). Koch inherited the financial difficulties that had plagued Beame but was able to restore the city's credit and put it on better financial footing. A gregarious man with a strong personality, he became famous for greeting constituents with the amusingly self-serving question, "How'm I doing?" Koch hoped to be NYC's first four-term mayor, but corruption scandals and revelations of his harsh dealings with other officials stopped him at three.

Rudolph Giuliani (1994–2001). A former U.S. Attorney, Giuliani became mayor with a pledge to help the failing city get back on its feet and improve the lives of all New Yorkers. He established a zero tolerance policy against crime and was influential in transforming some of the sleazier sections of the city into places where citizens and tourists felt safe. Terrorist attacks against the World Trade Center on September 11, 2001, propelled Giuliani into the national spotlight. Even though his tenure was ending, he quickly stepped up to reassure New Yorkers and help lead them through those trying times. A 2008 run at the GOP presidential nomination went nowhere, despite Giuliani's mention of 9/11 at every opportunity during his campaign.

The Mad Bomber

♥ ♥ ♥ ♥

*Sure, he wanted revenge, but he also wanted to protect
New Yorkers from their utility company.*

Ninety miles north of New York City, George Metesky, an amiable-
looking middle-aged man in a business suit, drove his car 80 feet
from his driveway to the garage workshop at his family's house. He
changed into coveralls and used gunpowder extracted from rifle
bullets to craft what he called "units." He wanted New Yorkers to
know that he had been wronged. When he meticulously packed
away his tools at the end of the day, Metesky's bomb was ready.

The man who would become familiar to New Yorkers as the
Mad Bomber nursed a grudge against his former employer, Con-
solidated Edison (Con Ed), New York's utility company. While
working for Con Ed in 1931, Metesky suffered an accident and came
to believe that he had been gassed and contracted tuberculosis as a
result. Some of that may have been fanciful thinking, but two things
were indisputable: The illness left him unable to work, and Con Ed
denied him workman's compensation. Metesky was angry.

A Little Attention, Please

More than 900 letters sent by Metesky to elected officials and newspapers failed to bring Con Ed to account. Frustrated, he devised an
alternative plan. In November 1940, he left a pipe bomb outside a
Con Ed plant on Manhattan's Upper West Side. A note read, "CON
EDISON CROOKS, THIS IS FOR YOU." He signed it, "F.P." The
bomb didn't go off, but Con Ed—and New York—had been warned.

The following September, an unexploded pipe bomb wrapped in
a sock with a note signed "F.P." was discovered near Con Ed's headquarters. However, before Metesky could scare the city a third time,
the nation entered World War II. New York City police received a
letter from "F.P." outlining his patriotic intentions:

"I WILL Make no more BOmB UNITS for the Duration of the
WAR . . . Later I WILl bring The con EDiSON to JUSTICE—THEy
will pay for their dastaRdLy deeds."

New York saw no more bombs from "F.P." for nearly ten years, although the threatening letters continued. Then, in March 1950, an intact bomb was found in Grand Central Station. "F.P." was back.

Clues

Metesky rapidly escalated his Con Ed war. A bomb blew up in the New York Public Library in April 1951, and another hit Grand Central. Between 1951 and 1956, Metesky placed at least 30 bombs. Although 15 people were injured by 22 that exploded, no one was killed.

The lead detective turned to a criminal psychiatrist. Dr. James Brussel studied the case and concluded that the "Mad Bomber," as the press now called him, was of Slavic descent, Catholic, and was burdened with an Oedipal complex. Detectives could find him outside the city living with a female relative. The NYPD was dubious, but Dr. Brussel assured them that when they found "F.P.," he wouldn't come along until donning a buttoned double-breasted suit.

To trap "F.P.," the *New York Journal-American* encouraged him to submit his story. Metesky bit, and the story was printed. A Con Ed clerk had previously sifted through files of "troublesome" former employees and discovered Metesky. All this information added up to an identification. In January 1957, the cops drove to Waterbury, Connecticut, where Polish Catholic Metesky lived with his sisters. He opened the door in his pajamas and cheerfully admitted to being "F.P.," explaining that the initials stood for "Fair Play." Before he was arrested, he changed into a doubled-breasted suit.

Just What Is Insanity, Anyway?

Metesky grinned throughout his arraignment. He was sent to Bellevue Hospital for evaluation and ruled insane. He was committed to Matteawan State Hospital for the Criminally Insane without trial.

On his release in 1973, Metesky told the *New York Times* that he wished he had stood trial. "I don't think I was insane," he said. "Sometimes . . . I wondered if there was something wrong with me, because of the extreme effort I was making." He reminded reporters that he was trying to help others. "If I caused enough trouble, they'd have to be careful about the way they treat other people." George "Fair Play" Metesky died in Waterbury in 1994 at age 90.

The Coney Island Mermaid Parade

♥ ♥ ♥ ♥

Where else can alien mermaids, lobsters, and sea monsters get together for a day of fun in the sun?

A woman dressed as a crab saunters down the boardwalk, waving her red, claw-shaped oven mitts in time to soul music that blasts out of a small amp in a child's red wagon. Crab-lady is flanked by a "dead sailor" (a skinny man covered in white body paint and dressed in a sailor suit), three more women (one with very hairy armpits), and little girls in elaborate homemade, sequined mermaid costumes. There's also a gentleman dressed as a seahorse. And rounding out this "Mermaid Soul Train" is a fellow in a blond wig and hula skirt who strums a ukulele. His coconut bra floats on copious tufts of red chest hair. It's just another unforgettable moment in the Coney Island Mermaid Parade.

Say Hello to Summer

Billed as the largest art parade in America, the Mermaid Parade has been a Coney Island tradition for three decades, held on the first Saturday following the vernal equinox, to welcome the official start of summer. Elaborate floats and antique cars glide down Surf Avenue as the marchers step off from the boardwalk. Although billed as family friendly (parade organizers send groups with children marching down the boardwalk first), some of the participants opt for costumes consisting of nothing more than body paint, G-strings, pasties, or just total nudity. Political statements are not uncommon.

The parade is overseen by a celebrity King Neptune and Queen Mermaid. The king and queen appease the gods by tossing fruit into the ocean, making the water safe for swimmers. They also judge the parade's floats and costumes. Such luminaries as Moby, Queen Latifah, David Byrne, and Patti D'Arbanville have performed this public service for New Yorkers. Later, hardy revelers dance the night away at the Mermaid Parade Ball.

Noteworthy Staten Islanders

♥ ♥ ♥ ♥

Here are some interesting and prominent
folk with close Staten Island ties.

Christina Aguilera (1980–) Sexy, much-publicized pop singer and Staten Island native.

Alice Austen (1866–1952) Photographer of the island's history; lived in Rosebank.

Joan Baez (1941–) Folk singer and antiwar activist; Staten Island native.

Ella Reeve Bloor (1862–1951) Women's rights and labor activist, Staten Island native.

Alfred Thompson Bricher (1837–1908) Hudson River School maritime painter, longtime New Dorp resident.

Aaron Burr (1756–1836) U.S. senator, third vice president; spent later life in Port Richmond and died there.

Roy Clark (1933–) A sweet-sounding country singer and picker from Great Kills? It's true!

Dorothy Day (1897–1980) Catholic social justice activist, longtime Staten Islander.

Ann Duquesnay (ca. 1957–) Tony-winning singer, Grammy-nominated lyricist; resides in Silver Lake.

Jennifer Esposito (1972–) Actress, Moore Catholic High School alumna.

John Frémont (1813–90) General, politician, and explorer; lived much of his later life on Staten Island.

Sammy "The Bull" Gravano (1945–) Organized crime turncoat, lived on Staten Island.

Marilyn King (1949–) 1976 Olympic pentathlete from Bay Terrace.

Rebecca Craighill Lancefield (1895–1981) Pioneering microbiologist and strep researcher; Fort Wadsworth native.

Alyssa Milano (1972–) Actress, grew up on Staten Island.

Frederick Law Olmsted (1822–1903) Designed Central Park, among many others; resided on Staten Island.

Antonio López de Santa Ana (1794–1896) General and president of Mexico, spent part of his later life of exile on Staten Island.

Patricia Buckley Moss (1933–) Noted painter of country scenes, Staten Island native.

Alan Seeger (1888–1916) Poet who perished in World War I fighting with the French Foreign Legion; grew up on Staten Island.

Elizabeth Ann Bayley Seton (1744–1821) First U.S.-born Catholic saint, summered with her father in St. George.

Robert G. Shaw (1837–63) Commanded the African American 54th Massachusetts, killed in action at Fort Wagner, South Carolina; lived on Staten Island in his teens.

Edward Stettinius Jr. (1900–1949) Secretary of state, first U.S. ambassador to UN; spent part of his childhood on Staten Island.

Theodore Sturgeon (1918–85) Science fiction author, screenwriter, and Staten Island native. Sturgeon's Law: *Ninety percent of everything is crap.*

Clive Thompson (1940–) Renowned Afro-Caribbean dancer who founded his own troupe on Staten Island.

Bobby Thomson (1923–) Hero of the 1951 Giants' pennant, lived on Staten Island.

Henry David Thoreau (1817–62) Poet and philosopher, spent a lot of time on Staten Island.

Amy Vanderbilt (1908–74) Etiquette author from Westerleigh and Curtis High School.

Cornelius Vanderbilt (1794–1877) Shipping magnate, founder of a university known for bad football (but strong academics), and a native.

Wu-Tang Clan (est. 1992) The martial arts–oriented rappers come from Clifton.

Paul Zindel (1936–2003) Playwright, children's author, Pulitzer Prize winner, Staten Island native.

Play Ball!

♥ ♥ ♥ ♥

Baseball and New York City are inseparably connected. In fact, it's almost impossible to imagine one without the other.

No discussion of New York City is complete without at least a mention of the national pastime. After all, the Big Apple has been home to what is arguably the sport's greatest team—the Yankees—since 1913, not to mention three other legendary franchises: the Dodgers, the Giants, and the Mets. Here's a brief overview.

The New York Yankees

Before they were the Yankees, they were the New York Highlanders. Established in 1903, the team sported its trademark pinstripes for the first time in 1912, a fashion trend the franchise would embrace from then on.

The Highlanders were officially renamed the Yankees in 1913 and, in the years that followed, quickly established themselves as a powerhouse team with some of the finest players ever to pick up a ball and glove. One of the team's first superstars was Babe Ruth, whom the Yankees purchased from the Boston Red Sox in 1920 for just $125,000. The next year, Ruth contributed to the Yankees' first American League pennant—and the Red Sox cursed their own stupidity.

In the decades that followed, the Bronx Bombers unleashed a steady stream of exceptionally talented ballplayers, including Lou Gehrig, whose record streak of 2,130 consecutive games played stood for 56 years; Joe DiMaggio, who wowed crowds with a still-unsurpassed 56-game hitting streak in 1941; slugger Mickey Mantle; Don Larsen, the only pitcher to hurl a perfect game in a World Series (October 8, 1956); and Roger Maris, who, in 1961, broke Babe Ruth's record of 60 home runs in a single season by hitting 61.

The Yankees are one of baseball's winningest teams with (at last count) 27 world championships. After 85 years at legendary Yankee

Stadium, the team moved to new digs across the street in 2009, where they continued their winning ways.

The Brooklyn Dodgers

Brooklyn baseball dates back to the mid-1800s, when the borough hosted its first team, the Brooklyn Atlantics. The franchise had numerous names over the years and permanently became the Dodgers in 1932. Throughout, Brooklyn fans remained as passionate about their team as those who rooted for the Yankees or the Giants. Little wonder that thousands of hearts were shattered when the team left Ebbets Field for California before the 1958 season.

The Brooklyn Bums produced their share of quality players, but one of the team's proudest moments occurred in 1947 when team president Branch Rickey broke baseball's long-standing color barrier by placing Jackie Robinson at first base. Robinson experienced horrendous racism as Major League Baseball's first black player, but he never lashed back, instead proving his worth on the field. During his first year with the Dodgers he batted .297 and won Rookie of the Year.

In the 1940s and '50s, the rivalry between the Dodgers and the Giants became one of the most compelling sagas in baseball history. The competition climaxed in 1951 when the teams found themselves tied for the National League pennant, forcing a three-game playoff. It remains one of baseball's most exciting series, with the teams splitting the first two games. The Dodgers were leading by two runs in the final inning of the tie-breaking third game when Giants outfielder Ralph Branca hit a home run off Bobby Thomson with two men on base. The so-called "Shot Heard Around the World" was a heartbreaker for Dodgers fans everywhere.

The New York Giants

The Giants are one of baseball's oldest teams and one of its most successful in terms of wins. The team got its start in 1883 as the New York Gothams and became the Giants in 1885.

Over the many decades, the Giants have given the world some astounding players. In 1895, for example, Cy Seymour pitched both games of a doubleheader—and won both. And in the early years of the 20th century, stellar players such as Christy Mathewson, who enjoyed multiple 30-win seasons and once pitched 68 consecutive

innings without giving up a walk, helped put fans in the bleachers at the Polo Grounds, where the Giants played from 1911 to 1957.

The 1930s and '40s were strong decades for the Giants, who won the NL pennant in 1933, '36, and '37. The team produced several star players during that period, including Mel Ott, Bill Terry, and Carl Hubbell, who wowed fans by striking out Babe Ruth, Lou Gehrig, Jimmie Foxx, Al Simmons, and Joe Cronin in the first two innings of the 1934 All-Star Game.

In 1951, the Giants brought aboard Willie Mays, who was batting .477 in the minor leagues. Mays was slow to start but eventually found his groove and hit 20 home runs that season to become Rookie of the Year—and, eventually, one of the best players in major league history.

At the end of the 1957 season, with the Polo Grounds scheduled for demolition and New York unwilling to finance a new park, the Giants packed up and moved to San Francisco. It was a sad day for all New Yorkers.

The New York Mets

The New York Metropolitans (forever after known as the Mets) were accepted into the majors in 1961 as one of four expansion teams. They played their first official game on April 11, 1962, losing to the St. Louis Cardinals 11–4. During their early, formative years the Mets played mediocre ball, which earned them the nickname "Lovable Losers." In 1966, however, the team acquired its first true star in pitcher Tom Seaver. During 12 seasons with the team, Seaver racked up an impressive 198 wins, 124 losses, and an ERA of 2.57.

The team played exceptional ball during the 1969 season, winning the National League Championship with a three-game sweep of the Atlanta Braves. The Mets then went on to win their first World Series, defeating the seemingly unstoppable Baltimore Orioles four games to one. Overnight, the team transformed itself from Lovable Losers to the Miracle Mets.

The Mets played up-and-down ball in the years that followed. Among the highlights, however, is the team's second World Series victory in 1986, when a soft ground ball hit by Mookie Wilson slipped between the legs of Boston Red Sox first baseman Bill Buckner in Game Six. It was an error that Buckner never lived down and one that still fascinates fans of New York baseball.

Eating for Nickels

♥   ♥   ♥   ♥

Where fresh meals were available, "quick as a click."

Spot the meal you want through a small glass door, insert some nickels into an adjacent slot, turn a chrome-plated knob, and then open the hatch to retrieve your food. Ah, satisfaction!

The Horn & Hardart Automats provided savory, self-service lunches and dinners ranging from salads, sandwiches, and mac & cheese to cakes, pies, and roast beef with sweet potatoes. At their height, these unusual places served more than 500,000 people a day, 350,000 of them in New York alone, annually selling more than 90 million cups of their famous fresh-brewed coffee. People of all social backgrounds and economic circumstances patronized the Automats. As Paul Hardart, the great-grandson of cofounder Frank Hardart, told the *New York Times* in 1998, "You had paupers and Rockefellers sitting next to each other. It was the great equalizer. A place you would go for good food, it was cheap and classless."

Nickel Throwers

New Yorkers still recall the assembly-line eateries where, in exchange for paper money and larger coins, "nickel throwers" in glass booths would give patrons the five-cent pieces needed to purchase cold meals. Employees behind the geometrically stacked rows of small compartments replenished each item as soon as one was purchased. Hot dishes were available at long serving counters.

Joseph Horn and the German-born Hardart based their initial Automat, opened in Philadelphia in 1902, on the Quisiana in Berlin. The first Automat in Manhattan opened in Times Square on July 2, 1912. Customers spent 8,693 nickels on that first day. During the 1940s and '50s, New York had about 50 Automats, but it eventually became impossible to compete with the fast-food giants. The last Horn & Hardart, on East 42nd Street, closed in 1991.

Mafia Buster!

♥   ♥   ♥   ♥

*Joseph Petrosino was one of the first New York cops to take
on the Mafia. He was clever, fearless—and effective.*

The name Joseph Petrosino means nothing to most New Yorkers—
unless they're police officers, who regard the guy as a legend. In the
first decade of the 20th century, Petrosino established himself as one
of the toughest, most effective detectives in NYPD history. His beat
was Little Italy, and he spent much of his career going toe-to-toe
with the Mafia. It was a war that ultimately cost him his life.

Takin' Names

Petrosino was brought into the department by Captain Alexander
Williams, who had watched Petrosino tangle with local thugs on the
city streets. Petrosino didn't meet the police height requirement, but
in addition to being tough as nails, he spoke fluent Italian and was
familiar with the local culture. Williams quickly realized that
Petrosino could be an invaluable asset to the force.

The NYPD put Petrosino to work as a sergeant in 1883. He
wasted no time making his presence known within the city's Italian
community. Strong and fearless, Petrosino became a brawler when
necessary, but he also knew the value of quiet detective work.
(Dedication and fearlessness eventually elevated him to the rank of
lieutenant.) To gather intelligence, for instance, Petrosino routinely
disguised himself as a tunnel "sandhog" laborer, a blind street
beggar, and other urban denizens who can slip around unnoticed.

Petrosino solved plenty of crimes during his career, but it was his
labor to eliminate the vicious gangs preying on Italian immigrants
that made him famous. Italian gangsters started setting up shop in
the city around 1900, bringing murder, theft, and extortion with
them. Petrosino made it his mission to end their reign of terror.

Unspeakable Violence

Foremost among Petrosino's gangland foes was Vito Cascio Ferro,
whom some consider one of the inspirations for Mario Puzo's

The Godfather. Ferro arrived in New York from Sicily in 1901, already a mob boss to be feared and respected. Petrosino made no secret of his desire to implicate Ferro in the gruesome murder in which a body had been dismembered and stuffed in a barrel. As Petrosino closed in, Ferro fled to Sicily, vowing revenge.

Meanwhile, Petrosino continued to battle the various gangs plaguing Little Italy. Kidnapping and murder were on the rise, as was the use of bombs. (In one terrifying incident, Petrosino managed to extinguish a bomb's fuse with his *fingers* just seconds before the bomb was set to explode.) Determined to stay ahead of the criminals, Petrosino established the nation's first bomb squad, teaching himself and his crew how to dismantle the deadly devices.

In 1908, Vito Ferro again attempted to reach into New York, this time through an intermediary—a murderous Sicilian named Raffaele Palizzolo. At first, clueless city officials embraced Palizzolo, who claimed to want to eliminate the Black Hand, as the Mafia was also called. But Petrosino was skeptical and tailed Palizzolo everywhere. This forced Palizzolo to return to Sicily, much to Ferro's anger.

All the News That's Fit to Blab

Petrosino's boss, Police Commissioner Theodore Bingham, was eager to eliminate New York's Mafia menace once and for all. Early in 1909 he sent Petrosino on a clandestine trip to Italy to meet with law enforcement officials there and gather intelligence. Because the underworld had put a price on his head, Petrosino made the trip disguised as a Jewish merchant named Simone Velletri. Unfortunately, his mission didn't remain a secret for long: While Petrosino was still in transit, the *New York Herald* ran a story that he was on his way to Italy specifically to gather information on Italian gangsters. The source? Bingham, who had stupidly confided in a reporter.

By the time Petrosino arrived in Italy, news of his mission had spread throughout the local underworld. Ferro ordered a hit. On March 12, 1909, two gunmen cut down Petrosino.

The detective's funeral was one of the largest in New York history. Thousands of police officers and citizens lined the streets as the procession traveled through the city to Calvary Cemetery in Long Island. The journey took five and a half hours—a fitting journey for a good man who lived and died for the rule of law.

Bragging Rights

Lincoln Center for the Performing Arts, located on Columbus Avenue between 62nd and 66th streets in Manhattan, is the largest performing arts center in the nation—and one of the most prestigious. Stretching over 16 acres, it is made up of 12 resident institutions that encompass pretty much all of the popular arts. Some of the most famous include the Julliard School (which has produced more artistically talented individuals than you can shake a baton at), the Metropolitan Opera, the New York Philharmonic, the New York City Ballet, and the Lincoln Center Theater.

President Dwight Eisenhower broke ground for the center on May 14, 1959, and predicted that it would become "a mighty influence for peace and understanding throughout the world." The center's first building, Philharmonic Hall—now known as Avery Fisher Hall—opened three years later. Total construction cost: $185 million.

A variety of auditoriums and halls, both expansive and intimate, host Lincoln Center's varied programs. The largest is the 3,900-seat Metropolitan Opera House, home stage of the Metropolitan Opera. Avery Fisher Hall, home stage of the New York Philharmonic, is the center's second largest facility with 2,738 seats. Smaller venues include the 268-seat Walter Reade Theater, which hosts screenings by the Film Society of Lincoln Center, and the 299-seat Mitzi E. Newhouse Theater, which showcases off-Broadway productions and other shows.

When New Yorkers are in the mood for top-notch entertainment, Lincoln Center for the Performing Arts is always at the top of their list. It presents more than 400 unique events each year, including American Songbook, Great Performers, the Mostly Mozart Festival, Midsummer Night Swing, and the Emmy Award–winning Live from Lincoln Center. So do yourself a favor and drop by the next time you're in town—your inner critic will love it.

Weegee Gets the Shot

♥ ♥ ♥ ♥

*Arthur Fellig's photographs of Depression-era and wartime
New York reveal an urban landscape that the great middle
class seldom observed: crime scenes, four-story fires, murder
victims, suicides, and showgirls' dressing rooms.*

With ears cocked toward his police radio scanner, Arthur Fellig
usually arrived first at any emergency call. He was a short, rumpled
figure who showed up so quickly some of his fellow photographers
(and even the police) joked that he could see the future. He earned
the nickname "Weegee," a phonetic spelling of the Ouija board. It
was a name he used on every book collecting his photography.

A City Laid Bare

Partly because Fellig had once been homeless, he felt a bond with
New York's underclass, and he photographed them with unmistak-
able empathy. His subjects included a knot of kids sleeping on their
fire escape for respite from their "stuffy tenement"; a homeless
woman leveling an unreadable stare at upper-class operagoers; a
family on the run from a tenement fire. But cleverly, Weegee created counterpoints to these affecting human-interest images with
stark shots of murder. In his flash-illuminated black-and-white shots,
the dead often resembled grimy dolls. Interiors of stores and cheap
apartments looked dirty and foreboding. His juxtapositions could be
striking. A dead body covered in newspapers dominates one photo-
graph. Above the corpse is a marquee that reads, "Joy of Living." In
his famous 1945 book, *Naked City*, Weegee included a shot of an
invoice. It reads, "Two Murders, $35.00."

Fellig stopped shooting late-night street photography a few years
after *Naked City* was published. He left crime and other mayhem
behind in order to shoot celebrities in New York and Hollywood,
travel across Europe, and work with experimental techniques (dis-
tortion lenses, melted negatives, prints exposed through warped
glass). His lasting impact, however, comes from his pitiless but
honest photographs of the city that made him famous.

Fast Facts

- *What is a Knickerbocker, anyway? One who can trace roots back to the old Dutch colonists. There actually was a Knickerbocker family, but the term owes its popularity to a fictional character created by Washington Irving.*

- *Famed publisher Joseph Pulitzer (1847–1911) liked Manhattan, but not its cacophonous dull roar. He was so sensitive to noise he had a soundproof bedroom added to his East 73rd Street home.*

- *John Roebling's cable company, which supplied the cable for the Brooklyn Bridge (as well as the Washington and Golden Gate bridges), was the primary supplier of wire for the Slinky children's toy during the 1950s.*

- *In May 1990, Bonwit Teller's art deco flagship building was demolished to make way for the Trump Tower. Located at 721 Fifth Avenue, the Tower initially housed a new Bonwit Teller that was subsequently replaced by the French department store, Galeries Lafayette—like the new Bonwit, it quickly went down the tubes. Sometimes the past just can't be duplicated.*

- *Think the city is polluted now? In the mid-1800s the streets of Manhattan got dirtied by 250 tons of horse manure daily, plus 45,000 gallons of horse urine and 30-odd horse corpses.*

- *Manhattan has skyscrapers because it's full of schist—that is, a metamorphic bedrock called Manhattan schist, which makes a stable construction platform. It is nearest the surface in Midtown and Lower Manhattan.*

- *In 1859, Manhattan native and future Civil War political general Daniel Sickles murdered the son of national anthem writer Francis Scott Key for having an affair with Sickles's wife. Pleading temporary insanity, Sickles was acquitted.*

- *One now-vanished Greenwich Village niche was Little Africa. This African American district, bounded by modern Bleecker, East Houston, and Sullivan streets and La Guardia Place, thrived from the Civil War era through the 1880s.*

NYC Timeline

Prior to 1524
Thirteen tribes occupy Long Island and other parts of present-day New York City. In what is now Manhattan, the Wappinger hunt, fish, and grow maize. When colonists begin to arrive, it's estimated that 15,000 Wappinger live in about 80 settlements around the region.

April 17, 1524
Giovanni da Verrazzano of France makes it to New York Harbor and observes the entrance to the Hudson. (His 1528 trip back to the New World goes badly. He makes his way to Florida, but during a land excursion in the Bahamas he's eaten by natives.)

September 10, 1609
Henry Hudson, an English subject working for the Dutch East India Company, arrives with his crew near what is now Coney Island. One of the crew, John Coleman, is killed by an arrow to the neck, making it the first murder in New York City.

September 11, 1609
Despite the advent of violence, Henry Hudson sails on to New York City.

September 12, 1609
Henry Hudson negotiates the Hudson River searching for the elusive (and, as it turns out, nonexistent) passage to Asia. (His crew will set Hudson adrift during a mutiny in 1610.)

1613
The fur flies with the founding of Lower Manhattan as a Dutch fur-trading settlement encourages a race for pelts.

1625
Dutch settlers call their new home New Amsterdam and set about building Fort Amsterdam.

1638
Willem Kieft becomes director general of New Amsterdam.

1641
Kieft and the Dutch combine forces in "Kieft's War" against Native Americans.

The Wooden Horse, the first tavern in New Amsterdam, opens its doors.

February 1643
Settlers ratchet up the violence against American Indians by crossing the Hudson River to present-day Jersey City, where they perpetrate the Pavonia Massacre. Eighty Native Americans are killed.

August 29, 1645
Thanks to reinforcements sent from Holland, the Dutch are able to hold out long enough to sign a peace treaty with the Native Americans.

May 27, 1647
Peter Stuyvesant becomes New Amsterdam's director general and immediately curtails the city's religious freedoms. Even worse, as far as some settlers are concerned, Stuyvesant closes all of the city's taverns.

February 2, 1653
New Amsterdam is formally incorporated as a city.

1664
The English attack by sea and conquer New Amsterdam, renaming it New York for the Duke of York.

1665
Thomas Willett, a British-born American merchant, becomes the first mayor of the city of New York.

(Continued on p. 75)

Famous Folks from Queens

♥ ♥ ♥ ♥

They all came from or lived in Queens, and there are many.

Ron Artest (1979–) NBA defensive standout from the Queensbridge projects. A noted physical player, he gained infamy when he slugged a taunting fan in Detroit.

Barbara Bach (1947–) Rosedale native, remembered as the "Bond girl" in *The Spy Who Loved Me* (1977); wife of Ringo Starr.

Gary Bettman (1952–) NHL commissioner, a Queens native who oversaw the league's expansion into the southern United States.

Jimmy Breslin (1930–) Born and raised in Jamaica; acclaimed journalist who once looked a little too closely into the Lucchese crime family and got badly beaten for it.

Dr. Joyce Brothers (1927–) Longtime advice columnist and TV personality from Far Rockaway.

Barbara Pierce Bush (1925–) Born in Flushing; first lady of the United States as wife of President George H. W. Bush and mother of President George W. Bush.

Peter Camejo (1939–2008) Born in Queens of Venezuelan descent; longtime Socialist Workers Party and later Green Party activist, as well as Ralph Nader's running mate in the 2004 presidential election.

Georgia Cayvan (1857–1906) Late 19th-century stage star who spent her last years under care in Flushing.

Julie Chen (1970–) Born and raised in the borough; best known as hostess of TV's *Big Brother* reality series.

"Gentleman" Jim Corbett (1866–1933) Heavyweight fighter and pioneer of scientific boxing; spent last 30 years of his life in Bayside.

Bob Costas (1952–) Queens native of Irish and Greek descent; longtime TV sports commentator and one of the most respected sportscasters of his era.

Renée Cox (1960–) Came to Queens as an infant; achieved fame with her women- and African American–themed photography and art.

Mario Cuomo (1932–) Influential politician, state governor, and oft-mentioned presidential possibility; Queens native and son of a Jamaica shopkeeper.

Nelson DeMille (1943–) Jamaica native, very successful thriller novelist.

Patty Duke (1946–) Elmhurst native, child actress; an Emmy, Oscar, and Golden Globe winner.

Susan Faludi (1959–) Queens native; Pulitzer Prize winner and feminist author.

Whitey Ford (1928–) From Astoria; career New York Yankee pitcher, winner of 236 regular season and 10 World Series games and member of baseball's Hall of Fame.

Margaret Heckler (1931–) Flushing native; U.S. representative (R-Massachusetts), then secretary of Health & Human Services under the Reagan administration.

Sheila Jackson-Lee (1950–) Jamaica HS alumna, and a U.S. representative (D-Texas) since 1995.

Ja Rule (1976–) Born Jeffrey Atkins from Hollis; popular hip-hop artist.

Cyndi Lauper (1953–) Native; quirky, big-voiced pop icon since the early 1980s.

LL Cool J (1968–) Came out of St. Albans to enjoy a hip-hop career for more than a quarter century at this writing; has also enjoyed writing, acting, and entrepreneurial success.

Ethel Merman (1908–84) Astorian; legendarily strong-voiced singer and actress, doyenne of musical theater for half a century.

Martin Scorsese (1942–) A native of the borough and one of the best and most influential filmmakers in history.

Jerry Springer (1944–) Family moved from England to Kew Gardens in his youth; famous mainly for his shocking TV talk show and guests' frequent confrontations and impromptu violence.

Donald Trump (1946–) Spent some of his youth in Queens; famous for many things: ostentation, real estate, financial crises, flamboyant failed marriages, and a wicked comb-over.

Tales from Central Park: The Zoo

♥ ♥ ♥ ♥

It took a battle to address Central Park's original squatters.

Renowned landscape architect Frederick Law Olmsted was mad as hell. When he and Calvert Vaux drew up the pastoral plans for Central Park in 1858, they made a point not to leave space for a zoo—Olmsted objected to any sort of public menagerie. Now, just after park construction began, the city decided it needed something for animals.

The need for a zoo became clear when a New Yorker abandoned a bear cub in the park. The little critter was just dropped off to wander around and, probably, die. More critters arrived not long after. They were collected and housed, in an ad hoc fashion, around the Arsenal, the park's main building. Obviously, that wasn't a long-term solution.

In 1861, the state legislature authorized "the establishment of a zoological garden." Construction was authorized for the North Meadow, but it was never finished. As dozens of new proposals were debated, the animals remained behind the Arsenal in Victorian-style buildings. The tiny zoo was popular, but the animals didn't fare well.

A Proper Home

In 1934, a newly constructed, modern zoo finally opened, and its residents flourished. Unfortunately, the zoo declined over the decades, and by the 1980s the city parks commissioner referred to it as "Rikers Island for animals." Many people, including those who favored Olmsted's original plans, wanted the animals out altogether.

The zoo was turned over to the Wildlife Conservation Fund, which demolished the painfully small cages and rebuilt the five-acre site around three so-called "biomes." The animals had more breathing room, which reduced the stench and noise their wealthy human neighbors across Fifth Avenue had complained about.

Now that the animals are upstanding park tenants with clean facilities, the Central Park Zoo is one of the most frequently visited places in the park. Maybe even Olmsted would be pleased.

Halls (and Walls) of Fame

♥ ♥ ♥ ♥

*Where does one of the most famous cities in the
world celebrate the famous? Right here!*

New York has the highest population density in the country, the
county boasting the most languages spoken, and the majority of
public transportation users. And throughout its history, the city has
been home to numberless people who achieved in a great variety of
areas. As befits one of the world's great cities, New York has several
archives and collections devoted to local achievers.

Nesuhi Ertegun Jazz Hall of Fame: Jazz lovers can rejoice in the
smooth atmosphere of the Nesuhi Ertegun Jazz Hall of Fame. It is
named for the Atlantic Records executive and located in the Jazz at
Lincoln Center complex. Photos of the honored musicians flash on
an 18-foot-long video wall comprised of 12 panels and accompanied
by pithy quotes. Jazz, of course, plays softly in the background. Those
who can't make it to 110th Street and 5th Avenue to admire the 25-
foot-tall statue of Duke Ellington and his piano lifted by nine muses
can study it in miniature at the hall. Multimedia booths and kiosks
provide facts about the inductees. Only four musicians are inducted
every year. Members include Louis Armstrong, Dizzy Gillespie,
Miles Davis, Gil Evans, Ella Fitzgerald, and Benny Goodman.

Hall of Fame for Great Americans: Billed as America's "original
Hall of Fame," this attraction was completed in 1900, on land that at
the time was part of New York University. Today, the site is on the
grounds of Bronx Community College. The hall displays bronze busts
of 98 notable Americans in 630 feet of space in an open-air colonnade
designed by architect Stanford White. The memorial was built with
spaces to feature 102 Great Americans, but four spaces remain unused.
Induction began in 1900 and continued at five-year intervals until
1970–73. No one has been added since 1976. Early busts were
arranged by category (authors, theologians, scientists, soldiers, and so
forth), as indicated by insets along the walkway, but later busts have no
pattern of placement. Beneath each bust is a plaque that might contain

a snippet of poetry, a line of music, or a brief biography. But who isn't already familiar with the likes of George Washington, the Wright brothers, Thomas Edison, and Robert E. Lee?

Masonic "Wall of Fame": Outside the executive offices of the Masonic Grand Lodge are several display cases that celebrate American leaders who were Masons, such as George Washington and Benjamin Franklin. Recipients of the Grand Lodge Award of Distinction (for example, Red Skelton, John Glenn, Gen. William Bratton, Gen. Douglas MacArthur, and Michael Richards of *Seinfeld* fame) are represented in a photo gallery. More can be learned about each famous Mason downstairs at the Chancellor Robert R. Livingston Masonic Library of Grand Lodge, which has one of the world's largest collections of Freemasonry books and artifacts.

Nathan's Wall of Fame: The Nathan's 4th of July Hot Dog Eating Contest is the Super Bowl of competitive eating, and Nathan's Wall of Fame honors the champs with a mural depicting the hot dog– devouring stars under the coveted "Mustard Belt." Beneath the motto, "They Came. They Ate. They Conquered. All in 12 Minutes," is a list of champions. Compare 2007's winner Joey Chestnut (66 hot dogs) to 1984's champ Birgit Felden (9.5) to see just how far we've advanced in the past few decades.

National Track and Field Hall of Fame: Housed in a onetime armory, this hall of fame celebrating the fleet and the fit is a riot of movement, primary colors, and sound that emanates from dramati- cally placed video screens. Visitors' heart rates rise right from the start. For those moved by such things, track shoes once worn by Olympians Carl Lewis and Mildred "Babe" Didriksen, as well as those of New York City Marathon record breaker Khalid Khannouchi, are on display. You'll also find other sorts of historic athletic gear, plus a scale map of the New York City Marathon. A movie loop highlights great individual achievements in track and field history. Inductees' names are etched into a 40-foot-long glass Wall of Fame overlooking a 65,000-square-foot track and arena. In addition to admiring the Fastest of the Fastest, the Highest Jumpers of the Highest Jumpers, and the Farthest Shot Put Throwers of the Shot Put Throwers, visitors can play with interactive features to learn about nutrition and how to develop an active, healthy lifestyle.

Queen of All Views

♥ ♥ ♥ ♥

How can you stick a toe in the Hudson and one in the Atlantic, or go from the Bronx to Coney Island in one step? By visiting the New York City Panorama, the world's largest architectural model of a city.

In 1964, controversial city planner Robert Moses decided to build a panorama of New York for the upcoming '64 World's Fair. His intentions were two-fold: Not only could he contribute a work of functional art to the city, he would emphasize his accomplishments in urban planning. In keeping with his style of doing things, Moses figured the bigger, the better—and the makers of the panorama delivered.

Measuring 9,335 square feet, the model represents the 321 square miles of the city. One inch equals 100 feet, which means that the Empire State Building, for example, is almost 15 inches tall, representing the nearly 1,500-foot-tall New York landmark. But it's just one of 895,000 tiny buildings, streets, parks, bridges, homes, and waterways that make up the panorama, which was constructed mostly of wood and plastic. Visitors to the fair were impressed and enchanted. At the time of the panorama's creation, the price tag was $672,000—not too bad for an intricate model of what many believe to be "the center of civilization."

A Tiny City Gets an Upgrade

After the World's Fair, the panorama found a home at the Queens Museum and has been there ever since. In 1992, it got a redo. By then, the city had changed considerably, and the panorama was face-lifted to reflect those changes. The freshening project cost more than the original (right around $750,000) but kept the work current for the crowds who make the trip to the museum every year. In 2006, museum officials added a multimedia accompaniment to the exhibit; now various neighborhoods can be lit separately, and audio-visual slideshows are adapted to presentations given on different aspects of the city.

The only things missing from this mini–New York? As of now, there aren't any figures of people—or trash cans.

The Metropolitan Museum: A Week Won't Do It Justice

♥ ♥ ♥ ♥

Try to see it all—just try.

It's entirely possible that even if you don't have attention deficit disorder, you can immediately develop something quite like it simply by walking into New York's vast Metropolitan Museum of Art. The mind-boggling variety of holdings—two million items!—can inspire and intrigue so thoroughly that although visitors might enter with the aim of seeing specific exhibits, they'll depart with heads sent spinning by unanticipated fascinations.

A Museum for the Ages

Widely hailed as one of the world's greatest museums (perhaps *the* greatest, with its only competition the Louvre in Paris), the Met, as it's familiarly known, hosts five million visitors every year. Now 20 times its original size, it occupies more than two million square feet and is almost a quarter of a mile long—the equivalent of four New York City blocks.

Despite the fact that the museum mounts about 30 special exhibitions each year, some of which are then sent on the road, at any given time it can display only a mere fraction of its holdings, which are divided into 22 different departments. Permanent displays include interiors from first-century Rome; paintings by almost all of the European masters (40 by Monet, 23 by Cézanne, 20 Rembrandts, a self-portrait by Van Gogh, works by El Greco and Botticelli, and five Vermeers, the largest collection of that artist's work anywhere in the world); as well as American modern art, which occupies part of the American wing.

There are also massive amounts of drawings, prints, and photographs, as well as a gigantic selection of weapons and armor (one of the museum's most popular collections) and a definitive assortment of

musical instruments. Other divisions include African, Asian, Oceanic, ancient Near-Eastern, Byzantine, and European sculpture and decorative arts; American decorative arts; Greek and Roman work; plus medieval and Islamic art. There are also extensive libraries available to serious students and scholars. Whew!

Let this preface, and the following, serve as warning that you cannot set aside only a few hours to even superficially explore the Met. But the act of *trying* is incredibly enjoyable.

From Small Acorns...

The Metropolitan Museum opened in 1872, two years after its founding by a consortium that included business leaders and artists. Back then, the museum attracted 800,000 guests annually to view its initial collection: a Roman stone sarcophagus (burial object) and an assortment of nearly 200 European paintings. Originally located at 681 Fifth Avenue (now a Tommy Hilfiger store), it moved to a 14th Street mansion in 1873. Those downtown digs soon proved inadequate as well, so a permanent home was finally found on the east side of Central Park. The first building's High Victorian Gothic style was already out of fashion by the time of its completion. Surrounded by newer construction, the original design was relegated to serve as the interior, and by the 1950s, its remnants had been almost entirely stripped away. The striking neoclassical facade still in place was completed in 1926.

The museum is simultaneously overwhelming and surprisingly intimate. Viewers are reminded that every single one of these objects was once created by human beings, many of whom walked the earth many millennia ago: The oldest items here are a set of flints dating back to the Lower Paleolithic period, between 300,000–75,000 B.C.

Jacqueline Kennedy's Temple

One of the museum's biggest draws is its Egyptian artifacts, with 36,000 pieces housed in a 40-gallery wing. The department of Egyptian art was founded in 1906 to oversee a collection that had been growing for decades. That same year, the museum received dispensation from the government of Egypt to excavate at specific sites, a 30-year program that resulted in one of the world's most comprehensive collections of prehistoric and Roman-era antiquities.

Among the most popular attractions are the spectacular mummy cases and, especially, the Temple of Dendur, built circa 15 B.C. as a shrine to the goddess Isis. It was dismantled by the Egyptian government in the mid-1960s before Egypt built the Aswan High Dam, which would have put the sandstone building and other major monuments underwater. A rescue mission mounted in 1960 under UNESCO (the United Nations Educational, Scientific and Cultural Organization) resulted in the reclamation of 24 important archaeological structures, including Dendur. Philippe de Montebello, a longtime Met director, notes that "it was Mrs. [Jacqueline] Kennedy who personally chose the Temple of Dendur... as Egypt's gift to the United States," and it was she who also insisted that it be installed in the Met. Reassembled in 1978 in its own gigantic room, complete with a reflection pond and floor-to-ceiling windows that overlook Central Park, the temple proves that even back in the 19th century, graffiti "artists" couldn't resist a blank surface.

Fashion! (Turn to the Left)

The Met is also home to a world-renowned costume institute, which holds a much-publicized annual fashion fund-raiser. The 700 tickets available (reserved for big-time fashionistas, celebrities, and socialite donors) run from $5,000 to $6,500 apiece. The institute, once helmed by imperious former *Vogue* editor Diana Vreeland, continues to inspire modern designers with over four centuries' worth of clothing and accessories collected from around the world. Past exhibits have included "Rock Style" (mounted in conjunction with Cleveland's Rock and Roll Hall of Fame, it included outfits worn by The Beatles, Mick Jagger, David Bowie, Elvis Presley, Madonna, and Bjork); "AngloMania: Tradition and Transgression in British Fashion" (everything from an outfit custom-made for the famous 19th-century roué Beau Brummel to a women's trouser suit by Stella McCartney, set in period English rooms); "The Model as Muse" (a comprehensive collection devoted to Coco Chanel), and an extremely popular tribute to "Jacqueline Kennedy: The White House Years," complete with the First Lady's inaugural-gala gown and famous pillbox hats.

The bad thing about the Metropolitan Museum is that even the most determined sightseer will only grasp a minute amount of its glories. The good thing is that it's always there to welcome you back.

Battle of Harlem Heights

♥ ♥ ♥ ♥

If you stroll the campus of Columbia University on the city's Upper West Side, the quiet walks and elegant buildings create a sense of tranquility and peace—but it hasn't always been that way.

Nothing about the area near Columbia suggests that it was once the site of a bloody battle, unless you happen to look for, or stumble upon, a bronze marker set in a grassy triangle on Riverside Drive at 121st Street. The modest plaque commemorates the September 16, 1776, Revolutionary War Battle of Harlem Heights, a fierce skirmish between green Continental Army troops under George Washington and a seasoned British Army led by General William Howe. An unplanned, unanticipated fight, the American victory there encouraged the ragtag Continental troops to believe that they could, just maybe, win a war with the greatest military power on earth.

A Surprise for Both Sides

While Washington expected to encounter British troops when they crossed from Queens to the north end of Manhattan Island, General Howe pulled a fast one. His troops, supported by a bombardment from five British frigates with some 86 cannons, landed far south, at Kips' Bay. The largely inexperienced American troops—hungry, underequipped, and, in many cases sick—retreated in a panic. General Washington was furious. Regrouping at Harlem Heights, Washington sent a party of Connecticut Rangers out to determine how far north the British had marched.

The party met with fire at today's West 106th Street, and in retreat the troops were taunted by a bugle call from the enemy that traditionally signaled the end of a foxhunt and the going to ground of the fox. Stung, Washington immediately sent a larger force to engage the British. After a bloody, daylong encounter, the British were sent flying—the first time, it's said, that Continental troops saw the backs of Redcoats and Hessians. Though the victory was short-lived—the Continental Army was soon pushed north—the Battle of Harlem Heights was a critical turning point in American morale.

Local Legends

It's no secret that New York City includes a reasonably sizable homeless population. According to the Coalition for the Homeless, for instance, every night of March 2010 saw more than 38,000 homeless people sleeping in municipal shelters. Thousands more were forced to sleep outdoors in parks, on the streets, and in the subway system.

Wait a minute—the subway system? One legend involving the city's have-nots remains a mystery. The labyrinthine tunnels of the subway system contain an awful lot of empty space. Sure, it's dark, dirty, and dangerous, but settlers in the area generally don't have their turf invaded. And some tunnels even have free electricity.

The homeless population inhabiting the subway tunnels is sometimes referred to as "the mole people," and years of study and a lot of speculation have yielded few facts about them. For starters, no one is sure how many homeless people live underground. Some say hundreds; others, thousands. The lore surrounding the mole people can get quite bizarre. Some of the more creative urban legends purport that underground dwellers have evolved webbed feet to navigate the mucky terrain and are cannibals preying on unobservant commuters.

In 1993, journalist Jennifer Toth published *The Mole People: Life in the Tunnels Beneath New York City,* a controversial book in which she claims to have visited mole people in the tunnels. The book details a complex underground society with a justice system and official governing powers. But many people, including public transportation experts, smelled a rat. Details didn't all add up, especially Toth's architectural descriptions of the tunnel networks.

So here's what we do know: Some homeless people live underground in the subway tunnels, especially around the transportation hubs of Penn Station and Grand Central Station. It can't be confirmed whether these people are living independently or if they've established hierarchical underground cities. But don't worry—if you doze off on the train, you're far more likely to miss your stop or get your wallet stolen than you are to be eaten.

Last Exit to Brooklyn

♥ ♥ ♥ ♥

Last Exit to Brooklyn *is a forlorn portrait of midcentury urban America. Although some today are obsessed with end-of-the-world scenarios and apocalyptic fears of meteors, mayhem, and Mayans, Hubert Selby Jr.'s scalding narrative is a reminder to us that nothing truly extraordinary needs to happen for life to go horribly wrong.*

Grove Press published *Last Exit to Brooklyn* in 1964, when Selby was 36 years old. It was his first novel. The book is comprised of six narratives, some of which had appeared earlier as individual pieces in literary journals. As a group, the tales revolve, if sometimes tenuously, around a place of business called The Greeks, "a beatup all night diner near the Brooklyn Armybase."

The Heart of Darkness

The story is set in the 1950s, a period generally recalled as one of America's sunnier decades. But according to Selby, it was a period of deep frustration that became the backdrop to failure. The book opens with the savage beating of a soldier by local punks and doesn't grow any more lighthearted as the story progresses. In the segment called "The Queen Is Dead," Georgette, a transvestite, shows up at a party of hoods and drag queens. She longs to be with Vinnie, one of the neighborhood thugs from the opening sequence. Such bad judgment runs wild in *Last Exit,* so there is a pitiless logic in the fact that, during the Benzedrine- and booze-fueled night of the party, backbiting turns to sexual violence. Similar tensions are at the core of "Strike," in which a witless fellow named Harry abuses his mid-level union position to ingratiate himself with money-hungry drag queens. At home, he resents and beats his wife.

"Tralala" follows the exploits of a female character of that name, who pursues a buck by using men and her body—and the occasional bottle over victims' heads. Drug abuse and the grind of growing older send Tralala into a spiral that climaxes in brutal, unreasoning violence.

There's no doubt that *Last Exit to Brooklyn* is an unpleasant book. Unadventurous readers may question its value. But the novel practically bursts with insights into people and the sorry consequences of poverty, stunted educations, and shriveled souls.

Beat godfather Allen Ginsberg declared that *Last Exit to Brooklyn* would "explode like a rusty hellish bombshell over America," and he was right. When "Tralala" appeared as a short story, it sparked an obscenity trial in the United States that was eventually thrown out of court. The book's influence stretched across the Atlantic, where an obscenity case surrounding its publication helped end literary censorship in the United Kingdom.

Raw and Uncut

Because *Last Exit to Brooklyn* dispenses with apostrophes or quotation marks, the novel has a peculiar, rushing urgency. Words tumble off the page. Dialogue runs amidst narrative text without any distinguishing marks. Swearing, street jargon, and other colloquial language of the '50s give the book a bleakly matter-of-fact feel.

Plot and structure are also unorthodox—all part of Selby's scheme to eliminate any sort of conventional device that might keep readers at arm's length. Pick up this harsh, New York novel, and you're not just an outsider, not just a witness, but a (possibly unwilling) coconspirator.

From the pathetic Tralala to skimming union organizers, from the drunken servicemen to the sugar daddy who hunts transvestites, Selby's characters shine a light into all the dark corners of Brooklyn. It's a harsh light. Everybody we meet wears deep scars picked up during life's daily grind. Few of the people are honest, even to themselves. *Last Exit to Brooklyn* is the dark, urban counterpart to the revelatory journey Jack Kerouac undertook and wrote about in *On the Road.* Kerouac's vision was reasonably optimistic, even exalted, but in Selby's Brooklyn, ideas are small, life is short, and people are quick to revert to their animal natures.

High-School Dropout

Selby was born in Brooklyn in 1928. His father was a coal miner and Merchant Marine. Selby left high school after just a year and then lied about his age in order to follow his father into the merchant marine. He contracted tuberculosis and had ten ribs removed as part

of experimental treatments. Recovering in
New York, he became addicted to morphine.
Doctors told Selby he wouldn't live long.

The TB and a string of dead-end jobs
didn't exactly suggest a bright and shining
future for Selby. Fortunately, he received
encouragement to write from childhood
friend and novelist Gilbert Sorrentino. Grove
Press had a long history of publishing contro-
versial manuscripts, so many readers were predisposed to be excited
by *Last Exit to Brooklyn.* The attempts at institutionalized censorship that followed were priceless publicity. The book brought Selby
notoriety and infamy. More significantly, it hasn't been out of print
since it was first published.

Selby followed up with 1971's *The Room,* about a prisoner who
dwells in his own heroic and violent revenge fantasies. Selby's other
notable work is 1978's *Requiem for a Dream,* which looked at heroin
addiction among three friends (and was later adapted into an acclaimed film by Darren Aronofsky in 2000). *Last Exit* made it to
the big screen, too, in 1989, as a hard-hitting U.S.-German
coproduction.

Selby was married three times and fathered four children.
Respectable and acclaimed at last, he taught creative writing at the
University of Southern California for two decades before his death
in 2004.

- *How cheap was Brooklyn Dodgers owner Charles Ebbets? In
  1913, he disrupted the Opening Day flag procession to look for
  15 cents he had dropped. Plus, he refused help, lest someone else
  find and keep the coins.*

- *Peter Stuyvesant (1612–72) tried to expel Jewish refugees who had
  landed in Manhattan after leaving Brazil.*

- *During the Revolutionary War, some 11,000 Continental prisoners
  of war died in British prison hulks (dismasted ships) moored in
  Wallabout Bay, off Brooklyn. A memorial in Fort Greene Park
  honors the fallen patriots.*

Fast Facts

- *The Lenape (Delaware) Native Americans on Manhattan mainly farmed in modern Harlem, East Harlem, Greenwich Village, and the East Village. Lower Broadway was part of a Lenape trail that stretched from the Battery to Inwood.*

- *The Bronx Bombers didn't start out either as Yankees or in the Bronx. Formerly the Baltimore Orioles, the New York Highlanders began play at Hilltop Park (Washington Heights) in 1903. The team became Yankees in 1913 and moved to the Bronx ten years later.*

- *Jackie Gleason was born on Brooklyn's Herkimer Street in 1916. He was an inveterate comedian even back then. One day he spread Limburger cheese on the radiators of P.S. 73, closing school for a day.*

- Phytophthora infestans—*better known as late blight of potato—actually appeared in New York (in 1843; also in Philly) before it crossed the Atlantic to send more than a million starving Irish fleeing to America.*

- *The 9-foot palisade the Dutch built along future Wall Street (thus the modern name) in 1653 proved useless against Native American raiders. They came by canoe. Whoops!*

- *Before New York had elevated trains and subways, it had horse-drawn railcars. From 1832 until 1871, these comprised the city's dominant mass transit system. The system's ground-bound inadequacies inspired the el trains.*

- *Julia Gardiner Tyler (1820–89) came from Gardiner's Island but spent about ten years living on Staten Island. She was the one who initiated playing of "Hail to the Chief" during husband John Tyler's presidency.*

- *Builders started on New York City Hall in 1803. It took more than seven years to finish and cost almost half a million dollars (not adjusted for inflation). Fee for the winning design: $350.*

The Fabulous Plaza

♥ ♥ ♥ ♥

"Nothing unimportant ever happens at the Plaza." Thousands of New Yorkers who love the legendary hotel stand behind that famous claim.

For the past 100-plus years, the Plaza Hotel on Central Park South and Fifth Avenue has stood as one of Manhattan's premier landmarks. Glamorous and luxurious, "the castle on the park," as its current owners call it, has been seen in movies from *North by Northwest* to *The Way We Were* and figures in F. Scott Fitzgerald novels, a particularly
notable children's-book classic, and thousands of weddings, birthdays, honeymoons, proposals, and parties. It's also been a temporary home to political and sports stars, countless members of royalty, and celebrities such as The Beatles, Marlene Dietrich, Marilyn Monroe, Jackie Kennedy Onassis, and Mark Twain.

For generations of New Yorkers, the hotel's luscious Palm Court restaurant was the place for an elegant brunch or lunch, and the Oak Bar was *the* place to meet for a cocktail—or for several after work or the theater. The Plaza's image as the epitome of luxury has been lovingly polished since it opened its doors in 1907. Built at a cost of $12 million—a true fortune at the time—it was a skyscraper at 19 stories and the talk of New York. Modeled after a French chateau, it was set in an upper-crust residential neighborhood and filled with imported European treasures, including 1,650 crystal chandeliers. That's impressive, but get this: The then-new hotel placed the largest single order in history for gold-encrusted china.

Misbehavin'

Originally conceived as a residence for the wealthy, the Plaza registered as its first guests Mr. and Mrs. Alfred Gwynne Vanderbilt. The hotel soon added a wing for "transients," who were charged the princely sum of $2.50 a night for a luxury room (rates now begin at more than $600).

According to Curtis Gathje, the Plaza's official historian, more than one famous guest has been the source of scandal—long before rowdy rock stars. A month after the hotel opened, Mrs. Patrick Campbell, a world-renowned British actress, came to stay. Known for her sometimes-outrageous opinions and conduct, she lit up an Egyptian cigarette after dinner in the Palm Court and sent the place into chaos. When she refused to extinguish the offending smoke, a screen was hastily brought into the dining room so she could misbehave without offending other guests. The incident made the papers.

Eloise Buys a Condo

The Plaza's most famous guest doesn't even exist. This is, of course, Eloise, the central character of delightfully funny books written by Kay Thompson and illustrated by Hilary Knight. Kay Thompson was a legendary actress and singer known for her cabaret act and for such films as *Funny Face,* in which she danced Fred Astaire's feet off as a force-of-nature fashion editor (remember the "Clap Yo' Hands" number?). In 1955, she wrote a small book based on a character that sometimes appeared in her cabaret act, a precocious six-year-old. A much-debated story has it that the high-spirited if badly behaved little girl, who lives at the Plaza with her nanny, a turtle named Skipperdee, and a dog named Weenie, was based on Thompson's goddaughter, Liza Minnelli. In any case, *Eloise: A Book for Precocious Grownups* became a classic and was followed by several more Eloise books, which in turn netted Thompson free rent at the Plaza for many years. A life-size portrait of Eloise still hangs in the hotel and is continually visited by many little and not-so-little girls.

Now an official national and New York historic landmark, the Plaza was bought by the El-Ad Group of Israel in 2004, which announced plans to turn the hotel into high-priced condominiums, much to the chagrin of many New Yorkers. The building reopened in 2008 after a $400 million facelift and redesign. It now contains 181 condominiums and 282 guest rooms, managed by Fairmont Hotels. Fortunately the Oak Room restaurant and the Oak Bar, where Cary Grant was kidnapped during *North by Northwest,* are back in grand style, as is the Palm Court.

Reggie! Reggie! Reggie!

♥ ♥ ♥ ♥

The Setting: Yankee Stadium; October 18, 1977

The Magic: Reggie Jackson earns the title "Mr. October" with three homers on consecutive pitches in the Yankees' World Series victory-clinching game.

Reggie Jackson didn't just crave the spotlight—he downright hogged it. Before he signed with the Yankees, he announced of New York: "If I played there they'd name a candy bar after me." (He was right—when he got there, they did.) Upon his arrival in 1977, he told a reporter, "I'm the straw that stirs the drink." And he proved it with one night of amazing power.

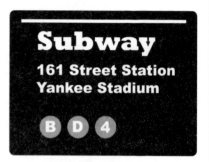

The Yankees had returned to the World Series in 1976 for the first time in 12 years (a mighty long stretch for the Yanks), only to get stomped in four games. In '77, they led the Series 3–2 over the Dodgers, but the men from L.A. had gone ahead in Game 6 on a solo homer by "the other Reggie," Reggie Smith. With one on and none out in the fourth, Jackson swatted the first pitch he saw from Burt Hooton over the right-field fence, and the Yanks were up 4–3. Jackson came to bat again in the fifth, with a Yank on first and two down. He cracked the first pitch he saw from Elias Sosa even farther back into the right-field stands. Two pitches, two homers for Reggie; Yanks up 7–3. Jackson batted again in the eighth, this time against Charlie Hough. Hough's first offering was his famous knuckleball, and Reggie creamed it. That made three homers on three swings. Jackson became only the second player to knock three dingers in one Series game (Babe Ruth was the other). On that night for sure, Mr. October didn't just stir the drink—he shook it.

Ach du Lieber, It's Jerry Cotton!

♥ ♥ ♥ ♥

*The best and most famous FBI agent in New
York has never even been in the city!*

German readers devour *krimi* novels—homegrown mystery and crime
thrillers bursting with hot women and unabashedly lurid violence. The
most popular *krimi* hero is FBI agent Jerry Cotton, whose first book,
G-Man, was published in 1954. Jerry Cotton has long been owned by
Bastei-Lübbe Publishing, which has issued Cotton novels and stories
created by at least 60 anonymous writers. (Jerry's creator and first
writer, Delfried Kaufmann, wasn't acknowledged until 1998!) Across
50 countries and nearly 20 languages, with more than 750 million
copies sold, Jerry Cotton risks everything to protect New York.

Give My Regards to *Broadway Strasse*

By 1965, Cotton was one of the most popular characters in Germany
and Europe, so a film adaptation was the next obvious move. Holly-
wood leading man George Nader traveled to Germany to play
Cotton in all eight films in the 1965–69 series. From the first one
(*Schüsse aus dem Geigenkasten* aka *The Violin Case Murders*) to the
last (*Todesschüsse am Broadway* aka *Dead Body on Broadway*),
Nader filled the bill: athletic and ruggedly handsome, with a
Brylcreem pompadour and plenty of well-cut suits and skinny ties.

Nader spoke English and was dubbed later; the other actors spoke
German. Second-unit crews in NYC filmed the skyline and streets and
made endless telephoto shots of Cotton's red Jaguar careening around
Manhattan. But nobody in the various casts ever went to New York.
Many "exterior" closeups of the city were faked in-studio, with the
actors in front of clumsy rear-projection screens showing the second-
unit footage. Genuine exteriors were shot in Hamburg and Berlin and
looked *nothing* like the Big Apple. Oh, but we quibble! In 2010, Jerry
Cotton enjoyed his first fake-New York film adventure in 41 years—a
spoofy, big-budget release from (where else?) Germany.

The Merchant's House Museum

♥ ♥ ♥ ♥

*Mind your manners around Gertrude. That's the best
advice one can receive before traveling to the East Village
to visit this 1832 structure—the city's only 19th-century
family home to be preserved intact, inside and out.*

In 1835, Seabury Tredwell, an importer
of metal hardware, paid $18,000 for
what is today the Merchant's House
Museum. Additions such as the cast-iron
stove notwithstanding (more about that
later), the house and its furnishings
remain pretty much as they were when
the Tredwells moved in.

   A prime example of the Greek-
Revival style, the Tredwell home was
eventually purchased by a cousin and
opened as a museum in 1935. It's notable for its original and renovated furnishings and details. The glass-globed chandeliers, installed
circa 1852, are believed to be the oldest domestic gas fixtures *in situ*
in the United States. Back in the Tredwells' day, the chandeliers
would have been lit only for special occasions.

Don't Turn Around: It's Gertrude

Five years into the family's occupancy, Gertrude, the eighth Tredwell
child, was born. Never married, she lived in the home until her
death in 1933. There are those who say she's stayed on ever since,
and she could certainly have her reasons for hanging around. Dad
Tredwell was a strict Anglican who allegedly refused to allow his
youngest child to marry her true love, a Catholic medical student
named Lewis Walton. (Henry James's novel, *Washington Square*,
may have been based on Gertrude's life.) Latter-day visitors have
seen Gertrude's apparition upstairs and in the kitchen. And late at
night, music has emanated from the front parlor, where Gertrude
was fond of playing the rosewood piano.

Public Life

That front parlor, where Gertrude's piano sits near a black-and-gold marble fireplace, is where the family would have entertained. Sliding mahogany doors separate this room from the rear parlor, where the gents smoked and investigated the liquor cabinet. Sometimes it seems as if the Tredwells have merely stepped out just for a moment.

There's much in the way of damask drapery, horsehair-stuffed sofas, and exquisitely carved mahogany, including a dozen hand-made "balloon-back" chairs attributed to renowned designer Duncan Phyfe (1768–1854); some of his other works are displayed in the Metropolitan Museum. The costume collection consists of over 400 items of clothing, with one dress dating back to 1815 and a complete wedding ensemble (including satin boots) from 1872.

Behind the Scenes

Beyond the parlors is the kitchen, where a "beehive" baking oven (so-called for its domed top) built into the brick wall is still employed almost daily to fill a perforated pie safe that stands nearby. The second floor, where the bedrooms are located, offers a privileged perspective, especially when you notice the chamber pots that did their duty in those days before indoor toilets. A novel selection of the pots' seats resides comfortably inside a glass cabinet.

One occasional exhibit, "Called by the Bell: The Life of a 19th-Century Domestic Servant," outlines the onerous duties once per-formed by the four-member household staff, mostly Irish women aged 18 to 41. Private family rooms, with canopied beds, cribs, and rather spare general furnishings, can induce an uneasy feeling of voyeurism in observers. These rooms were private spaces, and they feel like it.

Most Haunted?

But it's not strangers that seem to perturb Gertrude: The cast-iron stove, retrofitted into the kitchen in the mid-1970s, is the apparent focus of her ire. One caretaker claims that it has been shaken violently—more than once—by an unseen force. Well, the *New York Times* did say that this was "Manhattan's most haunted house."

So as long as you're polite when you visit, Gertrude should re-turn the favor. After all, she was brought up a lady, in a gentler time.

Famous People from Manhattan

♥ ♥ ♥ ♥

*Here's a sampling of noteworthy folks with
connections to Manhattan.*

Kareem Abdul-Jabbar (1947–) Grew up as Lew Alcindor in
Manhattan; one of basketball's all-time great "big men."

Jennifer Aniston (1969–) Grew up in Manhattan, alumna of the
High School of the Performing Arts; A-list actress.

Louis Armstrong (1901–71) Came to the Apple in his 20s; eventually came to define jazz with his rich voice and sweet trumpet notes.

John J. Astor (1763–1848) Immigrant to the borough who picked a
great time to put his fur fortune into Manhattan real estate.

Phineas T. Barnum (1810–91) Did much of his hokiest and most
entertaining showmanship in Manhattan; won't win any awards for
disability sensitivity, but people *did* flock to his circus and museum.

Angela Bassett (1958–) Harlem native and actress in films such as
How Stella Got Her Groove Back and *What's Love Got to Do with It?*

Harry Belafonte (1927–) Native, and a George Washington High
alumnus; known both for his long folk music career—first African
American Emmy winner—and strident civil rights activism.

Kurtis Blow (1959–) Harlem native, and one of hip-hop's first
successful artists; now a minister, he has become a strong force
against violence associated with hip-hop culture.

Humphrey Bogart (1899–1957) Native; iconic dramatic actor
famed especially for *Casablanca* and *The Maltese Falcon.*

"Diamond" Jim Brady (1856–1917) Native; pre–World War I
tycoon and financier who was famous for how much he could eat.

William F. Buckley Jr. (1925–2008) Famed Manhattan-born
author, columnist, and spokesperson for conservative thought.

Aaron Burr (1756–1836) Practiced law in Manhattan for a time
while living in Richmond Hill; became the nation's third vice
president—and the only serving VP—to kill a political rival in a duel.

James Cagney (1899–1986) Native of the Lower East Side; his tough upbringing led to a great career playing tough guys in film.

George Carlin (1937–2008) Native, raised in Morningside Heights; comic, social critic, and challenger of media censorship.

Richard Carmona (1949–) Harlem native; went to Vietnam with Special Forces and later became a doctor, then U.S. surgeon general.

Willa Cather (1873–1947) Acclaimed novelist who lived much of her later life in Greenwich Village.

Bennett Cerf (1898–1971) Native; cofounder of Random House and a noted humorist and TV personality.

Roy Cohn (1927–86) Native; a John Bircher who gained fame in the McCarthy era as a scourge of perceived Commies, and as a prosecutor in the Rosenberg spy trial.

Bob Cousy (1928–) From Yorkville; accelerated the pace of basketball with fancy ball handling, which led him to a Hall of Fame career.

Robert De Niro (1943–) His hugely successful and respected film career has spanned more than 40 years; grew up in Little Italy.

"Big Bill" Dwyer (1883–1946) Hell's Kitchen native who dominated Manhattan bootlegging during Prohibition.

Vincent "The Chin" Gigante (1928–2005) Native; had a notorious racketeering career and used to make a point of meandering around the Village in his bathrobe talking to himself.

Allen Ginsberg (1926–97) Major figure in the city's Beat movement for years; writer and poet.

Alan Greenspan (1926–) Washington Heights native who spent 19 influential years as Federal Reserve chairman.

Anna Roosevelt Halsted (1906–75) Born on East 36th Street; daughter of President Franklin D. Roosevelt and Eleanor Roosevelt.

Armand Hammer (1898–1990) Native; oil tycoon with a long, colorful and independent life.

Kitty Carlisle Hart (1910–2007) Lived in the borough for many years; best known outside the city for acting and TV, was beloved in NYC for personal grace and staunch support of the arts.

Nathan's Famous Hot Dogs

♥ ♥ ♥ ♥

*Eating as New Yorkers did back in 1916 is still
possible, even if it costs a bit more today.*

Every sunny summer day, the hungry, sweaty masses burst into
Nathan's Famous eatery on Coney Island's Surf Avenue, just as they
have done for almost a century. Steam from the kitchen adds to the
heat. The smell of grease weighs down the already humid air. Kids
clamor for crinkle-cut fries, elders want fried clams, and aspiring
professional eaters cram hot dogs down their gullets.

In 1916, Nathan Handwerker set up a stand in Coney and sold
frankfurters made from his wife's secret recipe. Soon he had enough
business to open a permanent restaurant. Nathan's Famous began
selling fizzy cold Coca-Cola that year, too. (In fact, Nathan's is one of
Coke's oldest customers.) It wasn't just everyday New Yorkers who
loved Nathan's beefy product—celebrities, athletes, and politicians
clamored for them, too. President Franklin Roosevelt even served
Nathan's to the king and queen of England when they visited the
United States in 1939.

The Contest

According to local legend, Nathan's annual July 4 hot dog–eating
contest was inaugurated in 1916, when four European immigrants
settled a bet about who was most patriotic by setting out to eat the
most franks. The winner of that first competition downed 13 dogs in
12 minutes. Today the contest is televised, and contestants gobble
more than 60 Nathan's Famous Frankfurters and fluffy buns in that
same amount of time.

A Nathan's Famous hot dog costs a lot more today than it did in
1916, but the taste of history is worth it. Only at Nathan's Famous
can people enjoy what Mayor Rudy Giuliani called "the world's best
hot dog." Nathan's franks were served at Walter Matthau's funeral,
and Barbra Streisand had a batch shipped to her in London. But the
most enthusiastic fans are the regular folks who make Nathan's a
must-visit destination.

Fast Facts

- *The single largest obstacle to the city's growth in the early 1800s was the water supply. New York solved this in the early 1840s with the Croton Aqueduct, which brought water from the mainland.*

- *Early Manhattan used to be quite hilly, with mounds as high as 100 feet above sea level. Most of these were graded flat and used as landfill. Of course,* manna-hatta *meant "hilly island" in Lenape.*

- *What did Manhattanites do with garbage before big scows existed to remove it? They threw it in the water to make new land. A good percentage of the Manhattan coast is built on garbage, or "landfill," as it's more politely called.*

- *When Ranger goalie Lorne Chabot went down in Game 2 of the 1928 Stanley Cup, 44-year-old coach Lester Patrick stepped into the goal himself. His men checked like fiends, and New York went on to win the game (in overtime) and the Cup.*

- *Manhattan native William Alexander (1726–83) was a general in the Continental Army and a trusted deputy of George Washington. He was also a British peer as Lord Stirling, though the soreheads in the House of Lords refused to recognize him.*

- *The Woolworth Building's roof used to have ornamental copper cladding. It may have become field telephone wire for the Army, because it was stripped and donated as scrap copper during World War II.*

- *A good percentage of the Civil War photos you see today came from Mathew Brady (1822–96), who had studios in New York. He ultimately went broke and died a pauper in a charity ward.*

- *William "Boss" Tweed may have been corrupt and dirtier than a Five Points alley, but he did establish the principle that Albany, the state capital, couldn't boss around New York City whenever it felt like it. That attitude helped Tweed gain control of many NYC institutions.*

Dearly Departed
Department Stores

♥   ♥   ♥   ♥

*Gone but not forgotten, many of Manhattan's most celebrated
shopping emporiums were indelible symbols of their era.*

The shopper's dream: a store that has "everything." In New York, it
all began in 1846 at 280 Broadway, between Chambers and Reade
streets in Lower Manhattan. There, inside a building whose
Italianate, marble-clad exterior earned it the sobriquet the "Marble
Palace," an Irish-born entrepreneur named A. T. Stewart offered
New Yorkers imported European merchandise at fixed prices. Select
pieces were displayed behind huge French plate glass windows and
in fashion shows that took place within the store's second-floor
"ladies parlor." It was a little bit of the Continent in New York.

Everybody Goes to Stewart's ... and Elsewhere

This innovative approach to retailing established A. T. Stewart as
America's very first department store and encouraged Stewart's
1862 construction of a larger, six-story, cast-iron-fronted structure
on a full city block at Broadway between Ninth and Tenth streets.
Inside the new store, shoppers were dazzled by extensive collections
of clothing, furniture, toys, and glassware.

Stewart's success led to the establishment of similar retail stores
such as R. H. Macy, B. Altman, Bergdorf Goodman, Lord & Taylor,
Arnold Constable, Siegel-Cooper, Simpson-Crawford, Stern
Brothers, McCreery's, and LeBoutellier, dotting lower Broadway all
the way from the aforementioned "Cast Iron Palace" up to 23rd
Street. This was a place to see and be seen, a fashionable stretch
known as "The Ladies' Mile."

Over the ensuing generations, some of the old, established
department stores have remained New York landmarks. These
include Lord & Taylor, the first such emporium on Fifth Avenue, as
well as the first to offer passersby eye-catchingly creative Christmas
windows; Bergdorf Goodman, the esteemed art deco home of

imported European fashions, where Doris Day enjoyed a shopping spree at Cary Grant's expense in the 1962 screen comedy *That Touch of Mink;* and Macy's, whose flagship Herald Square location was the setting for the classic 1947 Yuletide movie *Miracle on 34th Street.* Boasting more than one million square feet of retail space, Macy's was the world's largest store from 1924 until June 2009, when it was overtaken by Shinsegae Centum City in Busan, South Korea.

Into the Bargain Basement

Unfortunately, numerous other Big Apple retail giants are no longer around, but that doesn't mean that people who once shopped there don't still talk about them and mourn their loss. Take Gimbels, once Macy's main rival, located so close that, in *Miracle on 34th Street,* the latter store's Santa advises a mother to visit Gimbels for the roller skates that are sold out at his own establishment. The public loved that. Okay, so the more upmarket Macy's had its celebrated Thanksgiving Day Parade, but Gimbels had a bargain basement, the first in Manhattan, that underscored its slogan, "Nobody but nobody undersells Gimbels"—that is, until the store closed its doors in 1987.

Another dearly departed department store—particularly in the eyes of the fashion-conscious who shopped there—was Bonwit Teller, noted for its high-end ladies' apparel that attracted such clients as Marilyn Monroe, Jackie Kennedy, and Audrey Hepburn. Bonwit also supplied Grace Kelly's outfits for the 1955 Alfred Hitchcock thriller, *To Catch a Thief.*

Another store beloved by *fashionistas* was B. Altman, located just a short distance along Fifth Avenue, whose Christmas windows rivaled those of Lord & Taylor. One of Altman's most popular attractions, the Charleston Gardens restaurant, had ornate murals and a plantation-style facade that helped patrons enjoy the gentility and conservatism of a bygone age.

Many of the great NYC department stores had classy eateries as well as clothing, household necessities, beauty products, jewelry, and toys. In-store restaurants were fun lunchtime meeting places and handy stop-offs for busy shoppers who needed to recharge their batteries before continuing to assault their pocketbooks. Hungry shoppers were tempted by assorted home-style dishes that ranged from potpies, soups, and salads to club sandwiches and fat-friendly desserts.

42nd Street: Low and Lively

♥ ♥ ♥ ♥

Despite the recent cleanup, many New Yorkers still recall this famous street's down-and-dirty years with fondness and a sense of loss.

The United Nations Headquarters, the Chrysler Building, Grand Central Terminal, the New York Public Library, Bryant Park, Times Square—in a straight run from the East River to the Hudson, 42nd Street boasts many of the city's most celebrated landmarks. Nevertheless, this colorful thoroughfare has also experienced its fair share of twists and turns. Once the hub of vaudeville and the legitimate theater, it subsequently morphed into the showbiz-and-strip-joint haven whose name was celebrated in the popular 1933 Warner Bros. movie musical.

The Bad Old Days

"Where the underworld can meet the elite, 42nd Street," sang Ruby Keeler in the film's title number, alluding to the mixed bag of individuals who then regularly crowded the stretch between Broadway and Eighth Avenue that had attracted burlesque houses and cut-price movie palaces since the onset of the Great Depression. The elite largely kept their distance once the pornmeisters, druggies, and hookers had transformed this area into a crime-infested center of seediness by the early 1960s. Yet, some New Yorkers still yearn for the high-energy, down-and-dirty part of town that, since its sanitization in the mid-'90s, they have derided as a corporate theme park and midtown-suburban shopping mall.

The first theater came to 42nd Street in 1893, and by the early 1920s there were no fewer than 12 such establishments, including the New Amsterdam, where Sophie Tucker made her debut in the Ziegfeld Follies; the Republic, where the Irish-Jewish comedy *Abie's Irish Rose* became one of Broadway's longest running shows; the Selwyn, which staged the works of Somerset Maugham, George S. Kaufman, Edna Ferber, Noel Coward, and Cole Porter; the Lyric, where the likes of Fred Astaire and the Marx Brothers took to the stage; and the Apollo, which hosted performances by stars such as

Lionel Barrymore, Jimmy Durante, W. C. Fields, Ethel Merman, and Rudy Vallee.

Bump 'n' Grind

During the second half of the 1920s, the construction of newer theaters effectively relocated Broadway's epicenter to the area between 45th and 46th streets, and this, together with Prohibition and the Wall Street Crash of '29, forced many of the 42nd Street establishments to screen cheapo exploitation flicks or resort to the bump 'n' grind of burlesque in order to survive. The slide into sleaze had begun, and this reached its nadir—or, as fans might say, its height—during the 1960s, '70s, and '80s, when the neighborhood's crummy collection of flophouses, strip clubs, and adult bookstores, swarming with pimps, prostitutes, cross-dressers, mobsters, and thrill-seekers, gave rise to the quip that 42nd Street was so named because it wasn't safe to spend more than 40 seconds there.

The fact was many people were still willing to take the chance, including several million tourists who flocked there each year to gawk at the goods and often pay to sample them. Yet, others were not so impressed, including New York City Mayor Ed Koch (tenure 1978–89), whose closure of 42nd Street's "grindhouse" porn movie theaters in a series of late-night raids commenced the cleanup that continued during the next decade.

Back to the Mainstream

Today, the "New 42nd Street" has upscale shops and restaurants that have risen from the ashes of their dilapidated predecessors, as well as state-of-the-art Broadway theaters. These include the Hilton Theatre, constructed from the old Lyric and Apollo theaters; the five-story Forest City Ratner entertainment complex, which includes a 25-screen AMC theater and grew out of the old Liberty, Harris, and Empire theaters; the American Airlines Theater that stands on the site of the old Selwyn facility; and the totally renovated New Amsterdam, which is now operated by Disney Theatrical Productions. Who would have predicted that Disney, the purveyor of all things innocent, would base itself in *the* place with a storied history of selling the exact opposite?

The Literary Village

♥ ♥ ♥ ♥

Greenwich Village has always welcomed the offbeat. Here are a few of the great writers who once called these streets their own.

Storytelling seems to come easily in this part of town, with its cozy tangle of small streets. It's tempting to conjure up the vision of Washington Irving ensconced at his sister's home at 11 Commerce Street circa 1819, possibly writing "The Legend of Sleepy Hollow." Up the block at #38 is the Cherry Lane Theatre, established in 1924 by poet Edna St. Vincent Millay. She lived around the corner at 75 Bedford Street in "the narrowest house in New York"—still a highly coveted domicile, despite the fact that it measures just 9.5 feet at its widest. Originally constructed in 1873, the house's 1930s inhabitants included *New Yorker* cartoonist and "Shrek" creator William Steig, his first wife, and her sister, anthropologist Margaret Mead.

Down by the River

On the West Side, a couple of blocks east of the Hudson River, stands St. Luke in the Fields (487 Hudson Street), founded in part by church warden Clement Clark Moore, who wrote 1822's beloved "A Visit from St. Nicholas" ('Twas the night before Christmas . . ."). A bit farther north, at 567 Hudson and 11th Street, the White Horse Tavern occupies a wooden structure that dates to the mid-1600s. The tavern has served everyone from Jack Kerouac (who used to be thrown out on a regular basis) to John F. Kennedy Jr., but it is primarily known for the legend that Welsh poet Dylan Thomas drank himself to death here by downing 18 whiskeys in one go. In truth, Thomas imbibed a few beers at the tavern on November 9, 1953; he was already feeling ill and died a few days later at nearby St. Vincent's Hospital. (The myth makes for a better story, though.)

John Lennon to Emma Lazarus

Sinclair Lewis lived at 69 Charles Street for three years, beginning in 1910; Woody Guthrie had a brief 1942–43 tenancy at #74 (and wrote "This Land Is Your Land" while living on 14th Street—the northern-

most border of the Village). Maurice Sendak (*Where the Wild Things Are*) is thought to have lived at #92. In 1971, John Lennon and Yoko Ono moved into their first New York apartment together a few blocks north at 105 Bank Street.

Not all the Village's famous alumni actually *lived* here. Thomas Paine, the author of "Common Sense," passed away in 1809 at 59 Grove Street, off Seventh Avenue. The original building is long gone, but a plaque on the present structure notes its significance.

A few steps west of Tenth Street and Sixth Avenue is the little gated alley called Patchin Place, which at one point or another was home to poet e.e. cummings (for 40 years), critic Djuna Barnes, journalist John Reed *(Ten Days That Shook the World)*, and writer Theodore Dreiser. Across Sixth, just west of Fifth Avenue is 14 West Tenth Street, where Mark Twain is said to haunt the stairwell—even though he spent only a year here in 1901, enjoying far more time at 21 Fifth Avenue. Emma Lazarus dwelled a few doors down at #18; her 1883 sonnet "The New Colossus" ("Give me your tired, your poor") is immortalized on a bronze plaque at the Statue of Liberty.

Mid-Village

To the southeast lies Washington Square Park, hotbed of 1950s bohemia and 1960s rebellion. Henry James's 1880 *Washington Square* was inspired by visiting his grandmother at what was then 19 Washington Square North (the numbering system has changed). In 1882, James's friend Edith Wharton moved in a few steps away, with her mother, at #7. Wharton's keen observations of latter-19th-century New York society informed her 1920 novel *The Age of Innocence,* making her the first female recipient of a Pulitzer Prize.

Master of the Macabre—and Moving

Although Edgar Allan Poe spent his final New York years in a cottage in the Bronx, he was also a Village habitué. When living at Sixth Avenue and Waverly Place in 1837, Poe visited the Northern Dispensary—still at Waverly and Christopher Street—to treat a head cold. He later moved to 113 Carmine Street, 130 Greenwich Street, 15 Amity Street (now 15 West Third Street), 154 Greenwich Street, 195 East Broadway, and finally—in the fall of 1845—85 Amity Street

(now 85 West Third), where he began "The Cask of Amontillado" while revising "The Raven" and other poems. Preservationists were horrified when owner New York University, originally intent on demolishing the 1835 three-story town house, came up with a compromise "interpretive reconstruction" in the early 21st century that destroyed the original brick facade and moved the original site a half-block away. Northeast of Washington Square Park, at Broadway and East Tenth, is the Gothic-revival Grace Church, thought to have inspired "The Bells"; Poe was visiting family friends nearby when he wrote the first draft.

Across the Park

South of Washington Square Park, on MacDougal Street between West Fourth and Bleecker, is Caffe Reggio, the first place to serve cappuccino in the United States when it opened in 1927. Louisa May Alcott probably could have used a coffee break 60 years earlier, while she wrote *Little Women* across the street at 130–132, in row houses belonging to her uncle. Down the street at 113 MacDougal and Minetta Lane, the Minetta Tavern has been reinvented as an upscale bistro, but back in 1923, when *The Reader's Digest* was founded in the basement, this was a hangout for e.e. cummings, Ezra Pound, and playwright Eugene O'Neill, whose boarding house was on Washington Square South.

Heading East

Around the corner on Bleecker Street, the long-closed San Remo Café (#189) played host to the Beats: Kerouac, Burroughs, Corso, and Ginsberg. In the '70s, longtime Villager Ginsberg moved northeast to 437 East 12th Street, where he stayed for over 20 years; his neighbors included author/punk rocker Richard Hell.

After immigrating to New York in 1981, lavender-coiffed British transplant Quentin Crisp (*The Naked Civil Servant*) made his home at 46 East Third Street and Second Avenue—not far from Bill Burroughs's 222 Bowery "bunker," a windowless apartment in a former YMCA where the *Naked Lunch* author lived from 1974 to 1980.

By then, of course, the Village and a new cast of characters were already creating yet another chapter in the never-ending story: "The moving finger writes; and, having writ, moves on . . . "

NYC Timeline

(Continued from p. 42)

August 1673
The Dutch use 21 ships to regain control of New York. They rename the city, now part of a province called New Netherland, New Orange.

1674
Nearly bankrupt from two years of war with France, Britain, and factions in Germany, the Dutch cede New Netherland to the British, via the Treaty of Westminster. New Netherland's central city reverts to the name New York.

1685
James II ascends to the throne in England, and New York becomes a royal colony. Expatriate Brits in and around the city are not pleased.

1688
James II further ticks off New Yorkers by tossing New York and New Jersey into the previously established Dominion of New England.

April 18, 1689
James II is deposed during the Glorious Revolution in England, which helps encourage riots in New York.

1689
Shortly after chaos breaks out, Jacob Leisler, a German-born trader, seizes control of lower New York in what comes to be known as Leisler's Rebellion. Lieutenant Governor Francis Nicholson is tossed from office.

1689–1691
Jacob Leisler creates a new government with direct popular representation and establishes a legislative assembly that isn't dominated by wealthy merchants and landowners.

May 16, 1691
A replacement governor sent from England to New York by William III has Jacob Leisler beheaded.

March 13, 1698
The Anglican Trinity Church holds its first mass.

1700
Local population of the Native American Lenape, once 15,000 strong, now is just 200.

1702
Yellow fever kills 570 people in New York; that casualty figure represents 1 in 9 of the city's population.

1725
The first newspaper published in New York, a weekly called the *New York Gazette*, is established to tout the British government's view of the colony and the larger world.

1733
The *New-York Weekly Journal* is founded by John Peter Zenger to provide an alternative to the British-controlled *New York Gazette*.

August 5, 1735
A jury in New York decides a case that establishes the legal precedent for freedom of the press. The decision confirms the right of the anti-British *New-York Weekly Journal* to tweak the monarchy via news and satiric rhyme. In broader terms, the decision establishes that the truth is a defense against a charge of libel.

1754
Columbia University is founded as King's College.

(Continued on p. 116)

You Can Thank New York

Anyone who's ever spent August in New York—where the concrete and asphalt keep things steamy even in the wee hours of the—morning, will certainly understand why the city was the natural birthplace of what some say is the world's greatest boon to mankind: cool air on demand.

Changing temperatures and humidity inside the Sackett-Wilhelms Lithographing Company in 1902 Brooklyn were causing quite a problem. The varying conditions caused the printing plant's paper to expand and contract, and its colored inks became misaligned or out of register. Willis H. Carrier, just 25 years old and a year out of Cornell University with an engineering degree, was called upon to invent a system to stabilize the plant's interior air. His response to this problem—air conditioning—earned him the nickname, "The Father of Cool."

While many attempts had been made around the world to cool interior temperatures—one required using half a million tons of ice every two months—Carrier was the first to carry it off successfully. It wasn't yet called *air conditioning,* however—that term was later used by another inventor for his system that added moisture to the air in textile manufacturing plants.

Carrier's basic ideas revolutionized the fledgling field and still provides the foundation for modern air conditioning. He further refined his idea of how to condition, clean, dehumidify, and cool air, he claimed, on a foggy night while waiting for a train. The inventor patented his "Apparatus for Treating Air" in 1906, and in 1911 he unveiled his Rational Psychrometric Formulae, which is now known as the Magna Carta of the air conditioning industry.

In 1915 Carrier and several others in New York founded the Carrier Engineering Corporation—a company that today employs 45,000 in 172 countries. Among the milestones in Carrier's career were the first residential air conditioner (1914), the first air-conditioned department store (1924), and the air conditioning of such places as Madison Square Garden, Grauman's Chinese Theatre in Los Angeles, the Canadian Houses of Parliament, and the USS *Forrestal.* Carrier died in New York City in October 1950.

Beatlemania New York Style!

♥ ♥ ♥ ♥

In August 1965, the Beatles took New York by storm—and ushered in the British Invasion.

The Beatles owe New York City a huge debt for their popularity in the United States. *The Ed Sullivan Show,* one of the first American television shows to feature the Fab Four, helped introduce them to a music-hungry public early in 1964. But it was their concert at Shea Stadium on August 15, 1965, that sealed the deal.

It was a musical event unlike any other. The Beatles arrived in the United States on August 13 and the next day recorded a live segment for *The Ed Sullivan Show.* The concert at Shea Stadium, home of the New York Mets, was the first leg of their U.S. tour. The opening acts that day were the King Curtis Band, Cannibal and the Headhunters, Brenda Holloway, the Young Rascals, and Sounds Incorporated.

Getting the Beatles to Shea Stadium proved to be a logistical nightmare. Because of extraordinarily heavy traffic leading to the ballpark, the band was transported by limo to the Manhattan East River Heliport, where they boarded a helicopter that took them to the roof of the World's Fair building in Queens. There, the boys were loaded into the back of an armored Wells Fargo van for the trip to the stadium. When it was their turn to play, they raced through a tunnel to the stage, which had been erected at second base.

Play Louder, Mates, I Can't Hear You

Unfortunately, the crowd of 55,600 hysterically screaming fans produced such a din that the four musicians literally could not hear themselves play. This proved especially difficult for Ringo, whose drums were supposed to set the beat for each song. But positioned behind the others, he couldn't see or hear what the rest of the band was doing. Immediately after their 12-song set, the boys fled to the armored van for a quick escape.

The concert was filmed for a somewhat truncated documentary record of the event, *The Beatles at Shea Stadium,* which premiered on the BBC in England on March 1, 1966.

What Nellie Bly Found on Blackwell's Island

♥ ♥ ♥ ♥

If you visit Roosevelt Island, you'll notice a building called the Octagon. These days, it's a posh condominium, but it was once the site of human injustice and chaos, 19th-century–style. Crackerjack reporter—and beloved New Yorker—Nellie Bly uncovered the story.

A little slip of land in the East River, Roosevelt Island was called Blackwell's Island during the 18th and 19th centuries. It was just farmland and hunting ground initially, but a prison was built in 1832, and several years later it was joined by the New York Lunatic Asylum, which was dominated by the Octagon Tower. The structure was beautiful, with an enormous spiral staircase and a domed, octagonal roof, but from the start, the asylum was grossly mismanaged. More than 1,700 mentally ill inmates were crammed inside (twice as many as should have been there), and although nurses were on duty, inmates from the nearby prison handled most of the supervision.

Over the next few decades, more prisons, asylums, and work-houses were built on Blackwell's, helping to inspire the island's new nickname: Welfare Island. Mortality was high because the care was so poor. Infants born there rarely lived to see adolescence. Any time spent on Blackwell's Island was too long for most.

The Girl's Got Sass

Help was on the way. Born in Pennsylvania in 1864, Elizabeth Jane Cochrane was a spitfire from the start. As a teen, she wrote an angry editorial to the *Pittsburgh Dispatch* about an article she found insulting to women. The editor was so impressed he hired her. Elizabeth assumed the pen name "Nellie Bly" (after a popular song) and lobbied hard for juicy stories. Although she landed a few, newspaperwomen at that time were relegated to the fashion and arts beats, a fate Bly fought against. Yearning for more substantive work, she left the *Dispatch* for New York City in 1887. She had bigger fish to fry.

Bly got a job at Joseph Pulitzer's *New York World* in hopes of significant stories. She already had one to pitch: She would feign insanity and get into the Women's Lunatic Asylum on Blackwell's Island. Everyone had heard about the dastardly conditions there, but no one had dared check it out. Bly's editors were duly impressed and gave their new employee the green light.

That night, Nellie checked into a Manhattan boardinghouse and commenced to freak everyone out. She acted bizarrely, dirtied her face, and feigned amnesia. Before long, the police came and took her away—straight into the heart of Blackwell's insane asylum.

From Bad to Worse

What the 23-year-old reporter found when she got there was worse than she had feared. For the next ten days, she endured the terrors and neglect that long-term inmates knew all too well. Life in the asylum was reduced to the animal level. Rotten meat and thin broth, along with lumps of nearly inedible dough, were all inmates were given to eat. And to wash it all down? Unclean drinking water.

Everyone was dirty, surrounded by their own filth and excrement from the rats that had free reign over the place. Baths consisted of buckets of ice water poured over the head, and the residents passed their days on cold, hard benches in stultifying boredom.

Bly's editors rescued her after ten days, and Nellie wrote her exposé, called *Ten Days in a Mad-House.* The story blew up in the faces of the tin gods who controlled the prison and the asylum. Physicians and staff members tried to do damage control, but it was no use. A grand jury investigation commenced, and before long, new standards—many of which were suggested by Nellie herself—were implemented in institutions statewide. Moneys were allocated, and the asylum on Blackwell's received long overdue repair and rehabilitation.

As for the young reporter, she'd never have to go back to the fashion pages again. Bly continued to seek out adventure and remained a respected investigative reporter until she retired in 1895. Celebrated after that as an industrialist, Nellie remained in New York City until her death in 1922.

Bloody Angle: The Most Violent Place in New York?

♥ ♥ ♥ ♥

If you're looking for some NYC history but don't feel like hitting a museum, take a trip over to Chinatown and check out Bloody Angle. This infamous area at the bend in Doyers Street was the site of untold bloodshed for years.

Lower Manhattan today is quite the place to be. The East Village is full of restaurants and boutiques; SoHo offers high-end shopping and crowds of tourists; the Lower East Side is hipster central, and, of course, the crocodiles that inhabit Wall Street keep that area bustling. But not so long ago, the southern end of the island was rife with gangs, prostitution rings, corruption, and general debauchery.

Chinatown, a neighborhood that became "official" (and ghettoized) around 1882 with ratification of the Chinese Exclusion Act, was particularly active in terms of violence and chaos. Secret societies called "tongs" were formed to protect and support Chinese American residents, but before long the groups were simply gangs that spent their time dealing in criminal activity—and they weren't afraid to use violence against anyone who didn't like it. Many different tong gangs existed, and they didn't all get along. Unrest grew, and by the end of the 19th century and beginning of the 20th, the Tong Wars were on. Few participants made it through alive.

Doyers Street: A Bad Part of Town

Running more or less north and south between Pell Street and the Bowery, Doyers Street is just one block long. Halfway down the block, Doyers turns sharply—hence the "angle" part of Bloody Angle's name. This turn provided a great spot for ambush, and the battling gangs knew it. In 1909, the bloodiest tong war in Chinatown history began when a gang that called themselves the Hip Sings killed an On Leong comedian for being disrespectful. The ensuing war was ruthless, and its locus was the bend in Doyers Street. From then on, the spot would be known as the Bloody Angle.

Herbert Asbury, whose book *The Gangs of New York* was later made into a hit movie by Martin Scorsese, wrote, "The police believe, and can prove it as far as such proof is possible, that more men have been murdered at the Bloody Angle than at any other place of like area in the world." The tongs were vicious and showed no mercy: If you got in their way, you were a goner.

Adding to the danger of the area was a warren of underground tunnels. Connecting buildings and adjacent streets, the tunnels were frequented by gang members who used them to facilitate their dastardly deeds. An assassin would ambush and kill a victim and then disappear down into the tunnels. Several minutes later the killer would emerge, far from the scene of the crime.

Plenty of places near Bloody Angle offered killers opportunities to calm their nerves with a drink—and nail down an alibi. Gang hangouts included The Dump, The Plague, The Hell Hole, and McGuirck's Suicide Hall.

New Violence, and a Cleanup

Eventually, the Tong Wars quieted down, at least for protracted periods of time. By 1930, it was mostly safe to take Doyers if you were passing through Chinatown. But then in the late 1980s, crack cocaine gripped New York, and as a result, gangs grew once again, this time with astonishing wealth and savage violence. Bloody Angle returned to being the most dangerous block in the city as the Chinese Flying Dragon gang launched a turf war against the Vietnamese Born to Kill (or BTK) gang.

Successful anticrime crusades by mayors Giuliani and Bloomberg in the 1990s and 2000s cleaned up much of New York, including Chinatown. Today, Bloody Angle is more likely to be called "Hair Alley" because of the multitude of salons and barbershops located there. The local post office is there, too, nestled among restaurants and shops.

As for the hidden tunnels, most have either been closed up or repurposed by locals. A tunnel once used by criminals to escape capture in the 1900s is now a belowground shopping arcade—and don't worry, it's safe to shop there.

Tin Pan Alley

♥ ♥ ♥ ♥

A place that was once synonymous with songwriting is long gone, yet the popular music it produced will last forever.

If you're a student of classic popular music, you'll hear these in your head as soon as you read the titles: "In the Good Old Summertime," "Give My Regards to Broadway," "Shine on Harvest Moon," "By the Light of the Silvery Moon," "Let Me Call You Sweetheart." And try these: "Alexander's Ragtime Band," "Swanee," "Baby Face," "Ain't She Sweet," "Happy Days Are Here Again," "Take Me Out to the Ball Game," "God Bless America." These and many, many more hit songs of the late 19th and early 20th centuries sprang from the West 28th Street district in lower Manhattan between Fifth and Sixth avenues, which was once known as Tin Pan Alley.

Why *Tin Pan Alley?* Well, legend has it that newspaper writer Monroe Rosenfeld coined the name after hearing the dissonant sound of multiple composers simultaneously pounding pianos in music publishers' offices that were located practically on top of each other. Others attribute the name to Roy McCardell's May 1903 article in *The World,* titled "A Visit to Tin Pan Alley, Where the Popular Songs Come From."

Beauty and Business

Although the "tin pan" racket may have given some neighbors plenty of headaches, the music itself often provided a lot more pleasure, since it was created by such legends as Irving Berlin, Hoagy Carmichael, George M. Cohan, Scott Joplin, Jerome Kern, Cole Porter, and Fats Waller, as well as the songwriting teams of George and Ira Gershwin; Al Dubin and Harry Warren; Buddy DeSylva, Lew Brown, and Ray Henderson; Gus Kahn and Walter Donaldson;

Bert Kalmar and Harry Ruby; and Arthur Freed and Nacio Herb Brown.

Until the latter part of the 19th century, major publishers of American music were scattered throughout the country, with particular concentrations in New York, Chicago, Boston, Philadelphia, St. Louis, Cincinnati, Baltimore, Cleveland, Detroit, and New Orleans. However, when a post–Civil War boom in the purchase of pianos resulted in a massive increase in demand for sheet music of songs to play on them, the industry began to assemble in the city that was already the main center for the performing arts: New York. There, at 51 West 28th Street, M. Witmark & Sons initially led the way by providing new music for free to established performers as a means of plugging its song catalog. Soon others followed suit, including the Robbins Music Corporation, the Remick Music Company, the E. B. Marks Music Company, and Shapiro, Bernstein & Company, as well as the firms headed by Irving Berlin and fellow composer Harry Von Tilzer.

Writing to Order

During these early years, composers and lyricists of proven ability usually signed exclusive contracts with a particular company and then wrote to order, producing songs to suit current trends. These were often created for Broadway and vaudeville—escapist entertainment required upbeat numbers with catchy melodies. The music publishers were happy to oblige, especially in the wake of Charles K. Harris's 1892 waltz song, "After the Ball," which sold more than two million copies of sheet music during that year alone. This was big business, and pop songs of both commercial and—in many cases—long-lasting appeal were churned out to satisfy the public's appetite for romantic ballads, novelty songs, and dance tunes, as well as ragtime, jazz, and blues.

By 1907, most of the major publishers had relocated from West 28th Street to the West 30s and beyond, yet the Tin Pan Alley moniker prevailed until sheet music sales declined in line with the ascent of radio and the record player during the early 1930s. Thereafter, the Tin Pan Alley style and business model became anachronisms, and the scene was long gone by the time rock 'n' roll rose to prominence a quarter-century later.

How Marlon Brando Changed Acting Forever

♥ ♥ ♥ ♥

Marlon Brando revolutionized stage and screen technique by leading the influx of a new wave of actors after World War II. His role as Stanley Kowalski in Tennessee Williams's Broadway smash A Streetcar Named Desire *led to the Hollywood version, both directed by Elia Kazan, which catapulted Brando to mainstream stardom.*

The New York theater scene in the 1940s was rich ground for acting coaches. Lee Strasberg, Stella Adler, and Stanford Meisner were all disciples of Constantin Stanislavski. The Stanislavski System was a kind of "grammar" for actors. By breaking down a task or interaction into objectives and obstacles, an actor could better get "in the moment" of a scene. In New York, Strasberg and others adapted the Stanislavski System to focus more on the actor personally identifying with the character and using techniques to understand psychological motives. Students led the charge for a new kind of acting: The Method. In this new guard were Paul Newman, Marilyn Monroe, James Dean, and Marlon Brando.

Brando followed his older sisters to New York in 1943. He studied with Stella Adler and traveled to Massachusetts to do an in-person audition for Tennessee Williams for his new play, *A Streetcar Named Desire. Streetcar,* which would go on to win the Pulitzer Prize, tells the story of Blanche DuBois, an alcoholic Southern belle who moves in with her sister, Stella Kowalski, and Stella's abusive working-class husband, Stanley. Stanley and Blanche clash physically and emotionally, which leads to assault and Blanche's nervous breakdown.

Stanley

Brando wandered around the stage during rehearsals. He didn't know his lines. The ones he did remember he muttered softly. Director Elia Kazan encouraged his antics. Brando spent hours touching and examining every object on the set. By handling the objects, he used their familiarity to get himself into the emotional tenor of a scene. Repetition often brought staleness to performances, but Adler, Kazan, and Brando believed that spontaneity could reinvigorate a scene. Brando would ad lib and improvise to inject new life into the play. He didn't just act; he reacted.

His behavior frustrated costar Jessica Tandy, who came from the classical tradition: Hit your mark, know your lines, and say them. At one point Tandy shouted, "Speak up! I can't hear a bloody word you're saying." Costar Kim Hunter was more forgiving: "Some nights he made terrible choices, but they were always *real.*"

The play opened in three cities (New Haven, Boston, and Philadelphia) before hitting Broadway on December 3, 1947. Brando (as Stanley Kowalski), Tandy (as Blanche), Hunter (as Stella Kowalski), and Karl Malden (as Mitch) received standing ovations and 12 curtain calls. "In those days people stood only for the national anthem," said producer Irene Selznick.

The reviews were gushing. Brando's mumbling and habitation of the set during the weeks of rehearsal caged a sexuality and violence that, when released, fired the first shot of the "great revolution in American acting." The Actors Studio was founded just prior to the play's opening, and Method actors soon flooded Broadway and Hollywood, having been electrified by Brando's performance and Kazan's direction.

Imitators

Talents as bright as Montgomery Clift, Paul Newman, and James Dean were inspired by what Brando had achieved. But there was an inevitable downside to Brando's influence. Among many lesser actors, precise diction gave way to imitations of Brando's mumbling. T-shirts replaced neat attire. Some young actors struck poses or attitudes instead of truly acting their parts. "Lots of the actors were just slobs," said Alice Hermes, Brando's diction coach at Erwin Piscator's Dramatic Workshop. "Brando mumbled only when appropriate."

Quotables

"New York is an exciting town where something is happening all the time, most of it unsolved."

—Johnny Carson

"I think my favorite sport in the Olympics is the one in which you make your way through the snow, you stop, you shoot a gun, and then you continue on. In most of the world, it is known as the biathlon, except in New York City, where it is known as winter."

—Michael Ventre, *L.A. Daily News*

"New York now leads the world's great cities in the number of people around whom you shouldn't make a sudden move."

—David Letterman

"New York makes one think of the collapse of civilization, about Sodom and Gomorrah, the end of the world. The end wouldn't come as a surprise here. Many people already bank on it."

—Saul Bellow

"On a New York subway you get fined for spitting, but you can throw up for nothing."

—Lewis Grizzard

"No one as yet has approached the management of New York in a proper spirit; that is to say, regarding it as the shiftless outcome of squalid barbarism and reckless extravagance. No one is likely to do so, because reflections on the long narrow pig-trough are construed as malevolent attacks against the spirit and majesty of the American people, and lead to angry comparisons."

—Rudyard Kipling

"In New York, we had primary elections for mayor. To improve their chances, all five candidates changed their name to Rudy Giuliani."

—Conan O'Brien

Seeing Is Believing at Hubert's

♥ ♥ ♥ ♥

*A 42nd Street sideshow provided affordable offbeat entertainment,
as well as a professional haven for the disenfranchised and forgotten.*

Once upon a time (during the 1880s, for those of you keeping track),
the building located at 228 West 42nd Street was respectable.
Designed by the esteemed architectural firm of McKim, Mead &
White, it was originally a schoolhouse before its 1908 conversion into
New York's first themed restaurant, Murray's Roman Gardens. The
eatery was proud of the Egyptian peacocks and Libyan tigers that
were living complements to the place's atriums, galleys, temples, and
fountains. The splendor that was Murray's came at a time when the
surrounding neighborhood was part of the city's burgeoning theater
scene. Yet, by 1925, Prohibition had forced the closure of both this
exotic eatery and the luxury hotel upstairs. The reversal of fortune
paved the way for a veritable oddities' emporium that, in line with
42nd Street's famed slide into seediness, quickly established itself as
the epitome of the sideshow dive.

Oddities and Cootchy-coo

Founded by one Hubert Miller, Hubert's Museum and Flea Circus
had something for everyone—at least, for those whose tastes shaded
to the peculiar or impolite. During the early part of Hubert's existence, a pinball arcade dominated at street level. After Bill Schork
and Max Schaffer assumed ownership in the late 1930s, patrons
were invited down a flight of linoleum-covered stairs into a Bosch-
like basement netherworld. Inside, for just 25 cents a pop, patrons
gawked at the mammoth feet of Susie the Elephant Skin Girl; the
flipperlike arms of Sealo the Seal Boy; the armless torso of José de
Leon; the fetchingly furry face of Lady Olga Roderick (the bearded
lady in Tod Browning's classic movie *Freaks*), and the perplexing
hermaphrodite known as Albert-Alberta.

   If these attractions weren't sufficient to satisfy, there were
jugglers, strongmen, and exotic dancers, as well as "Voodoo Jungle
Snake Dancer" Princess Sahloo; sword swallower Lady Estelline

Pike; Presto the Magician; Lydia the contortionist; Azrad the fire-eater; and Congo the Jungle Creep (a self-invented "wild man" who had come from Haiti). During the late 1950s—when the museum was owned by Princess Sahloo's fire-eating husband, R. C. Lucas—crowds were entertained and amused by Larry Love, a falsetto-voiced, ukulele-playing "Human Canary" who eventually became world famous as Tiny Tim.

Whereas Tiny was on the way up when he appeared at Hubert's, other performers were, unfortunately, headed in the opposite direction. In 1939 and 1940, legendary baseball pitcher Grover Cleveland Alexander—middle-aged, fat, and fighting a losing battle with the bottle—earned his keep by sitting on a stage between a snake charmer and the slot machines, regaling the starstruck with his old stories about the game. A similar fate befell former world heavyweight boxing champ Jack Johnson, who recounted prize fights from long ago as he sipped red wine through a straw and sold signed photos for five cents.

Dancing Fleas

Perhaps the most famous and celebrated of all of Hubert's attractions was found in a cubicle toward the rear, where visitors could examine the uncommonly agile fleas trained by Professor William Heckler and, from 1933 to 1957, by his son, Leroy. Lively and acrobatic, the Heckler fleas walked a tightrope, played football, and rode a carousel made of toothpicks.

"Ladies and gentlemen," a carnival-style barker would announce, "Sixteen fleas, comprising six principals and ten understudies, will perform six different acts for you! In the first, a flea will juggle a ball while lying on its back; in the second, another flea will rotate a miniature merry-go-round; and in the third, three fleas will be placed on chariots, and the one that hops the fastest will, of course, win the race!" At this juncture, the pitchman paused for effect, and then added, "Nevertheless, ladies and gentlemen, the act that most people talk about is that in which three costumed fleas dance to music on a tiny ballroom floor! Hard to believe? Seeing is believing, ladies and gentlemen, seeing is believing..."

An anachronism by the time the Swinging Sixties rolled around, Hubert's was forced to fold in 1965, though some of its exhibits remained until the end of the decade.

Bragging Rights

Nobody in America moves more people daily than New York's Metropolitan Transportation Authority: Buses alone truck along 2.3 million, while the subway carries more than three times as many (7.8 million). As a result, many New Yorkers don't own cars or even learn how to drive. The city's extensive public transit gives it the distinction of having the lowest per capita emissions from automobiles of any metropolitan area in the nation. In fact, the city's petrol consumption compares to the national average of the 1920s.

When the system originally opened on October 27, 1904, it was made up of only 28 subway stations, all of them in Manhattan. Now, according to the MTA, the station count of 468 is just 35 short of the combined total of every other subway station in the United States. Approximately 660 miles of track are used for commuter service, out of 840 miles in total—if laid end to end, those tracks would span the distance from New York to Chicago.

The longest ride you can take without changing trains is the A line from 207th Street in Manhattan to Far Rockaway in Queens for a total of 31 miles, all for the same fare (unlike some other systems that charge by the zone). It should come as no surprise that, as of 2009, the busiest station of all was Times Square (with a staggering annual total of nearly 59 million passengers), followed by Grand Central, just crosstown east on 42nd Street, with more than 42 million. New York has the fourth most populated subway system in the world (super-crowded Tokyo tops the list), with an annual ridership of 1.563 *billion.*

And while tourists often fear becoming a crime statistic, especially on that very same subway (which runs 24/7/365, unlike—say—London's tube, which closes down after midnight), the odds have been consistently reduced ever since the time of Rudy Giuliani as mayor. In 2004, Mayor Michael Bloomberg was quoted as saying, "The subway system is safer than it has been at any time since we started tabulating subway crime statistics nearly 40 years ago." (Nonetheless, it's still advisable to avoid flashing cash.)

Fast Facts

- Queens got its name from Queen Consort Catherine of Braganza (1638–1705), wife of King Charles II of England. A Portuguese princess and a practicing Catholic, Catherine was always on the outs with the English.

- One of Chinatown's nastier periods was the early 1900s, when violent Tong wars shook the community. Two of America's most important Chinese "tongs" (gangs) turned Doyers Street into a dangerous battleground called "Bloody Angle."

- Brooklyn baseball had the following nicknames: Atlantics (1884), Grays (1885–87), Bridegrooms or Grooms (1888–98), Superbas (1899–1910), Trolley Dodgers or Superbas (1911–13), Robins (1914–31), and Dodgers (1932–57). Only the final name choice was official.

- Anticipating vandalism, the British built an iron fence around the lead statue of King George (Bowling Green Park) in 1771. It didn't help; on July 9, 1776, irate patriots hauled it down to melt into bullets.

- Geography partly accounts for the sordid reputation of the Manhattan Detention Complex, better known as the Tombs. It was built on reclaimed wetland and began sinking shortly after construction in 1838.

- In 1838, free blacks created a seven-block Brooklyn settlement called Weeksville. It thrived for nearly a century in the modern Bed-Stuy neighborhood then vanished within 20 years.

- Before Opening Day 1907, the Polo Grounds got a freak spring snowstorm. After eight innings, snowballs began to fly—first in the stands, then at the players. Umpire Bill Klem forfeited the game to Philly.

- The original Trinity Church's construction (1696) had an interesting benefactor: William Kidd. The rich seadog gave generously to the building fund. Of course, things went a little south for Captain Kidd after that…

Not Just a Train Station

♥ ♥ ♥ ♥

At the turn of the 20th century, a few blocks in Manhattan's East Midtown were home to a maze of warehouses, slaughterhouses, and tenements prowled by paupers, squatters, criminals—and even a herd of goats. It was soon to be transformed into a fabled venue that now services 700,000 commuters every day.

Railroads had been running through Manhattan since 1832, but a quarter-century on, steam locomotives were banned from crowded areas. This made the first Grand Central Depot, built in 1871 by mogul Cornelius Vanderbilt, obsolete overnight. The new version—which took a decade to construct and cost roughly $2 billion in today's money—opened on February 2, 1913, to a jubilant crowd of 150,000.

The Age of Rail

Grand Central anchored a frenzy of early 20th-century development, as hotels, apartments, and office buildings were built on "air rights" over Park Avenue. At the same time, skyscrapers—including the sublimely art deco Chrysler Building—sprouted along East 42nd Street. In part because of this development, the terminal became America's busiest train station, hosting more than 65 million passengers (40 percent of the U.S. population) in 1947 alone. Just a few years earlier, Grand Central had helped conceal President Franklin Delano Roosevelt's secret  disability—polio that confined him to a wheelchair—by building a special train car and station right under the Waldorf=Astoria Hotel, allowing the President to enter unseen. Grand Central, then, served larger purposes than merely getting people from here to there.

But as the 1950s dawned on a new world of suburbs and afford-able cars, long-distance rail travel faltered, while real estate values in midtown Manhattan rose higher than skyscrapers. Plans to sacrifice Grand Central for an office tower were first bandied about in 1954.

Four years later, the railroad allowed the destruction of a six-story office building at the rear of the terminal to make way for the 59-story Pan Am Building (as it was then known), which sealed off the station from Park Avenue and uptown Manhattan.

The Threat That Nearly Destroyed a Landmark

It was assumed by many that the terminal's recognition in 1967 by the city's new Landmarks Preservation Commission would save the Beaux-Arts structure and the wonders that came with it: the clock facing 42nd Street that boasted the world's largest example of Tiffany glass, surrounded by sculptures of Minerva, Hercules, and Mercury; the Gustavino-tiled "whispering gallery" outside the famed Oyster Bar restaurant; the private office and salon of rail tycoon John W. Campbell, later revived to its original 1920s grandeur as one of the world's most chic cocktail lounges; the terminal's 12,000-square-foot main concourse, with an arched ceiling featuring a spectacular hand-painted representation of the Zodiac; and the clock atop the information booth in the center of the concourse, with its four opal faces, valued at $10 to $20 million.

Not so fast. Penn Central, the terminal's owner, intended to construct a 55-story building atop the station, which would have required part of the structure to be demolished. When the Preservation Commission fought back, Penn Central filed an $8 million lawsuit. That, in turn, created a mobilization of concerned citizens—most notably Jacqueline Kennedy Onassis, who personally lobbied politicians, powerbrokers, and the press—to publicize the terminal's plight. "If we don't care about our past, we cannot hope for the future," the former first lady declared. The U.S. Supreme Court eventually settled the decade-long legal battle in favor of the preservationists.

Today, Grand Central Terminal is not only a commuter hub and a special piece of New York history but a thriving nerve center offering fine dining; a shoppers' destination with dozens of unique stores and stalls; and a venue for art events and exhibits, including the famed holiday light show. The reverse-Zodiac concourse ceiling has been restored to its former glory, save for a dark patch stained by cigarette smoke over the years and the small hole poked by a poorly managed 1957 rocket display. Oh, and it also has some trains, too.

Berkowitz's Reign of Terror

♥ ♥ ♥ ♥

For one year, a murderous madman who called himself the Son of Sam held New York City hostage. Terrified residents stopped going outside, and some women even changed their appearance for fear of provoking the mysterious serial slayer. At its height, the police effort to catch the killer involved more than 200 determined detectives.

Between July 1976 and July 1977, New Yorkers couldn't pick up a newspaper or turn on the television without hearing about the notorious serial killer who referred to himself in cryptic letters only as the Son of Sam. He struck seemingly at random, primarily attacking young women, and by the time he was finally captured on August 10, 1977, six people were dead and seven gravely wounded.

The Son of Sam turned out to be a troubled loner named David Berkowitz, who told investigators upon his capture that demons in the form of howling dogs had instructed him to kill.

The Seeds Are Planted

Berkowitz had led a distressed life almost from the beginning. Abandoned as a baby, he was adopted by Nathan and Pearl Berkowitz, a middle-class couple who gave him a loving home. But Berkowitz grew up feeling scorned and unwanted because he was adopted. He made few friends, was viewed by neighbors as a bully, and did poorly in school.

When Pearl Berkowitz died of breast cancer in 1967, her son fell into a deep depression, and his emotional problems steadily worsened. His father remarried in 1971, and the animosity Berkowitz expressed toward his new stepmother eventually caused the newlywed couple to flee to Florida. Berkowitz, just 18, found himself alone in New York.

On Christmas Eve 1975, Berkowitz's internal rage reached the boiling point, and he stalked the streets with a knife, looking for someone to kill. He later told police that he stabbed two women that night, though police could locate only one, a 15-year-old girl named Michelle Forman who survived multiple stab wounds.

Berkowitz fled the Bronx and moved into a two-family home in Yonkers, where his mental state continued to decline. Barking dogs kept him awake at night, and Berkowitz eventually perceived their howls as demonic commands to kill. He moved out of the house and into a nearby apartment, where he became convinced that his neighbor's black Labrador retriever was also possessed. After shooting the dog, Berkowitz came to believe that its owner, a man named Sam Carr, also harbored demons.

The Shootings

The voices in his head eventually encouraged Berkowitz to once again seek victims on the street. On July 29, 1976, he shot Jody Valenti and Donna Lauria as they sat chatting in a car outside of Lauria's apartment. Lauria died instantly from a shot to the throat; Valenti survived.

In the months that followed, Berkowitz continued his nocturnal attacks, using a distinctive .44 Bulldog revolver to dispatch his victims.

- **October 23, 1976:** Carl Denaro and Rosemary Keenan were shot while sitting in a parked car. Denaro was struck in the head, but both survived.

- **November 26, 1976:** Donna DeMasi and Joanne Lomino were attacked by Berkowitz as they walked home from a late movie. DeMasi survived with minor injuries; Lomino was left paralyzed.

- **January 30, 1977:** Christine Freund and her fiancé, John Diel, were shot as they sat in a parked car. Freund was killed, Diel survived.

- **March 8, 1977:** College student Virginia Voskerichian was shot and killed while walking home from class.

- **April 17, 1977:** Valentina Suriani and her boyfriend, Alexander Esau, were shot and killed. Police found a note signed "Son of Sam."

- **June 26, 1977:** Judy Placido and Sal Lupu were shot in their car after a night of dancing at a local disco. Both survived.

- **July 31, 1977:** Bobby Violante and Stacy Moskowitz were both shot while sitting in a parked car. Moskowitz was killed, and Violante lost the vision in one eye and partial vision in the other.

Sam Speaks Up

At the scene of the Suriani-Esau shootings in April, police found a rambling, handwritten letter from Berkowitz in which he referred to himself as "Son of Sam." In the note, Berkowitz revealed that he felt like an outsider and was programmed to kill. He told police that to stop his murderous rampage, they'd have to shoot him dead. Forensic psychiatrists used the letter to develop a psychological profile of "Son of Sam" and concluded that he likely suffered from paranoid schizophrenia and thought himself a victim of demonic possession.

As the daily papers splashed gruesome details of each new killing across their front pages, New Yorkers began to panic. Women with dark hair cut their locks short or bought blond wigs because the killer seemed to have a penchant for brunettes. Many New Yorkers simply refused to go outside after dark.

A ticket for parking too close to a fire hydrant finally led to David Berkowitz's capture. Two days after the Violante/Moskowitz shootings, a woman named Cacilia Davis, who lived near the murder scene, called police to report seeing a strange man, later identified as Berkowitz, loitering in the neighborhood for several hours before snatching a parking ticket off the windshield of his car and driving away.

New York police detectives, working with the Yonkers police, decided to pay a visit to Berkowitz. They examined his car, parked outside his apartment, and spotted a rifle on the back seat. A search of the vehicle also revealed a duffel bag containing ammunition, maps of the crime scenes, and a letter to a member of the police task force charged with finding the Son of Sam.

Arrest and Aftermath

Berkowitz was arrested later that evening as he started his car. He immediately confessed to being the Son of Sam, telling the arresting officers, "You got me. What took you so long?"

In court, David Berkowitz admitted to six murders and received six life sentences, though he later recanted his testimony and claimed to have pulled the trigger in only two of the killings. The others, he said, had been committed by members of a Satanic cult to which he belonged. Despite his claims, no one else was ever charged in association with the Son of Sam killings.

World's Fair Wonderland!

♥ ♥ ♥ ♥

*World's Fairs are celebrated international events—
and New York has hosted three of the best.*

World Expositions—more commonly known as World's Fairs—give
the international community the opportunity to strut its stuff and
fairgoers a fascinating glimpse of the world around them. New York
City has hosted three such events, in 1853–54, 1939–40, and 1964–
65, and millions turned out to see what all the fuss was about. Here's
some info about the two most recent ones.

The 1939 New York World's Fair

The 1939 fair was held in Flushing Meadows in Queens. Occupying
more than 1,200 acres, it was the largest World's Fair ever held,
attracting an estimated 44 million people over two consecutive April-
October seasons. It was birthed in 1935 when a group of business
leaders came up with a plan for an international exposition to lift the
Depression-weary spirits of New York and the rest of the world.
They established a committee and worked closely with the world's
nations to create a spectacular, two-year event unlike any other.

The exposition opened on April 30, 1939, the 150th anniversary
of George Washington's first inauguration. Paid admission that day
totaled 198,791 people, with tickets costing 75 cents for adults and
25 cents for children ages 3 through 14. President Franklin D.
Roosevelt gave the opening address.

The fair's theme was "The World of Tomorrow," and fairgoers
couldn't wait to see what the future held. At the heart of the venue
were the Trylon and Perisphere, two ultramodernistic structures that
together formed the fair's thematic center. Inside the Perisphere,
fairgoers could view a diorama depicting a utopian future city called
Democracity.

Like all world expositions, the 1939 New York World's Fair
featured a wealth of attractions and events, including Ford Motor
Company's Road of Tomorrow, AT&T's Demonstration Call Room,
the City of Light diorama, the "Frozen Alive Girl" show, and syn-

chronized swimming in the 10,000-seat Billy Rose Aquacade—
a production that showcased Tarzan star Johnny Weissmuller and
future movie queen Esther Williams.

Of special interest was the Westinghouse Time Capsule, which
contained writings by Albert Einstein and Thomas Mann, copies of
LIFE magazine, a Mickey Mouse watch, a Kewpie doll, and other
period artifacts. Don't expect to see it anytime soon, however—it's
not scheduled to be opened until A.D. 6939.

The 1964 New York World's Fair

New York's second exposition was held in the same location but was
smaller in scope, spanning just 646 acres. It ran from April 22 to
October 18, 1964, and from April 21 to October 17, 1965.

Because it was held as the United States was gearing up the
space race, the fair's theme was "Man in a Shrinking Globe in an
Expanding Universe." The event featured 140 pavilions, most of
which were sponsored by major U.S. corporations, including General
Electric, Ford, General Motors, IBM, U.S. Steel, and Pepsi-Cola.
There also were 21 state pavilions and 36 international pavilions.

Unlike the 1939 New York World's Fair, the '64 Fair wasn't
sanctioned by the Bureau of International Expositions, which had
formally approved the Seattle Worlds' Fair just two years earlier. As
a result, most European and Communist bloc nations decided not to
participate, though South America, the Middle East, and Africa were
all well represented.

An estimated 70 million people visited the fair over its two-year
run. A variety of attractions kept them entertained, including the
Vatican pavilion, where Michelangelo's Pietá was on display; a re-
creation of a medieval Belgian village; the 7UP International
Gardens Pavilion, where people could taste sandwiches from around
the world; and Dinoland, sponsored by the Sinclair Oil Corporation,
which featured life-size replicas of nine different types of dinosaurs.

Despite all it had to offer, the 1964 New York World's Fair lost
money, resulting in years of litigation from its creditors. A handful of
pavilions survived after the fair, but others were sold for other uses.
The Austria pavilion, for example, was turned into a ski lodge in western New York, and the Spain pavilion was transported to St. Louis,
Missouri, where it became part of a Marriott (now Hilton) hotel.

A Call to Action!

♥　♥　♥　♥

The Stonewall Rebellion wasn't the first salvo in the fight for gay rights—but it did help bring the issue to the public's attention.

In the early hours of June 28, 1969, members of the NYPD raided the Stonewall Inn, a popular gay hangout on Christopher Street. Such police raids were fairly common—transvestism was out and out illegal in New York—but this time things went differently. Rather than meekly disappearing into the night, as had happened so often in the past, the angry crowd fought back.

This confrontation has come to be known as the Stonewall Rebellion. While it certainly wasn't the first push toward the public recognition of gay rights, it remains a defining moment in that ongoing movement.

Enough Is Enough

The Stonewall Inn was a Mafia-owned bar where gay men met to mingle and have a good time. Police frequently targeted the Stonewall and other gay establishments, arresting transvestites and harassing other patrons. What sparked the rebellion on June 28 remains a mystery. Some cultural historians speculate that patrons were still upset over the recent death of gay icon Judy Garland. Others say the crowd had simply had enough and decided to push back. Regardless, police found themselves confronted by an angry mob that refused to be cowed. Rocks, bottles, and even an uprooted parking meter pelted the cops. Several patrons were beaten and arrested.

But the unrest didn't end that night. The Stonewall Rebellion struck a nerve, and the rights of gay men and women became as important (and as legitimate) as those of other minorities. More protests occurred in the days that followed, making public a cause that had always been kept quietly in the closet. Men and women who had previously kept their sexual identities closely guarded secrets "came out" to family, friends, and the world, consequences be damned. Gay pride was suddenly on the cultural radar.

Murder at the Garden

♥   ♥   ♥   ♥

*The world was fascinated when a skirt-chasing Gilded
Age architect died atop the landmark he designed.*

Concerts by superstars the likes of Jimi Hendrix, Elvis Presley, John
Lennon, Michael Jackson, Frank Sinatra, and Barbra Streisand;
legendary boxing matches featuring Joe Louis, Rocky Marciano,
Sugar Ray Robinson, Joe Frazier, and Muhammad Ali; home games
of basketball's New York Knicks and ice hockey's New York Rangers.
These are just some of the events that have taken place at Madison
Square Garden since the first of its four incarnations was constructed
in 1879. Yet, perhaps the most notorious Garden event was the cold-
blooded murder of the man who designed the second Garden,
located like its predecessor at 26th Street and Madison Avenue.

That man's name was Stanford White, and his 1906 Garden
shooting in front of a high-society audience led to the "Trial of the
Century." (A somewhat premature title? It would subsequently be
shared with court cases starring, among others, Leopold and Loeb,
John Scopes, Gloria Vanderbilt, the Nazis at Nuremberg and O. J.
Simpson). Indeed, the aforementioned witnesses were not only
elevated in terms of their social status but also in terms of their
location, since the crime took place at the venue's rooftop theater
during the premiere of the saucy musical *Mam'zelle Champagne.*
Soon, the general public was abuzz with gossip about the sex and
jealousy that gave rise to the murder.

Mirrors and a Swing

Stanford White was not only the esteemed architect of numerous
neoclassical New York City public buildings and private mansions, he
was also a notorious (and married) womanizer who enjoyed assigna-
tions at a downtown loft apartment where he had installed a red velvet
swing so that his girls could "entertain" him. A standout among them
was Evelyn Nesbit, a beautiful artists' model and chorus girl who had
met "Stanny" shortly after relocating from Pittsburgh to New York in
1901. At the time, she was 16; he was 47. As Nesbit would later recall,

it was during their second rendezvous at the apartment on West 24th Street, where some walls and ceilings were covered in mirrors, that the redhead "entered that room as a virgin" and emerged with a little more experience.

Thereafter, while White continued treating nubile girls to his swing and mirrors, Nesbit embarked on a relationship with—and was twice impregnated by—young actor John Barrymore. Yet, it was the details of her affair with White that tormented Harry Kendall Thaw, the man whom Nesbit married in 1905. The son of a Pittsburgh coal and railroad tycoon, Thaw was a violent, drug-addicted ne'er-do-well who also had a taste for chorus girls. When he met Nesbit, the stage was set for a tragic showdown.

White's first bad move was to make less-than-complimentary remarks about Thaw to some ladies they both were pursuing. When Thaw learned about these cracks, he wasn't exactly delighted. His annoyance turned to jealous rage when, after he somehow turned on the charm to woo Nesbit, she admitted that she kept declining his proposals of marriage because "Stanny" had taken her virginity. This only made Thaw more determined, and after forcing his marriage proposals—and himself—on the social-climbing Nesbit, the chorus beauty finally relented.

A Pistol in His Pocket

According to Nesbit, she was continually brutalized by Thaw, and his preoccupation with her deflowering at the hands of "The Beast" finally exploded in violence on the night of June 25, 1906. It was on that evening that the Thaws happened to dine at the Café Martin where White, his son, and a friend were also eating. Like White, the Thaws were planning to attend the play's premiere at the Madison Square Roof Garden, and at some point Harry must have learned about this. After dropping Evelyn off at their hotel so that he could arm himself, he reappeared in a black overcoat (despite the summer heat), whisked his young wife off to the show, and paced nervously up and down between the dinner-theater tables before White

arrived at around 10:50 P.M. Thaw continued to hover for the next 15 minutes, until an onstage rendition of a song unfortunately titled "I Could Love a Million Girls" inspired him to approach the seated architect and shoot him three times from point-blank range.

One bullet entered White's left eye, killing him instantly; the other two grazed his shoulders as he fell off his chair. However, since two stage performers had just engaged in a dueling dialogue, most audience members thought the shooting was all part of the fun—until several witnesses screamed. At that point, according to the following day's *Times*, the theater manager leapt onto a table and demanded that the show must go on. Yet, when "the musicians made a feeble effort at gathering their wits" and "the girls who romped on the stage were paralyzed with horror," the manager informed his audience that an accident had occurred and they should leave quietly.

Arrested near the venue's elevators, Thaw asserted that White "deserved it.... I can prove it. He ruined my life and then deserted the girl." According to another witness quoted in the *Times*, Thaw claimed that "Stanny" had ruined his *wife*, not his life.

Either way, after the jury at this first "Trial of the Century" was deadlocked, Thaw's plea of insanity at the second resulted in his imprisonment at a state hospital for the criminally insane. Released in 1913 and judged sane in 1915—the year he granted Evelyn a divorce—he was again judged insane and sentenced to an asylum two years later for assaulting and horsewhipping a teenage boy.

Some people never learn.

- *The 1955 movie* The Girl in the Red Velvet Swing, *starring Joan Collins as Evelyn Nesbit, Ray Milland as Stanford White, and Farley Granger as Harry Kendall Thaw, recounts the love-triangle murder. An even more fictionalized account was provided in James Cagney's final feature film,* Ragtime (1981) *with Norman Mailer as White and Elizabeth McGovern as Nesbit.*

- *Following the first two incarnations of the Garden that were constructed at 26th Street and Madison Avenue in 1879 and 1890, Madison Square Garden III opened at 50th Street and Eighth Avenue in 1925. The current version of the indoor arena, located at Eighth Avenue and 33rd Street, opened in 1968.*

Fast Facts

- The best example of what New York looked like before the Dutch landed is Van Cortlandt Park, aka "Vanny." It's quite possibly the least modified place in the four northernmost boroughs.

- When Brooklyn founded a Historical Society in 1863, it obtained its charter from the New England Historical Society in Boston. One reason: to make an abolitionist political statement in those Civil War years.

- Today's baseball players should be glad they didn't play for Tammany hack Andrew Freedman's 1895–1902 Giants. He punched out errant players, with Tammany thugs on hand to make sure the players didn't hit him back.

- The British built a seawall along the edge of modern Battery Park in the 1700s, possibly to contain landfill. Modern workers continually hit the buried wall when they dig to start new construction.

- The 1886 unveiling of the Statue of Liberty was meant to be a tremendous moment. However, the day was so wet and misty that onlookers couldn't see the statue from the Battery.

- The Collect Pond, Manhattan's earliest drinkable water supply, was completely nonpotable by 1800. A poor, piecemeal fill job was undertaken and finished by about 1812. The undesirable location later adjoined the Five Points, Manhattan's quintessential Victorian slum.

- Although playwright Arthur Miller recalled seeing feminist writer Valerie Solanas shoot Andy Warhol in the lobby of the Hotel Chelsea, the attempted murder actually took place at Warhol's nearby Factory on June 3, 1968. This was after Solanas had visited the Chelsea earlier that day, looking for erotic-book publisher Maurice Girodias.

- In the early Dutch days, there was a swamp just west of Frankfort and Pearl Streets, gradually filled in over time. Today the Southbridge Towers housing co-op occupies the 2 × 2 block area.

Taste of New York

If any kind of food screams "New York," it must be "deli," a surviving remnant of the Jewish-American immigrant experience. The word is shorthand for *delicatessen,* which is German for "fine foods." *Deli* also describes a store or restaurant where that food can be found. Staples include matzo-ball soup, knishes (dough pockets, baked or fried, usually filled with potato), blintzes (the Jewish version of a crepe), salami, corned beef, pastrami, lox (smoked salmon), varieties of pickled cucumber—and plenty of everything. Prices for quality *and* quantity tend to be on the high side, but then again, a stingy deli sandwich is an oxymoron. So is décor, unless you count the requisite wall photos of every notable who ever stepped through the doors.

In Midtown Manhattan, two famous delis opened in 1937 and continue to vie for ultimate supremacy today. The Carnegie, which smokes and cures its own meats, counts among its many fans fancy-pants chef Joel Robuchon (he favors the pastrami) and Zagat's, which calls it a "can't miss . . . NY icon." It has been featured in Woody Allen's *Broadway Danny Rose,* celebrated in Adam Sandler's "Chanukah [Hanukkah] Song," and called the "most famous" deli in the country in *USA Today.* Cash only, though.

Nearby, the Stage Deli—which once welcomed Mayor Fiorello La Guardia, Jack Benny, Milton Berle, Joe DiMaggio and Marilyn Monroe, George Burns and Gracie Allen—also has "ginormous" sandwiches and a celebrity clientele, including Leonardo DiCaprio, Prince William, and that *fresser* ("glutton" in Yiddish), former President Bill Clinton.

However, the great-granddaddy is Katz's, opened in 1888 on the Lower East Side. With a nonexistent décor and cafeteria-style service (get a ticket at the entrance, order at the counter, have ticket marked, bus your own table, then present ticket and cash on the way out), it still boasts its famed signs proclaiming, "Send a Salami to Your Boy in the Army." The clubgoing crowd hits Katz's on its way to or from the area's hot nightlife; clubgoers probably don't know or care that Meg Ryan's faked sexual satisfaction scene in *When Harry Met Sally . . .* was shot here, as was part of *Donnie Brasco* with Johnny Depp. *Ess gesunt* (eat in good health)!

Dusty Rhodes: One-Year Wonder

♥ ♥ ♥ ♥

Most of Dusty Rhodes's baseball career embodied mediocrity. Yet in 1954, he was the toast of the town—and a pitcher's worst nightmare.

James Lamar Rhodes of Mathews, Alabama, was a substitute outfielder. A career Giant (1952–59), he hit an underwhelming .253 during that time. His field play and throwing arm were comically bad. He stole only three bases. This devoted bourbon enthusiast often stayed out late to fully enjoy his intoxicating hobby. Disregarding 1954, Dusty's lifetime stats were even worse: .238, with only 240 career base hits. A handful of players have exceeded that *in one season*.

What Happened in '54?

In 1954 the United States test-fired its first H-bomb, and Dusty—well, Dusty went nuts. Maybe it was radiation, or maybe he was upset because Joe DiMaggio married Marilyn Monroe. Whatever, Rhodes hit .341 with 15 homers and put together a Ruthian .695 slugging average. When Giants manager Leo Durocher looked down the bench for a pinch hitter, most of the guys would look away. Dusty would be loosening up with a bat, saying: "Ah'm your man, Skip."

In the World Series, it got ridiculous. Dusty hit .667 with seven RBI. He won Game 1 in extra innings with a pinch homer. He tied Game 2 with a pinch hit, stayed in, and hit another homer. In Game 3, Dusty singled in two runs with the bases loaded and had six at-bats, four hits, and two homers. The Giants swept Cleveland, and Dusty manned the broom. He won the Babe Ruth Award for best Series performance.

In 1955 Rhodes hit a sweet .305 in 187 plate appearances, but by '56 he was regular Dusty again, hitting an anemic .217 in 244 at-bats.

Rhodes the Person

Less well-known is Dusty's camaraderie with his African American teammates in those days of tense national race relations. Giant teammate and Negro League veteran Monte Irvin said, "He was like a brother to all the black players."

Manhattan's "Death Avenue": Look Both Ways Before Crossing the—Aaagghh!

♥ ♥ ♥ ♥

It's hazardous to cross a street in New York City. Cabbies barrel through yellow lights, and buses don't hesitate to intimidate pedestrians right back onto the sidewalk. But from about 1840 to the late 1920s, those crossing on a section of 11th Avenue had to avoid a hazard that may have been unique to American city streets. Say hello to "Death Avenue."

It's 1900. The concrete and bricks of New York's 11th Avenue are crowded today, but with just the usual sorts of bottlenecks: horse-drawn wagons and carriages, clots of pedestrians, pushcarts. You step from the curb... and promptly get run over by a train. And we don't mean a streetcar, either. No, *a real train* has just flattened you.

Maybe Not the Best Idea Ever

How could such a thing happen? (And it happened a lot—2,000 times in one ten-year period.) In the early part of the 19th century, the New York Central freight line was a main rail artery that carried much of New York's booming commerce. One of the first permanent railroads in the United States, the line connected much of the Northeast and would eventually expand to link the region to other parts of the country, too.

One section of this railroad ran through New York City itself, and was, unwisely enough, situated smack dab at street level. The tracks served the Hudson River line and ran along the west side of Manhattan on 11th Street. They were placed directly in the street without any kind of elevation or railing to separate the trains from

people or from the horse and buggy traffic on the typically crowded avenue.

It gets worse: Even as late as 1910, the trains' stopping power was limited to handbrakes that were operated by brakemen who rode the tops of closed cars. Because the brakemen engaged the brakes after a signal from the engineer, tardy stops were virtually guaranteed. As you can imagine, this led to continual collisions, many of which resulted in critical injury or death.

In a peculiar irony, the steam locomotives were shrouded at the front and sides with dummy panels that disguised the standard drive wheels. This was done so that horses wouldn't be frightened. It may also have encouraged people to ignore oncoming trains!

Take the High Road

In order to provide some semblance of safety, a group of men got together and called themselves the West Side Cowboys. These guys rode on horseback ahead of the trains to signal their arrival to anyone out and about on Death Avenue. But the Cowboys didn't work around the clock, and the death toll continued to rise. For people who lived in the area, and for all those who needed to do business there, a dull sort of terror was an ingredient of daily life.

It wasn't until 1930 that the city decided it would be best to take the huge train off the street. The High Line was built, and 11th Avenue was immediately a safer place. The High Line was used until 1980, when it fell into disrepair.

In 2004, New York invested $50 million to turn much of the High Line into a now-beloved city park. These days, tourists and locals who enjoy the park can look down over the cross streets and envision what used to be the most dangerous strip of pavement in the city.

- *Did you know that Roger Maris and Mickey Mantle did a movie together? It was called* Safe at Home *(1962). Here's a straight-to-the-point capsule review: Good thing both Yankees had other career options when Hollywood didn't pan out, because both Roger and the Mick came across as stiff and artificial. Well, who said acting is easy?*

Where They Played

♥ ♥ ♥ ♥

The Paramount Theater, at 1501 Broadway, was built in 1926.
By the 1940s it was one of the city's leading music venues.
The Paramount no longer operates as a theater, but a handful
of old-school Manhattan musical venues still stand.

How do you get to Carnegie Hall? The joke about arriving at Carnegie Hall (881 Seventh Avenue, at 57th Street) via practicing still holds true. This fabulous venue was built in 1890 and contains three halls; today, most concerts take place in the Isaac Stern Auditorium. President Theodore Roosevelt, Maria Callas, Leonard Bernstein, and Yo-Yo Ma have all walked upon this stage—as did The Beatles, who played two sell-outs here on February 12, 1964, with a top ticket price of $5.50. Unfortunately, plans to record and release the shows were thwarted at the last minute by a union dispute.

It's Showtime!

The equally legendary Apollo Theater opened in 1914 at 253 West 125th Street and has launched the careers of almost every R&B/soul/pop icon imaginable—although at first, African Americans weren't allowed in the audience! That had changed by 1934, when 17-year-old Ella Fitzgerald won one of the first Amateur Night contests. Among other Amateur Night winners: The Shirelles, Jackie Wilson, Gladys Knight and the Pips, and The Isley Brothers. The seemingly endless parade of stars even includes Buddy Holly and the Crickets, the venue's first all-white group, booked sight unseen in 1957 because Apollo management thought the group was black. This is where James Brown—whose 2006 return consisted of his lying in state—recorded his 1963 breakthrough, *Live at the Apollo,* a lofty No. 24 on *Rolling Stone's* "500 Greatest Albums of All Time."

Greenwich Village

Several important spots still function downtown, notably The Bitter End, which opened in 1961 at 147 Bleecker Street. Peter, Paul & Mary got started here; other future stars who have graced the brick-wall backdrop of the tiny stage include Bob Dylan, Billy Joel, James Taylor, Patti Smith, Norah Jones, Jackson Browne, Neil Young, and Hall & Oates, as well as comics Woody Allen, Dick Cavett, and Richard Pryor. In January 2006, singer Stefani Germanotta performed here, before reinventing herself as Lady Gaga.

Just a few steps away, at 157 Bleecker, sits Kenny's Castaways, where Bruce Springsteen made his Manhattan debut with the E Street Band in 1972. Other Kenny's alumni who went on to greater fame and fortune include Aerosmith, The New York Dolls, and The Ramones. Open since 1967 (although originally built in the 1820s), the room that houses the nightclub once earned the enviable sobriquet, "the wickedest place in New York."

Around the corner at 115 Macdougal Street is the Café Wha?, opened in the 1950s by Manny Roth, uncle of singer David Lee Roth. Those who cavorted on the original stage (located next door) include Lenny Bruce, Joan Rivers, The Velvet Underground, Springsteen, Dylan, and Jimi Hendrix.

Not Just the Rockettes

Radio City Music Hall (1260 Sixth Avenue) was the brainchild of Samuel "Roxy" Rothafel. The venue opened in 1932, during the depths of the Great Depression, as "a palace for the people." Some 300 million have since passed through a hall whose art deco splendor provides a show all its own. With a capacity of 6,000, Radio City manages to feel simultaneously grand and intimate. The Hall has hosted many historic film premieres (including the original *King Kong* and *Breakfast at Tiffany's*), as well as stars ranging from Sammy Davis Jr., Frank Sinatra, and Count Basie, to Ray Charles, Tony Bennett, Sting, and Paul Simon. Radio City has frequently been the venue of choice for the Grammys and MTV Video Music Awards; and the holiday shows featuring the renowned Rockettes are perennially popular.

Meet Me at the Beacon

The Beacon Theatre, at 2124 Broadway, is the "older sister" to Radio City, as it too was created by Sam Rothafel. The Beacon, boasting a similarly over-the-top deco style, opened in 1929 as a venue for vaudeville, other live performances, and films. Designated a national landmark in 1979, the 2,600-seat, three-tiered theater has had a consistently strong run, with artists such as the Allman Brothers Band (173 shows here since 1989), Jerry Garcia, Radiohead, Aerosmith, Michael Jackson, and Queen. The historic concert house, which still employs its original sound system, was the first to be outfitted by IMAX for the 1991 film, *The Rolling Stones at the Max.* On October 29, 2006, the Stones were also the "house band" for President Bill Clinton's 60th birthday celebration. Even the Dalai Lama has gotten into the act, teaching classes here in August 1999.

"The World's Most Famous Arena"

But the Big Kahuna of them all, the place where a sell-out show says you've really made it, is Madison Square Garden, at Four Pennsylvania Plaza (Seventh Avenue, between West 31st and 33rd streets). This is home to the New York Rangers and Knicks (retired team jerseys flutter from its rafters) and other sports/cultural spectacles. Its current site, set atop commuter hub Pennsylvania Station and holding almost 20,000, is actually the Garden's fourth incarnation.

In 1971, MSG hosted the first rock benefit concert when ex-Beatle George Harrison headlined "The Concert for Bangladesh." The Garden was also a special place for John Lennon, because on November 28, 1974, he allowed himself to be cajoled on stage there by Elton John, not long after Lennon's "Whatever Gets You Through the Night" became America's No. 1 single. Later that evening, Lennon reconciled with estranged wife Yoko Ono. The couple had previously performed here at 1972's "One to One" benefit, recorded and eventually released in 1986 as "Live in New York City."

Finally, in the Gone-But-Not-Forgotten department, Madonna performed her first single, "Everybody," live at club Danceteria back in 1982. The 30 West 21st Street address is now home to a stack of multi-million-dollar condominium apartments—as previously noted, New York's not big on sentimentality!

A Little Denmark in the Big Apple

♥ ♥ ♥ ♥

Each Sunday in Brooklyn Heights, the Danish
Seamen's Church celebrates its unique service.

At 102 Willow Street in Brooklyn Heights, both the American and
Danish flags are flown. This is the Danish Seamen's Church. Inside,
a large ship's model and a brass ship's bell suggest the church's
mission: ministering to Danish seamen who dock in New York. In
the course of a year, church members travel to the nearby harbor to
visit crews aboard the more than 300 Danish ships that briefly berth
in NYC annually. And on a larger scale, Danish Seamen's Church is
simply the heart and soul of the city's Danish-American community.

More than a Century of Service

A Danish preacher named Rasmus Andersen founded *Den danske
Sømandskirke* in 1878. The church moved to its current home in
1957. A $900,000 reconstruction that kept the church shuttered for
most of 2005 resulted in an airy, light-filled space that's now used
regularly for church and community activities.

Lutheran by denomination, the Danish Seamen's Church is part
of the National Church of Denmark and is supported in part by the
Danish government. Though this is the only one of its kind in New
York, Danish Seamen's churches are in cities around the globe.

If you think the uniqueness of the Brooklyn church means the
place must be small, well, *nej, slet ikke*. The Danish Seamen's Church
estimates that more than 10,000 people are involved in its events
annually. Its Christmas Fair draws folks from around the city for
Danish hot dogs, a distinctive mulled wine called *gløgg*, sweets, and
Christmas ornaments and other craft goodies. The church also hosts
get-togethers for Danish and American young people, teaches Danish
language classes, helps ease Danish newcomers' transitions to the city,
arranges talks by Danish artists and celebrities, and tries to cement
bonds between the American and Danish cultural communities.

Diggin' Dirt!

♥ ♥ ♥ ♥

Many of the nation's juiciest scandals have sprung from the Big Apple. Here is a notorious quartet.

New York City is no stranger to scandal. In fact, over the centuries it probably ranks second only to Chicago in terms of politicians who get caught in compromising positions, the public revelation of high society's dirty little secrets, and assorted other embarrassments. Here are some highlights from among New York's worst scandals.

Eliot Spitzer's sexual shenanigans. Spitzer was the governor of New York and a promising up-and-comer in the Democratic Party until 2008, when he was fingered in a federal investigation that publicly revealed his penchant for high-priced call girls. Eliot!

The revelation had a devastating effect on Spitzer's political career, which had been built on his reputation as a squeaky-clean foe of organized crime and political corruption. The fact that the governor had been cheating on his wife was bad enough, political analysts noted, but more damning was the obvious fact that he was a bald-faced hypocrite.

Caught red-handed, Spitzer may have felt he had no choice but to resign as governor. After more than a year of lying low, he reentered the public eye as a political commentator. Observers' opinions are mixed as to whether he might one day seek political office again.

Miss America's political downfall. In 1945, Bess Myerson broke barriers as the first Jewish Miss America. Forty-two years later, the Bronx-born beauty was forced to resign from her job as New York City's commissioner of cultural affairs under a dark cloud of scandal. Among the allegations: that Myerson had used her political clout and winning personality to sway the judge overseeing the divorce of her paramour, Andy Capasso, a business executive 21 years her junior. Capasso, a wealthy sewer contractor, was later convicted of tax evasion and sentenced to four years in a federal prison.

According to an investigative report leaked to the *Village Voice*, Myerson, who was appointed by Mayor Ed Koch in 1983, manipulated Judge Hortense Gabel by placing that jurist's emotionally disturbed daughter, Sukhreet, on the city payroll as her assistant. Once Gabel had ruled in Capasso's favor, the newspaper reported, Myerson fired Sukhreet, initiated a cover-up, and lied about the entire affair. It was a sad end to the career of a woman who had given the city so much.

The Queen of Mean takes a fall. Everyone loves it when the obnoxiously rich fall from grace, and few wealthy New Yorkers have fallen as hard as hotel magnate Leona Helmsley. The wife of billionaire Harry Helmsley, who owned the lease on the Empire State Building, among other holdings, Leona Helmsley was convicted of tax evasion and sentenced to prison in 1989 following a widely publicized trial. Among the revelations: that she often terrorized her employees and routinely tried to stiff those who did work for her, including the contractors who renovated the couple's Connecticut mansion.

Perhaps most damning of all, however, was the testimony of a housekeeper who told the jury she had heard Helmsley comment, "We don't pay taxes. Only the little people pay taxes." Helmsley denied making such a statement but was never able to live it down. She died in 2007.

The humiliation of the *New York Times*. Since its founding in 1851, the *New York Times* has enjoyed a reputation as the newspaper of record. But that reputation received a vicious black eye in 2003 when it was revealed that one of its star reporters, Jayson Blair, was guilty of plagiarism and of making up many of the stories he filed.

Blair was a promising young journalist when he joined the *Times* as an intern in 1998. However, within two years he had been repeatedly called on the carpet by his editors for making too many errors in his reporting. Nonetheless, Blair was promoted to the national desk in 2002. A year later, Blair's conduct as a reporter had became so egregious that the *Times* was forced to conduct its own investigation, which found numerous instances of plagiarism, falsification of information, and outright lying. As a result, Blair was let go, and the *Times* published a 7,239-word mea culpa detailing Blair's errors and the newspaper's response.

Where the Heroes Hang Their Hats—and Capes

♥ ♥ ♥ ♥

Look out, bad guys! New York City is home to many of the world's most popular comic-book crimefighters.

Superman lives in the fictional city of Metropolis (which is somewhat similar to NYC), Batman in Gotham City (ditto). But plenty of other costumed heroes maintain digs in the real-life Big Apple.

- **The Avengers** (Stark Tower, Manhattan). This team was founded by Iron Man, the Hulk, Thor, Ant-Man, and the Wasp.

- **Luke Cage** (Times Square). Born and raised in Harlem, Cage went on to become a crime-fighting "hero for hire."

- **Captain America** (Brooklyn; Stark Tower, Manhattan). An experimental serum turned weakling Steve Rogers into one of the most recognized superheroes in the world.

- **Daredevil** (Hell's Kitchen). When Matt Murdoch was blinded by radioactive waste, his other senses and physical abilities were honed to superhuman levels.

- **Dr. Strange** (Greenwich Village). A twist of fate turned surgeon Stephen Strange into one of the world's most powerful sorcerers.

- **Hourman** (NYC). A special steroidlike pill gives chemist Rex Tyler superhuman powers for exactly one hour.

- **Iron Man** (Stark Tower, Manhattan). Behind the high-tech armor, Iron Man is really billionaire industrialist Tony Stark.

- **Justice Society of America** (greater NYC). Formed during World War II, the JSA's original roster included Flash, Green Lantern, Hawkman, Hourman, Doctor Fate, and Wildcat.

- **Spider-Man** (Forest Hills, later Manhattan). A bite from a radioactive spider gave young Peter Parker astounding abilities.

- **Wonder Woman** (greater NYC). Born on Paradise Island, the Amazonian crime fighter later made NYC her home base.

Ed Sullivan's "Really Big Shew"

♥ ♥ ♥ ♥

A horse-faced newspaper gossip columnist somehow managed to find consensus among the audience about what comprised a "variety show." Sunday nights from 8 to 9 P.M., 40 to 50 million citizens watched CBS-TV's The Ed Sullivan Show.

Ed Sullivan found acts Americans did not want to miss. In the pre-VCR, pre-Internet mid-20th century, he broadcast to the nation weekly. The show went out *live,* showcasing entertainment veterans and newcomers alike. Celebrities in the audience were invited to stand up and be recognized, and overseeing it all was Sullivan; stiff, hunch-shouldered, and yet somehow *perfect.*

Sullivan mixed high and low culture in a way that could only have happened in New York. Older viewers enjoyed Catskills comedians, vaudevillians, and plate-spinners. For the kiddies, there were dog acts, bicycling chimpanzees, and puppets (the charming Italian mouse Topo Gigio, with whom the famously uptight Sullivan made chit chat, first appeared in 1963). Ed also featured selections from opera and ballet and entire musical numbers from current Broadway shows.

"And Now, for the Youngsters in the Audience..."

Not simply the host, Sullivan was also the show's executive producer. He had a keen feel for the zeitgeist. He wasn't hip, but he knew hip when he saw it. He was one of the first TV hosts, for instance, to give airtime to young Elvis Presley. A stellar performance on Sullivan could make a career overnight. This was the so-called "water cooler" effect: Monday morning at the office, everybody talked about what they'd watched the previous evening. Early in 1964, *The Ed Sullivan Show* became *the* water-cooler topic across America.

"Here They Are!"

There are divergent stories about how Sullivan came to book a buzzed-about British band called The Beatles. Sullivan said that, while at London's Heathrow airport, he spied a crush of fans welcoming the lads home from a tour. Alternatively, anchor Walter Cronkite noted that he featured a puff piece about Beatlemania on his CBS News show in December 1963 and was subsequently contacted by Sullivan. Whatever the truth, Sullivan wasn't the first American TV personality to feature The Beatles: A performance clip of the band appeared on NBC's *The Jack Paar Show* in January 1964.

But Sullivan was the anointed kingmaker, and he hosted the group for three consecutive weeks. During that first appearance on February 9, 1964, the show drew a record-breaking 73 million viewers—38 percent of the American population—with a broadcast that literally changed the world.

A Weekly Fix of Rock

From that point on, the Sullivan show inadvertently became a stealth missile in the service of rock 'n' roll. As Mom and Dad enjoyed the Russian folk dancers, the kids gathered every week for a dose of Motown, the British Invasion, or homegrown rock. Before the fall of 1964 (when the teen music show *Shindig!* premiered on ABC) there was no other place to see rock acts at home. Everybody who was anybody appeared on the Sullivan show; the Rolling Stones, the Dave Clark 5, even the Doors, who ran afoul of the censors and were banned "for life." But by 1971, the American television audience had become segmented. The once-invincible *Ed Sullivan Show,* by then out of the top 20, was canceled. Sullivan himself passed on in 1974.

Bringing It All Back Home

By 1993, the studio had been renamed The Ed Sullivan Theater and was home to late-night TV host David Letterman. Will Lee, Letterman's bassist who also plays in The Beatles tribute group the Fab Faux, was delighted when Sir Paul McCartney visited the show. Lee told McCartney, "Welcome home," before the former moptop brought it full circle by playing a live set on the marquee for adoring fans who mobbed the streets below.

(Continued from p. 75)

1765
The British Parliament passes the Stamp Act. New Yorkers are not pleased, and the act is later repealed.

The Sons of Liberty is founded.

1766
New York mounts its first St. Patrick's Day Parade.

British troops begin what will be a 17-year occupation of New York City.

St. Paul's Chapel is completed.

1767
King's College (later Columbia) establishes the College of Physicians and Surgeons, becoming the second new world college to grant an M.D.

1775
The American Revolution begins.

July 9, 1776
New York officially endorses the Declaration of Independence.

July 10, 1776
New York's state constitution is framed.

August 27, 1776
The Revolution's first major clash, the Battle of Long Island, is waged. The British win and make New York their headquarters during the war.

September 21–22, 1776
The Great Fire of New York starts (most likely) at the Fighting Cocks Tavern at Whitehall Street, eventually destroying 400–500 buildings. Not surprisingly, some blame the British.

September 22, 1776
Nathan Hale, America's first notable spy, is hanged (at modern-day 66th Street and Third Avenue). He is just 21 years old.

April 20, 1777
New York's legislature passes its state constitution.

July 30, 1777
George Clinton is inaugurated as the first governor of New York.

November 25, 1783
Evacuation Day—when the British end their occupation of New York—is widely celebrated (and will become one of the city's most important holidays). General Washington marches triumphantly in from the north.

June 9, 1784
Alexander Hamilton opens the Bank of New York.

1786
The first directory of New York is published.

November 4, 1786
St. Peter's Catholic Church is consecrated. It will become known as the "Church of the Bells."

1787
City newspapers begin running *The Federalist Papers* by Alexander Hamilton, John Jay, and James Madison.

September 13, 1788
New York City becomes the first capital of the United States.

April 30, 1789
Washington is inaugurated in New York as the first U.S. president.

1790
More than 33,000 people live in New York City.

(Continued on p. 165)

The *Titanic* of New York

♥ ♥ ♥ ♥

Although the PS General Slocum *was smaller than the RMS*
Titanic *and acquired less notoriety after its tragedy, its demise
brought with it a substantial loss of life. Yet, quite unlike the fate
of the doomed White Star liner, the* Slocum *disaster occurred
scant yards from shore in full view of horrified onlookers.*

The Best Laid Plans

It was supposed to be a day of fun. The PS *General Slocum,* a 235-
foot side-wheel passenger ship owned by New York's Knickerbocker
Steamship Company, had been chartered for June 15, 1904, by St.
Mark's Evangelical Lutheran Church to take parishioners up the
East River to a church picnic. Onboard were over 1,300 people
anxious to flee the hot, noisy, metropolis. The outing had become
familiar. The largely German congregation had enjoyed this cruise
for 17 consecutive years and knew what to expect. As in the past, the
ship would cruise north up the turbulent river and then track east
across the vast blue expanse of Long Island Sound. When the vessel
made landfall, revelers would find themselves at bucolic Locust
Grove, on Eatons Neck, Long Island. But this year would be different. Tragically different.

Disaster in the Making

Many believe that the *General Slocum* was doomed from the outset.
During its trouble-plagued life, the craft had run aground no fewer
than three times and had suffered three serious collisions with other
ships. At least these mishaps might be explained away by bad luck.
Not so easy to defend was the frightful shape that the *Slocum* was in.
It's as if the vessel's owners were tempting catastrophe. How else to
explain rotted life preservers so brittle that they crumbled when
handled, and fire hoses so seriously decayed that they'd burst if put
to task? Then, as now, ship safety demanded a regular infusion of
capital. From the look of things, this was a commitment that the
Knickerbocker Steamship Company wasn't willing to make.

Fanning the Flames

Just half an hour into the journey, trouble arose when a 12-year-old boy alerted Captain Van Schaick to an onboard fire. Unfortunately, the captain dismissed the boy's words as a prank. It would be ten full minutes before Van Schaick would learn the truth. The *Slocum* had indeed caught fire and by now was almost consumed by it. Even as panicked passengers tried to flee the flames by flinging themselves into the treacherous East River, floors began to collapse upon those unfortunate souls riding below deck. A full-scale disaster was underway.

Inexplicably, Van Schaick chose to proceed at full speed upriver rather than beach the craft along the riverbank. The captain would later claim that he was trying to keep the fire from spreading to riverside oil tanks and flammable buildings. Whatever Van Schaick's motivation, the decision literally fanned the flames into an even deadlier firestorm. When the vessel eventually beached at North Brother Island, tremendous carnage had occurred. Of the more than 1,300 people on board, an estimated 1,021 had burned or drowned. On the other hand, the vast majority of crew members—including the seriously injured Van Schaick—survived. This outcome invited condemnation later from people seeking answers to the whys and wherefores.

Retribution

After a major tragedy plays out, the blame game begins. In Captain Van Schaick, his crew, and the steamship company, the public had the perfect villains. Had the accused not created a ridiculously unsafe condition by ignoring safety equipment? Had regular fire drills routinely been skipped? Above all, why had the captain not grounded his boat alongside the riverbank? Such a move would certainly have enabled more to escape.

In the end, Van Schaick was the only one tried in court. He was convicted of criminal negligence and misconduct and was sentenced to ten years at New York's Sing Sing Prison. Today, a marker in Tompkins Square Park serves as the only memorial to the *Slocum* tragedy, which is surpassed in number of deaths in the city's history only by 9/11.

New York Sports Icons

♥ ♥ ♥ ♥

No metropolis has produced more major team championships or more iconic athletes than New York. Here are a few of the latter.

- **Mike Bossy:** Only one New York team of the past half-century has won four straight championships—Bossy's 1980–83 Islanders. The NHL record-holder of goals per game with 0.76, his airborne score in the 1982 Stanley Cup Finals is legendary.

- **Joe DiMaggio:** The "Yankee Clipper," baseball's first $100,000 man, set what may be an unbreakable record with his 56-game hitting streak. And eloping with Marilyn Monroe is *so* New York.

- **Gertrude Ederle:** Raised by a Manhattan butcher, this early-20th-century woman was a gold medal-winning Olympian and the first of her gender to swim the English Channel. New York was so thrilled it gave Gertrude a ticker-tape parade.

- **Patrick Ewing:** Ewing went title-less in his 15 years as the Knicks center, but he is by far the franchise's career leader in points, rebounds, and blocked shots.

- **Walt Frazier:** "Clyde" was flamboyant on the court while he point-guarded the Knicks to a pair of NBA crowns. Off court, he rocked a Rolls-Royce, full-length furs, colorful suits, and velour fedoras.

- **Lou Gehrig:** No baseball moment is more poignant than when the seemingly indestructible "Iron Horse" informed the Yankee Stadium faithful of his premature retirement. Before his terminal illness, Gehrig rivaled Babe Ruth as the game's greatest hitter.

- **Althea Gibson:** Reared on the mean streets of Harlem, the "Jackie Robinson of tennis" was a pioneer of equality not only as a great champion in that sport but also as the first black woman on the LPGA Tour.

- **Reggie Jackson:** Jackson's 1977–81 tenure in the "Bronx Zoo" was deliciously tumultuous and delectably successful. The self-proclaimed "straw that stirs the drink" stirred up unrelenting controversy—and two Yankees World Series crowns.

- **Derek Jeter:** There's real estate reserved in Yankee Stadium's Monument Park for this classy captain, still in the game after 16 years, five championships, and a team-record hits total.

- **Mickey Mantle:** "The Mick" melded unfussy charm, irresistible charisma, and an ability to hit a ball as far as anyone to become Gotham's icon of icons. He was high achieving but imperfect—like the city itself. New York venerated him—and still does.

- **Don Mattingly:** "Too small" and "too slow," Mattingly never appeared in a World Series, but his popularity rivals that of any Yankee. An MVP Award, a batting title, and a hard day's work won hearts.

- **Willie Mays:** By the time a 26-year-old Mays left town with the Giants in 1958, he already was an institution. Some claim he's the purest baseball machine ever to have lived.

- **John McEnroe:** The *New York Times* dubbed this tennis badboy "the worst advertisement for our system of values since Al Capone." Still, the caustic Queens product spent most of the early '80s as the world's No. 1-ranked player.

- **Mark Messier:** In 1994, Messier delivered the beloved but star-crossed Rangers their only Stanley Cup since 1940. Images of their captain's emotional meltdown after the win are indelible.

- **Joe Namath:** The course of pro football changed forever in Super Bowl III. Namath, the brassy, pantyhose-hawking quarterback, publicly guaranteed a Jets upset of the monstrously favored Colts. He delivered and effectively equalized the AFL and NFL.

- **Bill Parcells:** Parcells's can-do (as long as it's his way) attitude played well in the gritty city, and the Giants played well under his coaching. He made a flagging franchise into a two-time Super Bowl champ.

- **Mike Piazza:** Playing to a traumatized town, Mets catcher Piazza stroked a winning homer in the first game after the 9/11 terrorist attacks—the most cathartic swing in the annals of NYC baseball.

- **Willis Reed:** Reed literally limped onto the court for Game 7 of the 1970 NBA Finals and—despite a torn thigh muscle—inspired the Knicks to triumph over the Lakers for their first ring.

- **Mariano Rivera:** With Zen-like reliability, Rivera has been the fail-safe closer for more than 500 Yankees victories. Through 2009, he'd recorded the final out of 14 postseason series—almost triple the previous major league record.

- **Jackie Robinson:** Baseball's color barrier was shattered by a man in a Brooklyn uniform—a circumstance that remains a source of pride to that diverse borough. In 1955, Jackie helped deliver Brooklyn's first 20th-century National League championship.

- **Sugar Ray Robinson:** The ostentatious but consummately cool Robinson endured a troubled adolescence in Harlem, then manned up to capture world titles in two weight classes and earn broad support as the greatest boxer of all time.

- **Babe Ruth:** Ruth practically "invented" the home run, stamping New York as the center of the baseball universe in the process. His every swat, word, and deed was larger than life.

- **Tom Seaver:** Seaver transformed baseball's most piteous franchise into the Miracle Mets of '69, pitching them to an improbable World Series win. Entering the Hall of Fame with the highest percentage of votes ever, he's also the only one wearing a Mets cap.

- **Phil Simms:** His 15-season body of stats suggests he's the preeminent Giants quarterback, but it was Simms's near-perfection as MVP of Super Bowl XXI that reserved his place in this pantheon.

- **Casey Stengel:** At his best (winning seven World Series as Yanks manager), worst (helming the Mets), or mostly mediocre (playing for the Dodgers and Giants), Casey was singularly loopy and lovable.

- **Michael Strahan:** Strahan anchored numerous suffocating defenses, piling up the fifth-most sacks (141.5) in NFL history— every one of them in a Giants uniform.

- **Joe Torre:** Torre came of age in Brooklyn and blew into the Bronx decades later to manage the Yankees to a dozen consecutive postseason berths and four world championships.

- **Mike Tyson:** "Iron Mike" hooked and jabbed his way out of a chaotic childhood in the city's roughest 'hoods to fashion an equally chaotic career as world heavyweight boxing champ.

- **Grete Waitz:** Her native Oslo is 3,656 air miles from what was her greatest stage, but Waitz is at the core of Big Apple athletics for winning a record nine New York City Marathons from 1978 to 1988.

Saturday Night Live Alumni

♥ ♥ ♥ ♥

That show in Rockefeller Center is an incubator of talent. At this point, generations of performers have passed through these walls. Most were unknown when they arrived, although a few already had healthy careers by the time they joined the cast. But all of the following performed week in and week out, live from New York.

Chevy Chase (on show 1975–76)

Dan Aykroyd (1975–79)

John Belushi (1975–79)

Jane Curtin (1975–80)

Gilda Radner (1975–80)

Paul Shaffer (1975–80)

Bill Murray (1977–80)

Harry Shearer (1979–80, '84–85)

Al Franken (1977–80, '86–95)

Gilbert Gottfried (1980–81)

Eddie Murphy (1980–84)

Julia Louis-Dreyfus (1982–85)

Jim Belushi (1983–85)

Billy Crystal (1984–85)

Christopher Guest (1984–85)

Martin Short (1984–85)

Joan Cusack (1985–86)

Robert Downey Jr. (1985–86)

Anthony Michael Hall (1985–86)

Randy Quaid (1985–86)

Damon Wayans (1985–86)

Jon Lovitz (1985–90)

Dennis Miller (1985–91)

Dana Carvey (1986–93)

Phil Hartman (1986–94)

Ben Stiller (1989)

Mike Myers (1989–95)

Chris Rock (1990–93)

Rob Schneider (1990–94)

Julia Sweeney (1990–94)

Chris Farley (1990–95)

David Spade (1990–96)

Adam Sandler (1991–95)

Sarah Silverman (1993–94)

Chris Elliott (1994–95)

Michael McKean (1994–95)

Will Ferrell (1995–2002)

Molly Shannon (1995–2001)

Tracy Morgan (1996–2003)

Jimmy Fallon (1998–2005)

Tina Fey (2000–2006)

Amy Poehler (2001–8)

Local Legends

Whether you're a fan of gangster movies or not, you've undoubtedly heard the phrase "sleep with the fishes." It may come as no surprise to find that the concept started with real, grisly events in New York City's East River.

The East River is a tidal strait spanned by eight bridges and thirteen tunnels separating Long Island from Manhattan Island and the Bronx on the mainland. The lower portion, which flows between Manhattan and Brooklyn, was once one of the busiest shipping channels in the world. Although the East River is known for being filthy, experts claim it's not as polluted as it once was.

At one time, when New York City had more than its share of organized crime, it wasn't uncommon for gangsters—both the Mob and the Westies, an Irish gang from Hell's Kitchen—to murder their enemies and dump the bodies into the East River. This could be done in a few ways, none of which were for the faint of heart. Sometimes bodies were dismembered and chopped into pieces so they couldn't be identified if, and when, they washed ashore. (Intimidating the departed's survivors with bloody appendages was also effective, apparently.) Other times, entire bodies were disposed of in the water.

Legend has it that some gangs gave their victims—alive or dead— "cement shoes," literally encasing their feet in concrete so they sank to the bottom of the river and stayed there. We refer to it as a legend, however, because it doesn't appear to be true. There's no evidence of any gangster turning anyone into a human sidewalk (although they weren't against sometimes using cement or heavy rocks as an anchor).

Bodies occasionally still turn up in the East River as a result of murder or suicide, mostly in the warmer months from April to August. As the waters warm up after the winter, corpses decompose faster and produce gases that bring the bodies floating to the surface.

The Best of Broadway!

♥ ♥ ♥ ♥

*The Great White Way boasts a million lights—and nearly
as many memorable shows and performances. Here's a look
at the ten longest-running shows in Broadway history.*

On Broadway, success is measured in many ways, such as rave
reviews and boffo box-office. And then there's the length of time a
show can attract an appreciative audience. These are Broadway's
top ten longest-running shows, with a tally of their single-run performances (which includes a few shows still running as this book is
published).

1. *The Phantom of the Opera* (9,000+ performances). Andrew Lloyd Webber's musical
version of the Gaston Leroux classic is the
longest-running and most financially successful production in Broadway history, and shows
no signs of slowing down. It crossed the 9,000
barrier in September 2009. Touring productions have brought the show to every major
city, and the play was even adapted as a motion
picture. On Broadway, they don't get any bigger.

2. *Cats* (7,485). Another Andrew Lloyd Webber musical hit, *Cats*—
based on *Old Possum's Book of Practical Cats* by T. S. Eliot—ended
its run in 2000 after 18 continuous years on Broadway, making it one
of the most popular productions ever. If you missed it, don't worry—
a road production will almost certainly make it to your town
eventually.

3. *Les Misérables* (6,680). Based on the novel by Victor Hugo, this
wildly successful production closed in 2003, only to reopen three
years later to satisfy demand from audiences who missed it the first
time around.

4. *A Chorus Line* (6,137). A Broadway production about, naturally
enough, the chorus line of a Broadway production, *A Chorus Line* is
one of the most acclaimed shows in Broadway history. In its first year

it won nine Tony Awards, in addition to the 1976 Pulitzer Prize for Drama. Like *Les Misérables,* it closed its doors only to reopen in 2006 as a very successful revival.

5. *Oh! Calcutta!* (5,959 as a revival). *Oh! Calcutta!* got its start Off Broadway because of its then-startling presentation of full frontal nudity. The staid Great White Way wasn't ready for that when audiences first saw *Oh! Calcutta!* in 1969. However, in 1976 the play reopened on Broadway and played continuously for the next 13 years.

6. *Chicago* (5,500+ as a revival). First produced in 1926 as a play, *Chicago* hit Broadway in 1975 as a musical, closed, then reappeared in revival in 1996. In 2002, a movie version of the play, starring Renée Zellweger and Catherine Zeta-Jones, helped generate even more interest, resulting in a production that still has legs. It tallied its 5,500th performance in February 2010.

7. *Beauty and the Beast* (5,461). Based on the 1991 Disney animated hit, this musical production was a surprise hit on Broadway, where it ran for an impressive 13 years. And like most Broadway successes, touring companies still bring it to appreciative audiences.

8. *The Lion King* (5,200+). Another musical based on an elaborate Disney cartoon feature, *The Lion King* hit Broadway in 1997 to instant acclaim and a rabid desire for tickets. A favorite of young and old alike, it won a Tony Award for Best Musical. It achieved 5,200 performances in May 2010.

9. *Rent* (5,124). When it premiered on Broadway in April 1996, *Rent* created huge buzz over its story of a group of poor, young artists who struggle with life in the shadow of AIDS. *Rent* received immediate critical acclaim and went on to win four Tony Awards, including Best Musical, as well as the 1996 Pulitzer Prize for Drama.

10. *Miss Saigon* (4,092). An updated version of Puccini's *Madame Butterfly* set against the Vietnam War, *Miss Saigon* took Broadway by storm when it premiered in April 1991 following a successful run in England. Audiences were wowed by the musical's extravagant sets, and many in the original cast impressed critics. Indeed, *Miss Saigon* won Tonys for Best Actor in a Musical, Best Actress in a Musical, and Best Featured Actor in a Musical.

Quotables

"Broadway has been very good to me. But then, I've been very good to Broadway."

—Ethel Merman

"There's nothing that can match Broadway for stature and dignity."

—Sammy Davis Jr.

"Being on Broadway is the modern equivalent of being a monk. I sleep a lot, eat a lot, and rest a lot."

—Hugh Jackman

"Broadway is a main artery of New York life—the hardened artery."

—Walter Winchell

"Broadway is a tough, tough arena for singing."

—Julie Andrews

"But it's a Broadway show, so even if you're Christine in *Phantom,* you're still a princess. All female leads are princesses whether they're Disney princesses or not."

—Christy Romano

"It's better to star in Oshkosh than to starve on Broadway."

—James Gleason

"You bet I arrived overnight. Over a few hundred nights in the Catskills, in vaudeville, in clubs and on Broadway."

—Danny Kaye

"My one ambition was to go to Broadway, and I never gave up on that dream."

—David Hasselhoff

"In New York I was always offered the hot, sexy roles. But in L.A. I was offered the plain, dowdy roles. It says a lot about the difference between the coasts."

—Bebe Neuwirth

The Triangle Shirtwaist Fire

♥ ♥ ♥ ♥

A tragic conflagration near Washington Square Park turned the spotlight on factory conditions and sweatshop practices in the garment industry and, by extension, most other early 20th-century industries. The calamity sparked reform in labor laws and working conditions, but at an extremely high price.

On a Saturday afternoon in March 1911, workers at the Triangle Shirtwaist Factory in New York City were getting ready to go home after a long day. They were tidying up their workspaces and brushing fabric scraps off the tables and into large bins. Someone on the eighth floor carelessly threw a match or cigarette butt into one of those bins, and within minutes, flames took over the factory floors. Panicked workers rushed to evacuate, and many on the ninth floor became trapped. That floor had two exit doors, but one was blocked by fire and the other was locked—a precaution owners deemed necessary to prevent thefts by workers. The terrified people on that floor—mostly women and girls—were faced with two choices: wait for rescue (and likely die in the fire) or jump from the windows. Many chose to jump. Overall, 146 workers died in the tragedy.

The Last Survivor

Austrian Jewish immigrant Rose Rosenfeld survived the tragedy by figuring out how the executives were handling the situation. Rose hopped a freight elevator to the roof, where she was rescued by firefighters. When the bosses tried to bribe her to testify that the doors hadn't been locked, Rose refused. Her anger at the needless death lasted a very long lifetime.

Rose married Harry Freedman in 1927. Two of their three children had polio; Rose helped them regain the ability to walk. Rose Freedman promoted reform by retelling her story of the fire throughout her life. She was a diehard L.A. Lakers basketball fan, and her numerous friends knew never to phone during games. Rose died February 15, 2001, age 107, the last survivor of the Triangle Shirtwaist fire.

One Amateur's Night at the Apollo

♥　♥　♥　♥

*Some might call it a testing ground. Others will say it's more
like a cauldron. Whatever your point of view, everybody agrees
that Amateur Night at Harlem's famed Apollo Theater has
produced heartbreak, as well as generations of new stars.*

Lauryn waited anxiously backstage as
the host promised the full house an
exciting Amateur Night at the Apollo.
As she walked onstage, she made
sure to put on a brave smile and rub
The Tree of Hope, a piece of tree
trunk on the side of the stage that
Apollo Theater performers have
considered a good luck charm since
1934. The tree had been a Harlem

landmark near the old Lafayette Theater, then the premiere venue
for African American singers, dancers, and actors. It was cut down
when New York City construction widened Seventh Avenue and the
Apollo Theater first opened.

It was Wednesday night in not just one of the city's toughest
neighborhoods, but one of its toughest performance spaces. The
Apollo audience held nothing back. If they didn't like what they heard
or saw right away, they booed. If the performance didn't get better,
they booed louder. Sometimes performers walked offstage in defeat.
A few were jeered so much they had to be dragged off by the emcee.

"Who's Lovin' You?"

"How old are you, Lauryn?" the host asked, putting a microphone in
her face.

She kept her eyes on the fans she could count on, her friends
and family cheering from their seats. "I'm 13."

"What song are you singin'?"

"'Who's Lovin' You?'" Lauryn had picked a Smokey Robinson classic she thought the crowd would appreciate.

The host gestured to the center of the stage. "'Who's Lovin' You?' Well, come on, Lauryn. We're gonna love you." The crowd broke into encouraging applause as the youngster took her place behind the microphone and under the spotlight.

A Little History

The famous Apollo Theater on Harlem's 125th Street is not merely a venerable and important launchpad for up-and-coming performers. It was also one of the first theaters in the city to welcome an African American audience. Ever since Amateur Night was founded in 1934, it's attracted ambitious unknowns from all over the United States. Jazz legend Ella Fitzgerald was one of the first Amateur Night winners at the tender age of 17. Stevie Wonder, Billie Holiday, Michael Jackson, and James Brown are a few other legends who braved the raucous Apollo stage as unknowns, hungry for their big break. Imagine all the famous fingerprints on The Tree of Hope!

Back to the Show

Lauryn swayed behind the microphone. Although she felt things were going well, the audience began to grumble. The nervous singer was standing skittishly far from the mic. She was hard to hear. A chorus of boos drowned out Lauryn's cover of the Smokey tune.

"Stand up to the mic!" the crowd screamed.

Lauryn did as she was told. She pulled the microphone off its stand and walked upstage. She couldn't make out the audience in the bright lights, but she could hear them clap to the rhythm.

Amateur Night at the Apollo was a life-changing experience for young Lauryn Hill. Yes, *that* Lauryn Hill. Her beautiful voice and quick instincts didn't end in victory that night, but she did go on to win international fame as a member of the hip-hop group The Fugees, along with five Grammy Awards for her debut solo album *The Miseducation of Lauryn Hill.* (Years later, she returned to the Apollo to perform with The Fugees. Nobody booed then.)

Lauryn Hill isn't the only famous performer who initially came up short at the Apollo. Other "losers" who would go on to redeem themselves include Luther Vandross, Dave Chapelle, and Ne-Yo.

Fast Facts

- *Visiting New York? Want to feel more welcome on the sidewalks? Stay right, don't stop abruptly, avoid walking several abreast, and don't be a "meanderthal"—a person who walks as if shopping at a department store.*

- *Carly Simon (born 1945, in the Bronx) grew up as a huge Dodgers fan. In fact, young Carly even became a team mascot. (It couldn't have hurt that her father helped found Simon & Schuster.)*

- *When Grand Central Terminal got a facelift in the mid-1990s, workers found 2,500 ornate stars on the ceiling. No one living seemed to know about them, since they'd been obscured by many decades of accumulated dirt.*

- *Many assume that Rikers Island is in Queens because the bridge connects it to Queens. But the big jail complex that incarcerates 14,000 inmates maintained by over 11,500 police and civilians is actually in the Bronx.*

- *In Tammany's heyday, it wasn't rare for a ward to tally twice as many Democratic votes as registered voters. Who was its first major political leader? A man accused of treason and murder: Aaron Burr.*

- *In 1924 a Times commentator complained that New York's 18,000 taxis amounted to far more than were needed. Twelve thousand would suffice, he said. Patience pays: By 2009 the number was down to 13,000.*

- *Whitey Ford (Yankees 1950–67, 236 wins) owed part of his pitching success to his magic ring. You see, he welded a piece of rasp onto it, which enabled him to nick the ball to enhance movement.*

- *The Columbia University Marching Band has long enjoyed outraging people. In 1989, they depicted a burning flag in response to the controversial flag-burning Constitutional amendment debate. It earned them some bomb threats.*

Any Place to Hang Your Hat: NYC's Smallest and Largest Dwellings

♥ ♥ ♥ ♥

About 8.3 million people live in New York City, and there's really space for only about half of them. But New Yorkers make it work.

Here are some of the city's more remarkably sized domiciles.

Home Sweet Microstudio

The smallest apartment in the city, as of December 2009, is a 175-square-foot "microstudio" located in Morningside Heights. Christopher Prokop, his wife, and two cats live in the tiny space—which, by the way, is on the 16th floor and accessible by staircase only!

Winner Takes All (That Fits, Anyway)

Since 2004, the online interior design magazine *Apartment Therapy* has held the annual "Smallest, Coolest Apartment" contest. Kevin Patterson won the 2009 prize with his West End Avenue apartment that totaled a cramped 210 square feet. (Kevin's tips for enlarging a space included using furniture with built-in storage space and painting walls white.)

Poor Little Rich Guy

The most expensive townhouse ever sold in Manhattan is a five-bedroom, 8,300-square-foot penthouse at the Time Warner Center. It was sold by investor Gerhard Andlinger for $37.5 million in 2009. The bad news? He initially put it on the market at $65 million.

Upper West Side: Where Do I Sign Up?

For the biggest apartments in Manhattan, you should probably be looking on the Upper West Side. Buildings such as the fabled Dakota or Ansonia—where pads are as large as 2,500 square feet—boast spectacular views and plenty of room to enjoy them.

Da Verrazzano and New Angoulême

♥ ♥ ♥ ♥

In 1524, the famed Italian explorer brought Europe its first eyewitness description of New York Harbor and its friendly natives. And he hadn't even been mugged!

Giovanni da Verrazzano's New York stopover was part of a lengthy seagoing effort to find the ever-elusive passage to the Pacific Ocean for King François I of France. What land should France claim? Only by knowing the sea passages could François decide.

The expedition originally included four ships and departed Normandy in 1523. Two of the original ships turned back off Brittany with storm damage, however, and one went privateering. Only the multimast carrack *La Dauphine* made it to the Portuguese archipelago of Madeira, where it wintered and took on supplies for the next leg of the voyage across the Atlantic.

Aboard *La Dauphine,* the expedition made its first North American landfall in early spring 1524 off modern-day North Carolina and then followed the coast northeast. Da Verrazzano somehow missed Chesapeake Bay on his way to modern New York Harbor.

But He Didn't Get His "I ♥ NY" T-Shirt

The explorer's entry into the harbor indeed passed through the narrows (yes, those with the bridge bearing his name today). Loath to risk *La Dauphine* in tricky exploration of the shoreline, however, da Verrazzano set out across Upper New York Bay in a small boat. He mistook the Hudson for part of a lake and didn't explore further, but he did meet with cordial Lenape Native Americans. His recollections about their dress and agriculture remain valuable today.

Da Verrazzano continued northeast to what later became New England and finally returned to France in July. He named the NYC area *Nouvelle-Angoulême,* which means New Angoulême. (Didn't stick, but nice try.)

Aftermath

Da Verrazzano's quick-and-dirty tour of the modern northeast U.S. coast eventually faded into obscurity, which is unfortunate given its pioneering nature. The explorer glossed over numerous inland waterways (none of which actually led to China, of course, but he failed to confirm this). Unluckiest of all, da Verrazzano had the misfortune to operate shortly after Cortez and Magellan, whose feats upstaged his.

Had he been thorough and written more, we might remember da Verrazzano differently. But as New York's first European visitor, a distant kinsman of some who would one day call the city home, Giovanni da Verrazzano has a secure parking place in New York's history.

- *The Abenaki American Indians of Maine were far less friendly than those around New York Harbor. They mooned da Verrazzano.*

- *His brother Girolamo, brought along as cartographer, jumped to the conclusion that North America was two halves divided by (what we now call) a mythical "Sea of Verrazzano." The error wasn't cleared up for more than a century.*

- *Two other bridges are named for da Verrazzano: one in Rhode Island's Narragansett Bay and one connecting Assateague Island to the mainland of Maryland.*

- *The correct spelling of the explorer's name is definitely "da Verrazzano." The I-278 bridge that stands in his honor spells the name wrong, as does the bridge in Maryland. Rhode Island's bridge spells it correctly, though everyone leaves out the "da," which is like referring to the famous NYC mayor as "Fiorello Guardia."*

- *Some believe da Verrazzano's letter to King François I describing the voyage was a fake and that he never came to America at all. However, most historians accept his travels as genuine.*

- *"Old" Angoulême is a pleasant but unremarkable region in south-western France about an hour's drive east of Bordeaux.*

John "Muggsy" McGraw

♥   ♥   ♥   ♥

Thankfully, he can't hear us call him "Muggsy," because if he could, John McGraw would beat us senseless for using a nickname he hated. Over a span of 30 years, as a player and later as a manager, McGraw dominated New York Giants baseball.

Let's see: son of an Irish immigrant, one of eight kids, dirt poor, living through upstate winters, mother died when he was 11, father beat him until he left home at 12. You'd be tough too. But John McGraw loved baseball—and he could hit one. He became the heart and soul of the old Baltimore Orioles of the 1890s, one of the most notorious, rule-bending, profane, dirty, scrappy teams of all time. In 1902 McGraw became player-manager of the New York Giants, and an era began.

Field Chieftain

You can't argue with 2,763 career victories (second all-time), ten NL pennants with 11 more runner-up finishes, three World Series rings, and only two losing records. Two-thirds of the time, McGraw's teams were serious pennant contenders. From 1921 through '24, with four straight pennants and two World Series wins, his Giants achieved dynasty status.

His former players are unanimous: If you made a manual error, he would forgive you. If you made a mental mistake, however, "Mr. McGraw" would rake you over the coals like you'd never been raked before. He demanded thoughtful baseball, and he loathed losing. No wonder McGraw stayed so long in New York, where savvy fans knew how to applaud a well-executed hit-and-run.

"Hit the Showers!"

McGraw received that order from umpires 131 times in his career, a record that stood until 2007. In his day, a single season was 154 games, so in essence, he was ejected for nearly a full season when all added together. He finished playing in 1906 with a .334 lifetime average, which would have reserved his place in the future Hall of Fame even had he never gone on to success as a manager.

The Musical Brill Building

♥ ♥ ♥ ♥

In the 1950s and '60s, the Brill Building at 1619 Broadway
was a one-stop shop for the American record business.

This art deco structure is perhaps the
only building that has lent its name to
an entire genre of popular music.
The "Brill Building Sound" of the
1950s and '60s didn't emanate
from this address exclusively, however, but also from similar "hives" at
nearby 1650 and 1697 Broadway. The
"girl group" epoch began and ended here, as
did the careers of a clutch of teen idols. Activity at the Brill flourished at a time when producers and songwriters, not artists, created
and controlled the music. The "artists," in fact, were often semi-
anonymous entities that could be—and were—interchanged at will.
Fabian, Jimmy Clanton, and the other pompadour boys—who was
who? What was the difference between a Crystal and a Cookie?

From the 1950s through the late 1960s, with a few regional
exceptions such as Detroit's Motown, the Brill Building was the sound
of Young America. One smash hit after another was churned out by
songwriters Carole King & Gerry Goffin, Ellie Greenwich & Jeff Barry,
and Barry Mann & Cynthia Weil. There were others, too: Mike Leiber
& Jerry Stoller, Doc Pomus & Mort Shuman, Tommy Boyce & Bobby
Hart, Phil Spector, Neil Diamond, and Neil Sedaka. All were employed
here. The string of compositions turned out by Burt Bacharach and
Hal David for Dionne Warwick—beginning with 1962's "Don't Make
Me Over"—caused Dionne to be ubiquitous on the 1960s charts.

The Assembly Line

Every day, songwriters toiled in tiny piano-equipped cubicles. The
best of their output was distributed to local singers, musicians, and
producers, who booked time in recording studios on other floors to
cut demonstration records. The demos were played for publishers,

who then matched the material to producers and/or artists, in *their* offices. It was a model of vertical integration (as well as literal integration, since the songwriters were Caucasian and many of the artists were African American). Al Kooper, who went on to revolutionize rock organ playing on Bob Dylan's "Like a Rolling Stone," began here, writing "This Diamond Ring" for Gary Lewis, son of comedian Jerry. Even the eternally hip Lou Reed paid Brill Building dues (with a would-be dance craze, "The Ostrich," recorded by The Primitives) before achieving iconic status with The Velvet Underground and a long-running solo career.

He Hit Me (And It Knocked Me Off the Radio)

Eva Narcissus Boyd, the 15-year-old babysitter for King and Goffin, became "Little Eva" after recording "The Loco-Motion," a 1962 dance track written by her young employers. Even though songwriters would use anything and anyone for inspiration, results were sometimes misguided or misunderstood: When Boyd explained bruises caused by her boyfriend by saying he smacked her only because he cared so much, King and Goffin wrote "He Hit Me (And It Felt Like a Kiss)." Phil Spector recorded the song with The Crystals; but even in those unenlightened days, a woman making excuses for being punched around proved too off-putting for a public that "complained" the single right off the airwaves.

But It's All Over Now

When the British Invasion rolled ashore early in 1964, the Brill Building was practically put out of business overnight by artists who followed The Beatles' lead by writing and controlling their own songs. Bob Dylan and The Beach Boys' Brian Wilson were at the head of that pack, and many others would follow. Performers were now expected to express their own thoughts and feelings, not those cooked up by faceless scribes locked in cubicles.

Nowadays, the Brill—which in 1962 held nearly 200 music-related businesses—is just another office building, albeit one with the fabled Colony Record and Radio store located at street level. But if you listen very closely, you might still hear echoes of a golden era when New York contributed a majority of singles to America's hit parade.

Make the Scene!

♥ ♥ ♥ ♥

*New York City is home to hundreds of music clubs and
other cultural venues, yet only a handful can claim iconic
status. Here are a few of them. If you weren't "there"
during the '70s and '80s, you weren't anywhere.*

New York City has been the flashpoint for an immense number of
cultural movements over the years, from Beat literature to tagging,
gay rights to punk music. People naturally seek out the like-minded,
and on rare occasions the venues at which they meet take on both
historic and iconic status. Here are four that people still talk about:

- **CBGB & OMFUG,** 315 Bowery, Manhattan. When Hilly Kristal
  opened his new club in December 1973, he had little idea that it
  would become ground zero for the American punk rock scene.
  And yet, within a few short years, CBGB's reputation as the place
  for new and emerging bands made it one of the best-known music
  clubs in the world.

    An acronym for Country, Blue Grass, Blues & Other Music
  For Uplifting Gormandizers, CBGB & OMFUG showcased some
  of the nation's most influential bands long before they made the
  pages of *Rolling Stone,* including The Ramones, Blondie, Talking
  Heads, Television, The Patti Smith Group, Dead Boys, and The
  Dictators. The place looked like hell (and don't even ask about the
  bathroom), but true aficionados of cutting-edge music, found
  CBGB's to be their home away from home. A rent dispute closed
  the club in October 2006, but the legend lives on.

- **Studio 54,** 254 West 54th Street, Manhattan. Created by Steve
  Rubell and Ian Shrager, Studio 54 was much more than just a
  disco; it was a scene that had to be seen to be believed—*if* you
  were allowed past the velvet rope. Yes, admission was very selec-
  tive. From 1977 to 1986, celebrities such as Andy Warhol and
  Brooke Shields, as well as cool "nobodies," flocked to the club,
  where rampant drug use and clandestine sex were as big a draw as
  the place's huge, strobe-lit dance floor.

Rubell and Shrager found fame and fortune, but their free-wheeling lifestyle eventually caught up with them, and they both served time for a variety of tax infractions. Rubell died of hepatitis in 1989; Shrager went on to make even more money in the hotel biz.

- **The Continental Baths,** 2107 Broadway & 73rd Street, Manhattan. Located in the basement of the Ansonia Hotel, the Continental Baths was one of the largest and most famous gay bathhouses in New York. It had a disco dance floor, cabaret lounge, and sauna and swimming pool. Up to 1,000 customers could be accommodated at once. Because the Baths was a frequent target of police raids, its owner, Steve Ostrow, finally installed a secret light system to warn patrons when the cops were approaching.

   The Continental Baths was one of the first gay bathhouses to feature a live DJ, and it also hosted performances by entertainers who would later go on to much bigger things, including Bette Midler, Barry Manilow, and The Manhattan Transfer.

- **Plato's Retreat,** 2107 Broadway & 73rd Street, Manhattan. When the Continental Baths closed in 1975, entrepreneur Larry Levenson reopened the venue as a straight swingers' club. It didn't take long for word to spread, and Plato's Retreat was soon frequented by such celebrities as Richard Dreyfuss and Sammy Davis Jr., as well as everyday people who were eager to energize their sex lives.

   Plato's Retreat came complete with a swimming pool, buffet, Jacuzzi, and a large "mat room" for amorous couples—with handy windows for those who liked to watch. But unlike Studio 54, which strived to maintain an air of exclusivity, Plato's Retreat was open to everyone willing to pay the admission—famous or ordinary, gorgeous or homely. "Once you take your clothes off, everyone's the same," Levenson explained to journalist/documentarian Jon Hart. "Nudity is the great equalizer. Bus drivers were partying with doctors and Wall Street people."

   In 1981, Levenson and his partners were sentenced to prison for financial fraud. When Levenson returned in 1984, AIDS was in the headlines, and the club's attendance plummeted. Plato's never fully recovered, and the place closed its doors on New Year's Eve 1985. Larry Levenson passed away in 1999 following heart surgery.

The Mighty Pen!

♥ ♥ ♥ ♥

Thomas Nast was one of the most important editorial cartoonists of his day—and an unrelenting foe of political corruption.

When he picked up his pen, he drew beautifully. He invented Santa Claus as we know him today, created the Republican elephant and the Democratic donkey, and used his skilled pen to fan the fires of patriotism during the Civil War. But it was his efforts to draw attention to New York City's corrupt political system for which cartoonist Thomas Nast is best known today.

Nast was born in Landau, Germany, in 1840 and emigrated to New York City with his mother and sister at the age of six. (His father followed three years later.) A natural talent, Nast studied art, and at age 15 he was hired as a reportorial artist for *Frank Leslie's Illustrated Newspaper.* He later went to work for the *New York Illustrated News,* which sent him to Europe to cover, among other things, Giuseppe Garibaldi's military campaign in Sicily.

A National Audience

In 1862, Nast accepted a full-time position with the prestigious *Harper's Weekly,* for whom he had previously freelanced. The magazine sent him to the battlefields of the Civil War, where his artistic talent shone. An avowed Union supporter, Nast unabashedly used his pen to criticize, with dramatic flair, the Confederate war effort and rouse support for the North.

His gig with *Harper's Weekly* made Nast nationally famous, and after the war he was solicited to illustrate books. Nast enjoyed such work and accepted numerous illustration jobs while he continued to work for *Harper's Weekly.* It is estimated that over the course of his career, Nast provided drawings for more than 100 volumes.

Tweed in the Crosshairs

In 1868, Nast turned his pen against William Magear "Boss" Tweed, the corrupt leader of New York City's Tammany Hall political machine. Tweed used his influence to put almost all of city government and much of the state legislature in his pocket. Tweed was the worst kind of political crook, and Nast was unrelenting in his artistic attacks against Tweed's administration. The cartoonist's campaign in *Harper's Weekly* and the *New York Times* lasted nearly three years.

Tweed and his cronies quickly felt the effects of Nast's drawings, which depicted the politician and his followers as sleazy scum with their hands in the public till. Legend has it that Tweed became so incensed over Nast's illustrations that he told his underlings, "Stop them damn pictures. I don't care what the papers write about. My constituents can't read. But, damn it, they can see the pictures."

At one point, intermediaries for Tweed visited Nast and offered him a $100,000 "gift" to study art in Europe. Naturally, Nast realized he was being bribed, so he played along, upping the payoff amount until it reached $500,000—which Nast declined.

The End for Tweed

Nast's cartoons helped bring an end to Tweed's culture of corruption. In 1871, Tweed was kicked out of office by angry voters and eventually jailed. However, he managed to escape in 1876 and tried to flee to Spain. In an ironic twist, he was recognized and arrested by a customs official who could not speak English but who recognized Tweed from Nast's dead-on caricatures!

In the years that followed, Nast's relationship with *Harper's Weekly* began to sour. Nast left the magazine in 1886. He freelanced for various magazines until 1892, when he established his own, *Nast's Weekly*. Unfortunately, the publication lasted only six months. Nast had difficulty finding substantial illustration work in the years that followed, and in 1902 he accepted an appointment from President Theodore Roosevelt as consul general to Ecuador. In a sad irony, Nast contracted yellow fever while abroad and died on December 7, 1902.

To this day, Thomas Nast is revered as one of the most influential political cartoonists who ever lived, demonstrating every time he put ink on paper that the pen really is mightier than the sword.

You Can Thank New York

Ever since the dawn of humanity, people have searched for ways to cleanse themselves after the inevitable, if rather unmentionable, process of elimination. Ancient Romans used communal sponges (which were then replaced in a bucket of saltwater—*eww*). Over the centuries, different countries and cultures used, literally, whatever came to hand—leaves, hay, fruit skins, or even (ouch) corncobs; the wealthier had rags. Circa A.D. 589, the Chinese were reportedly the first to use something akin to what we now know as toilet paper, and by 1393, the imperial court was going through 720,000 sheets annually, at a massive two by three feet each. The emperor's family itself had its royal rumps massaged by perfumed paper. But it was almost 500 years later before a New Yorker named Joseph Gayetty introduced the first prepackaged tissue for the masses in 1857.

Marketed as "therapeutic" or "medicated" paper, Gayetty's invention—which sold in packs of 500 for 50 cents—was ahead (no pun intended) of its time in that the "unbleached pearl-colored pure manila hemp paper" also contained aloe vera (an ingredient still employed in some  "luxury" toilet tissues), for "the prevention of piles." Gayetty was so proud of his innovation that each loose sheet was watermarked with his name.

Unfortunately, not only was Gayetty's product ultimately not very successful (although it remained available until the 1920s), it soon had competition. Seth Wheeler, of Albany, New York, obtained a patent in 1871 for perforated toilet tissue on a roll (said to have been previously invented by someone from England, whose version flopped). Philadelphia brothers Thomas, Edward, and Clarence Scott adopted the idea of sheets on a roll from an inventor in Great Britain. They began selling it through intermediaries such as drugstores in 1890, privately labeled (they didn't want their name on the actual product) and cut to specifications.

But if it hadn't been for Joseph Gayetty's first attempt at improving the state of the nation's bottoms, we might all still be eagerly awaiting our next mail-order catalog.

There Was Max's—and There Was Everyplace Else

♥ ♥ ♥ ♥

"Max's Kansas City was the exact spot where pop art and pop life came together in the Sixties—teenyboppers and sculptors, rock stars and poets . . . Hollywood actors . . . boutique owners and models, modern dancers and go-go dancers—everybody went to Max's."

—Andy Warhol

Once upon a time, as all good fairy tales begin, New York City had a pulsing *scene.* The epicenter to this creative vortex, a place where artists and auteurs came together to cross-fertilize and check out everybody else, was Max's Kansas City, a bar/restaurant that opened in December 1965 on Park Avenue South, just north of Union Square Park. There was no "Max": The owner was Mickey Ruskin, a patron of the arts and restaurateur who wanted to create a new hangout for those whose work he admired. And as Dorothy might say, at Max's, we were definitely not in Kansas any more.

Wild

Mickey favored painters, so among the first to run up tabs (some later bartered for art) were future masters such as Robert Rauschenberg, Larry Rivers, and Roy Lichtenstein. But things really started to take off circa 1968, when Andy Warhol, who had recently moved his Factory from midtown to 33 Union Square West, began to come in. Warhol brought his "superstars" and The Velvet Underground, *the* rock group of the moment, with its songwriter Lou Reed. Reed's 1972 solo hit, "Walk on the Wild Side," is a literal recounting of the goings-on in Max's infamous back room.

Democracy of Cool

"Billy Wilder used to tell me about the coffeehouses in Vienna, and Max's was like that for me. I never knew any other place you could talk with writers, performers, various wandering gypsies, and [BS] about the ways of the world."

—Mel Brooks

Each table had a small bowl of hard, inedible chickpeas, used primarily as missiles during aggressive flirting. A couple of bucks brought a bowl of salad and brown bread with butter. Then the evening really got underway, and the alcohol began to flow. Someone else always picked up the bill.

Max's had a definite pecking order, yet the club and its patrons were oddly democratic in a way that had never happened before: Nobodies who might become somebodies mixed with those who had already arrived. Iggy Pop, Alice Cooper, David Bowie, and KISS held court at various tables as William Burroughs may have dined with Mick Jagger, as a pre-Blondie Debbie Harry waited tables, and as Roger Vadim and Jane Fonda stared at one Warhol acolyte's tabletop "showtime" striptease. Drag queens drifted by the Duke and Duchess of Windsor while fashion designer Betsey Johnson, then wed to the VU's John Cale, made her way to the ladies' room (next to the phone booth, whose minuscule confines were periodically defied by acrobatic, semipublic sexual activities).

Running on Magic

While downstairs was hopping, upstairs was reserved for live music, in a room that held a couple of hundred if strained to utmost fire-hazard occupancy. If you weren't on the guest list—and almost everybody was—it cost about $3 to catch the New York Dolls, NYC's early punk-rock answer to the Rolling Stones; Aerosmith (whose Max's showcase led to a contract); Patti Smith, who had previously frequented downstairs with boyfriend Robert Mapplethorpe; Willie Nelson or Bruce Springsteen sharing a bill with Bob Marley or Hall & Oates. As Mickey Ruskin once declared, it was "magic."

It couldn't last, and so it didn't. Ruskin filed for bankruptcy in 1974. Max's came under new ownership. Other soon-to-be-notable acts played upstairs, but the crowds thinned, and the luminaries dispersed. Some habitués died; others moved on. There would be new hot spots, fresh places to see and be seen. But there would never be another Max's. Jimi Hendrix said it was a place where "you could let your freak flag fly."

But that was then, and now this particular fairy tale was over. Mickey Ruskin died in 1983. The site where Max's stood is now occupied by a café and delicatessen.

Canny Coyote!

♥ ♥ ♥ ♥

Central Park is home to a variety of birds and animals—
though usually not coyotes. But over the past few years,
at least two of the canny canines have striven to move
from the surrounding wilds into the big city.

Pet dogs are a common sight in New York City, coyotes less so.
There's no surprise in that, of course, but in March 2006, a coyote
nicknamed Hal loped into the Hallett Nature Sanctuary with the
apparent intention of calling the place home. Park workers tried to
capture the cagey critter, but Hal proved to be an adept escape
artist. He eluded his pursuers by jumping into a lake and then led
them on an exciting two-day chase before finally being taken down
with a tranquilizer dart near the Wollman Rink ice skating facility.

How Hal managed to make his way into Manhattan had wildlife
officials scratching their heads. Coyotes are much more common
upstate, so it's a good assumption that that's where he came from,
moving unnoticed along the Hudson River and through the Bronx.
But how did he get into Manhattan? Did he cross a railway bridge
over the Harlem River? Did he swim? No one can say for sure.

New Yorkers became enamored with the gutsy coyote and
closely followed his saga in the newspapers and on the local news.
Cheers went up when he was captured alive and apparently well, but
the story ended on a sad note when Hal died while being tagged and
prepared for release into California Hill State Forest in Putnam
County, New York. A necropsy revealed that he probably died of
internal hemorrhaging from the ingestion of rat poison, complicated
by an advanced case of heartworms.

Hal wasn't the first coyote to have a run through Central Park. In
1999, another one was captured there and given to the Flushing Zoo
in Queens.

Though coyotes in Central Park inevitably make the front pages,
city officials don't consider them a serious threat to people. The
animals are shy by nature and tend to avoid humans whenever
possible, say wildlife experts. So what got into Hal?

Fast Facts

- In a 1938 boxing match very much tinged with politics and race, Joe Louis handed Nazi Germany's Max Schmeling a brutal first-round knockout at Yankee Stadium. The referee didn't even bother counting to ten.

- The 1863 Civil War Draft Riots showed city leaders that they had a serious urban problem on their hands. This eventually led to the Tenement House Acts, progressive attempts to alleviate squalor and the frustration it caused among residents.

- City College began in 1847 as a combination prep school and college called the Free Academy. It opened on 23rd Street and moved to Harlem in the 1890s.

- The copper plating over the Statue of Liberty's steel framework is quite thin: only $3/32$ inch thick. That's a thickness halfway between the old Eisenhower dollar coin and the Kennedy half-dollar.

- Mae West, born in Woodhaven in 1893, developed her signature walk of necessity. Standing only five foot one, she had to wear heels of six inches or so to enhance her stage presence, and the swaying walk naturally followed.

- On October 27, 1904, the New York subway system opened. Some 150,000 people gave it a try, and it began to supersede elevated trains. Manhattan's last el train shut down 51 years later.

- In 1910, the Lower East Side had 182 known synagogues between Houston Street, the East River, and the Bowery. Most blocks had one house of worship, some as many as six.

- The first New York Marathon (1970) consisted of laps around Central Park run by 127 marathoners. In 1976 it expanded to include all five boroughs; today it has to limit runners to 37,000.

The 1962 Mets, by the Numbers

♥ ♥ ♥ ♥

Casey Stengel's first-season Mets not only cratered in wins vs. losses, but they flopped in so many creative ways that some of their team and individual stats are downright entertaining. Check 'em out.

- **Winning percentage:** .250 (last), 60 games out of first place, 4th worst of all-time
- **Wins vs. losses in extra innings:** 4–13, worst in either league
- **Record vs. right-handed starters:** 26–92, worst in either league
- **Runs scored vs. runs allowed:** 617 vs. 948, worst in either league
- **Team batting average:** .240, lowest in either league
- **Batters used during season:** 44, most in either league
- **Catchers used during season:** 7, none of whom batted more than 160 times
- **Saves:** 10, fewest in either league
- **Home runs allowed:** 192, second highest in either league
- **Shutouts:** 4, tied for fewest in either league
- **Opposing players hit by pitch:** 52, most in either league
- **Staff ERA:** 5.04, highest in either league
- **Home and road records:** 22–58 and 18–62, respectively, both the worst in either league
- **Wild pitches:** 71, second highest in either league
- **Most errors:** Utility infielder Rod Kanehl, 32 in 117 games, a .936 percentage
- **Most positions played by one player:** Rod Kanehl, every position but pitcher and catcher
- **Best-hitting pitcher (20 or more at-bats):** Jay Hook, .203
- **Worst-hitting pitcher (20 or more at-bats):** Bob Moorhead, .045

- **Youngest player:** Ed Kranepool, 17 (born 11/8/44, debuted 9/22/62)

- **Worst batting average (50 or more at-bats):** Don Zimmer, .077

- **Worst on-base percentage (50 or more at-bats):** Don Zimmer, .127

- **Worst ERA (20 or more innings pitched):** Sherman "Roadblock" Jones, 7.71

- **Worst pitching record (20 or more innings pitched):** Craig Anderson, 3–17 or Bob L. Miller, 1–12 (you be the judge)

- **Most wins by pitcher:** Roger Craig, 10

- **Most losses by pitcher:** Roger Craig, 24

- **Only pitcher with a winning record:** Ken Mackenzie, 5–4

- **Most pitchers named "Bob Miller":** 2, Bob L. Miller (starter/reliever) and Bob G. Miller (relief)

- **Highest frequency of home runs allowed by pitcher (20 or more innings pitched):** Wilmer "Vinegar Bend" Mizell, 10 in 38 innings, or 2.4 dingers per 9 innings

- **Wildest pitcher (20 or more innings pitched):** Wilmer Mizell, 25 in 38 innings, or 5.9 freebies per 9 innings

- **Best manager at working the media:** Casey Stengel (had everyone in both leagues beat hands down)

- **Best quote:** Richie Ashburn, to "Marvelous" Marv Throneberry, mobbed by reporters: "Tell them how you're going to throw a party for your fans—in a phone booth."

- **Loopiest trade:** Acquired Harry Chiti from the Indians for a player to be named later—then shipped Chiti back to Cleveland as the "player named later."

- **Dumbest play:** Marv Throneberry's two-run triple, in which he failed to touch either first or second base and was called out.

- **Funniest play:** To end field miscommunication with Spanish-speaking infielder Elio Chacon, outfielder Richie Ashburn started to call for the ball in Spanish. The first time Ashburn did so, he was trampled by outfielder Frank Thomas, who didn't speak Spanish.

The Buoyant Pachyderm

♥ ♥ ♥ ♥

In an "only in New York" manner, an imprisoned elephant flees her Coney Island keepers. The catch? She makes her escape by water, not land. It gets better: She makes it as far as Staten Island by swimming six miles. Or does she?

To call Coney Island's escaped elephant "determined" would be like calling Babe Ruth a good hitter, at least in the most famous telling of this offbeat tale. On June 4, 1904, the hulking animal named Fanny took flight from her captors at Coney Island's Luna Park. Inexplicably, Fanny launched her bid in a westerly direction, across water, ignoring a far easier land path to the north. Five miles of open bay lay between the elephant and Staten Island's New Dorp Beach. Could the grey beast make it to the other side, where the Savannah-like grass might offer a life similar to that of her African home?

The Scheme

The above telling of the tale may or may not be true. An alternative holds that the elephant's Coney Island handler was angry that his enormous charge was no longer generating profits. Hatching a scheme to float Fanny by barge to a point just off New Dorp Beach, he allegedly pushed the beast into the drink during a deep fog and crossed his fingers. Certainly the publicity elicited by "the elephant who swam five miles!" would restore Fanny's earning power.

One fact is beyond dispute. The elephant *did* swim completely unaided to New Dorp Beach for at least half a mile. Fishers who sighted this unlikely swimmer were dumbfounded. Police "apprehended" Fanny when she reached shore. Charged with vagrancy, the elephant was lassoed and whisked off to a police stable, where she'd remain until her handler retrieved her. Crowds rejoiced when the now-famous Fanny was returned to Coney Island via boat and trolley car. Published reports suggest that business at Coney was especially good that season. And why not? The "New Dorp Elephant" was holding court beside the amusements and sideshows. *Ka-ching, ka-ching.*

Up in Flames: The "Fireproof" Crystal Palace

♥ ♥ ♥ ♥

How New York's attempt to emulate a London architectural triumph ended in financial and physical ruin.

In London in 1851, the first ever World's Fair was held. Opened by Queen Victoria and officially titled the Great Exhibition of the Works of Industry of All Continents, it was more commonly referred to as the Great Exhibition or the Crystal Palace Exhibition because of the vast, architecturally daring glass and cast-iron structure in which the expo was held. Two years later, New York City followed suit, staging the Exhibition of the Industry of All Nations inside its own Crystal Palace, a building whose glass and iron structure rendered it fireproof—or so its designers thought.

International Cachet, Domestic Glory

Located on 42nd Street between Fifth and Sixth avenues, on the Reservoir Square site that is now known as Bryant Park, the Palace was designed by Danish architect Georg Carstensen (who had helped develop Copenhagen's famed Tivoli Gardens) and his German compatriot, Charles Gildemeister. New York wanted to prove it could hold its own among the greatest cities on earth, and indeed, following the fair's grand opening in July 1853, Gotham enjoyed one of its first major tourist booms as more than a million people took in the artwork, consumer goods, and industrial products of no fewer than 4,000 exhibitors.

From house paint to fine paintings, farm tools to precision steam engines, the wares were ostensibly displayed to showcase the global fruits of the Industrial Revolution. However, like its London predecessor, the NYC exhibition clearly promoted domestic product and ingenuity above anything else. More than 15,000 panes of glass and 1,800 tons of iron were used to construct the giant cross-shaped structure, whose central 100-foot-diameter dome towered 123 feet above the city. If that sounds a little like London's centerpiece

structure, well, imitation is the sincerest form of flattery. Unfortunately, what the New York fair *couldn't* duplicate was the first one's huge profits.

May 1, 1853, was scheduled to be the public opening of the New York Crystal Palace, but major construction setbacks delayed the launch for more than two months. Finally, on July 14, U.S. President Franklin Pierce unveiled the highly anticipated "Temple of National Industry." After opening festivities in which poets sang psalms and philosophers cited industry as the source of humanity's greatest accomplishments, relatively modest numbers of people shelled out $10 for season tickets to the exhibition, while others paid the single-day admissions of 50 cents for adults and 25 cents for the kiddies.

The Embarrassment of Destruction

Several hotels were built to accommodate the visitors, yet after the initial burst of enthusiasm, there wasn't sufficient continuing public interest to avert a financial disaster. By March 1854, the expo's financiers were $100,000 in debt, and their attempt to correct this by recruiting the leadership of circus huckster P. T. Barnum was clearly a desperate move. Barnum may have been a successful businessman, but his carny expertise hardly lent itself to the requirements of a prestigious industrial exhibition. By the time the fair closed on November 1, 1854, the deficit had risen to around $300,000, and Barnum was deriding himself as "an ass for having anything to do with the Crystal Palace."

Thereafter, the huge glass cathedral was leased out as a concert venue and a convention center. But that came to an end when, just after 5:00 P.M. on October 5, 1858, during the 30th Annual Fair of the American Institute, fire broke out in a room storing wood patterns that had been used in the building's construction. Forget all of the iron and glass: Courtesy of high winds and ineffective extinguishers, the dome collapsed within 15 minutes, and just five minutes later the entire Crystal Palace was in ruins. To ensure there were no major injuries, New York firefighters evacuated about 2,000 people, but roughly half a million dollars of merchandise and machinery were destroyed—along with the last vestiges of a sparkling "fireproof" structure that had been intended to elevate a nation's pride.

Five Fun Forts in New York City

♥ ♥ ♥ ♥

Rarely do people associate military bases with New York City. Yet New York is home to more than 20 historic forts and Army bases. Here are capsules of some particularly tourist-friendly forts, as well as a still-active military base—one in each borough.

Blockhouse #1 (Manhattan): At the northern end of Central Park, the remains of Blockhouse #1 tower over the landscape, flag flying high. Built by volunteers in 1814 to protect New York from the British, the stone building never saw action.

Fort Hamilton (Brooklyn): An active Army base and site of the Harbor Defense Museum, Fort Hamilton played key roles in the Revolutionary War (although just as a position for guns) and the War of 1812. The current fort was constructed in 1825, and Robert E. Lee was stationed there in 1841. Two decades later, it served as a training site for volunteers fighting Lee's forces during the Civil War.

Fort Schuyler (Bronx): Currently home to SUNY Maritime College and the Maritime Industry Museum, the site was bombarded by the British during the Revolutionary War. Construction on the current gray stone fort began in 1833. It was used as a prison during the Civil War and as a training ground for World War I doughboys.

Fort Tilden (Queens): Now an arts center, nature reserve, and the anchor of the most unpopulated stretch of beach in New York City, Fort Tilden was established in 1917 to defend against attack by air or sea. Before it was decommissioned in 1974, the fort housed Nike Ajax and Hercules air defense missiles.

Fort Wadsworth (Staten Island): This fort occupies real estate that has seen the longest continuous military use in the United States. Fortified by the Dutch in the 1600s, the site was occupied by the British during the Revolution and then run by various branches of the U.S. military until it closed in 1994. Today, Civil War reenactments, tours, and great views of New York Harbor await visitors.

Where Science Is Fun!

♥ ♥ ♥ ♥

*The American Museum of Natural History is one
of New York City's best-known landmarks.*

Many people first saw the American Museum of Natural History in the movie *Night at the Museum* (2006), a comic fantasy in which a spell brings everything in the museum to life after viewing hours. The real museum may not be quite as raucous, but it *is* just as much fun.

Located in the Upper West Side of Manhattan, the museum was founded in 1869. Construction started in 1874, and over the decades the facility has grown to become one of the largest natural history museums in the world. It comprises 25 interconnected buildings that span several city blocks and boasts 42 permanent exhibits and several temporary ones, as well as a planetarium, research laboratories, and a massive library. With so much to offer, it's no surprise that the museum is one of the Big Apple's most popular tourist attractions.

A Lot to See

"Natural history" is the phrase to remember when visiting the museum. Its collections total nearly 32 million specimens that transport visitors from modern-day wonders all the way back to the very origins of the universe. Every discipline of human science is extensively covered, including biology, geology, astronomy, ecology, and anthropology.

Here are some of the most popular exhibition halls:

- The Anne and Bernard Spitzer Hall of Human Origins, formerly known as the Hall of Human Biology. Here, visitors find an in-depth examination of human evolution, with several life-size dioramas that illustrate human progress through the ages.

- The Harry Frank Guggenheim Hall of Minerals, a showcase for unique geological specimens, such as the 632-carat Patricia Emerald and the 563-carat Star of India sapphire, the largest ever found.

- The Arthur Ross Hall of Meteorites, which houses, among other things, Ahnighito, a 34-ton section of the massive 200-ton Cape York meteorite that landed in Greenland thousands of years ago.

- The Milstein Hall of Ocean Life, famous for containing one of the museum's most beloved exhibits, a 94-foot model of a blue whale.

- Hall of Saurischian Dinosaurs, home of the largest collection of dinosaur fossils in the world, only a portion of which are on display for public viewing. Not surprisingly, this hall is a favorite among young people, who can't seem to get enough of the massive Tyrannosaurus rex and Apatosaurus (formerly known as Brontosaurus) skeletons, both of which have been revised to reflect current 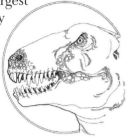 understanding of how these massive beasts stood and walked. (Fun Fact: The T-rex skeleton was assembled using the bones from two different skeletons discovered in Montana six years apart.)

Universal History

An especially popular attraction among museumgoers is the Rose Center for Earth and Space, which has replaced the old Hayden Planetarium. Ultramodern in design, the center features a spiral walkway off the planetarium theater from which patrons can view scale models of stars, planets, and other heavenly bodies hanging from the ceiling. The center also offers a history of the universe narrated by actress Jodie Foster, an ecosystem fully contained within a glass sphere, and a variety of space-related displays.

One of the most amazing aspects of the American Museum of Natural History is that there is no fixed admission fee—patrons may pay whatever they wish (though the suggested donation for adults is a very reasonable ten dollars). There are, however, admission fees for special programs such as the Sky show, the IMAX Theater, and certain temporary exhibits.

The Smithsonian Institution in Washington, D.C., may get more publicity, but folks with even a passing interest in the world around them, not to mention our past and future, owe it to themselves to pay a visit to the American Museum of Natural History at least once in their lives. It's the kind of place guaranteed to bring out the wondrous child in us all. And don't forget to pick up a keepsake dinosaur in the gift shop!

More than They Bargained For

♥ ♥ ♥ ♥

When Marilyn Monroe's skirt fluttered high into the air from the whoosh of a passing subway car, red-blooded men took notice. Hubby Joe DiMaggio was equally aroused, but in a far different way.

During the making of *The Seven Year Itch* (1955) actress Marilyn Monroe became an American icon playing every man's sweet, compliable fantasy come to life. Although nobody would call the gags in *Itch* sophisticated, Monroe and writer-director Billy Wilder present them with a delightful, unexpected innocence. The Girl (the character has no other name) is sexy, but utterly sweet. She gives every impression of having no idea how she affects men.

A Picture Lasts Forever

The concept of the film's most famous image was simple. The beautiful Girl stands above a subway grate on a hot NYC night, enjoying the breeze of the passing underground train. The rush of air "accidentally" lifts her white skirt, revealing Monroe's gorgeous gams and her, um, underthings. When the sequence hit movie screens, males went bonkers. To Wilder, the combination of exhibitionism, voyeurism, and blithe innocence was a home run.

The scene was shot at 52nd Street and Lexington Avenue, which was choked with gaping onlookers—including Monroe's husband and former Yankee slugger Joe DiMaggio. He observed the goings-on from the back of the crowd, his face an icy mask, his ears ringing with the hoots and hollers of hundreds of men ogling his wife.

"What the hell's going on here?" demanded Joe. Monroe was already Hollywood's "IT" girl, and DiMaggio had long battled with her over her cheesecake image. Joe stalked off, and he and Marilyn later argued wildly about her "bad behavior." Not long after that, they were divorced. Their marriage had lasted a scant nine months.

That was a personal tragedy for both, but in the abstract, Billy Wilder's instincts were right all along. The skirt-blowing sequence is one of Monroe's signature moments, a snippet of her cinematic magic that entices to this very day.

New York City's Oldest Restaurants

♥ ♥ ♥ ♥

Ten places to feast on New York history.

Because 70 percent of restaurants in New York close or change hands after just five years, the ten restaurants noted below have performed a miraculous feat: Each opened for business prior to 1900. Savor the past along with a steak, a pastrami sandwich, a burger, or a pint at:

Fraunces Tavern® (1762): New Yorkers owe many debts to Samuel Fraunces, founder of The Queen's Head Tavern. Not only did the Fraunces kitchen establish a take-out service (to go to Gen. George Washington's camp during the Revolution), the place also provided a home to colonialists who wanted to knock back a pint while griping about the Stamp Act and other hot political issues of the day. In a particularly big moment, the Fraunces hosted Washington's postwar gala and farewell speech to officers of the Continental Army. Just as significant is the structure itself, the oldest in Manhattan. Today, diners enjoy a colonial setting and browse the Revolutionary War artifacts in the museum upstairs.

Bridge Café (1847): The space currently occupied by the Bridge Café was built in 1794 and has offered some type of food or drinking enterprise ever since. However, it wasn't officially designated as a drinking establishment until 1847. In 1879, the place got into some trouble when it was classed as a "disorderly house" (a brothel, that is). The Bridge took its current name in 1979.

Pete's Tavern (1864): Pete's Tavern has been in the same location since it opened, making it the longest-lived continuously operating bar and restaurant in the city. The booths haven't changed in 100 years, so lucky (and imaginative) diners can share a table with the spirit of O. Henry, who wrote *The Gift of the Magi* at the booth by the front door. The original bar spans 30 feet and survived Prohibition disguised as a flower shop.

Old Homestead Steakhouse (1868): The Old Homestead has seen many changes in its neighborhood since it first opened. The formerly grimy meatpacking district is now home to hipsters and even an elevated park that was constructed on an abandoned freight rail. Amidst all this upscale development, the giant cow tethered to the restaurant's marquee ("We're the King of Beef") makes Old Homestead hard to miss, as does the neon sign notifying the public of its status as New York's oldest steakhouse. This was one of the first American restaurants to offer Kobe beef, and because that apparently went over big, the Homestead is now comfortable offering a $41 hamburger.

Landmark Tavern (1868): Farther up the west side, the Landmark Tavern originally perched on the shores of the Hudson River (there was no such thing as 12th Avenue in 1868). Its Irish founders tended to the needs of the

waterfront workers on the first floor, serving nickel beer on a bar carved from a single mahogany tree. Those original owners raised their kids and subsequent generations on the two upstairs floors until Prohibition, when the tavern closed for 30 minutes while the whiskey barrels were relocated to a speakeasy on the third floor. The speakeasy is long gone, but the Landmark's bar, stamped tin ceiling, floor tiles, and maybe even a Confederate soldier remain.

P. J. Clarke's (1884): Although the two-story building surrounded by high-rise towers on the northeast corner of Third Avenue and 55th Street has proudly stood in the neighborhood since 1864, the first restaurant opened on the site 20 years later. Serving celebrities (Frank Sinatra "owned" Table 20), businesspeople, and everyday folks alike, the checkered tablecloths give the bar and restaurant a homey feel. It hosted genius, too: Johnny Mercer supposedly worked out the melody for "One for My Baby (And One More for the Road)" while sitting at the bar. Clarke's is infamous (or beloved, depending on who you ask) for the gigantic urinals that dominate the men's room.

Keens Steakhouse (1885): This English chophouse is famous for its muttonchops and, in its early years, for the now-defunct Herald Square Theater District actors who hung out there. Women, however, were not permitted inside until 1905, when famed actress Lillie Langtry sued for admittance. In keeping with 17th-century British tradition, Keens allowed Pipe Club members to store their fragile clay pipes on its premises. The Club has had more than 90,000 members and now houses the world's largest collection of church-warden pipes, as well as pipes that once belonged to Albert Einstein, John Pierpont (J. P.) Morgan, Babe Ruth, and Teddy Roosevelt.

Peter Luger Steakhouse (1887): The German steakhouse that was to become Peter Luger opened in Williamsburg before there was a Williamsburg Bridge. The wood-paneled décor of ledges lined with steins hasn't changed much since then, but the steaks have been voted the best in the city by the Zagat Survey for more than 25 years in a row. Cows are selected by the present owner's granddaughter, who personally attends the meat market, looks each beast in the eye, and gives a thumbs up or down.

Katz's Delicatessen (1888): When the Katz family opened its delicatessen after arriving from Russia, they had to compete with dozens of Jewish delis that crowded the teeming streets of the Lower East Side. It was a tough fight, but in the end, the Katz's special way of smoking and pickling won out. During World War II, the owners sent salamis to their sons serving in the army, launching what has been Katz's slogan ever since: "Send a Salami to Your Boy in the Army." According to local lore, the U.S. Army bombarded the enemy with nicely aged salamis, which were then so enjoyed by the besieged that they surrendered.

Old Town Bar and Restaurant (1892): Chock full of original fixtures, the Old Town Bar and Restaurant has the oldest functioning dumbwaiter system in New York City. Its marble and mahogany bar is 55 feet long and is backed by a beveled-edge mirror that fills more than 250 square feet. The Old Town's tin ceilings tower 18 feet above patrons' heads. The enormous urinals, however, weren't installed until 1910. The bar lived through Prohibition as a speakeasy protected by Tammany Hall, New York's powerful Democratic political machine.

Movie Manhattan

♥ ♥ ♥ ♥

The best movies about New York? Well, that's a subject that provokes heated discussions, even among folks who've never been to the city.

Here's a fun tip for movie buffs. Ask your friends to name the ten best films made about New York and then leave the room—a lively conversation will still be going strong hours later. It seems everyone has a favorite New York flick. Here are some of our favorites.

- *After Hours* (1985), directed by Martin Scorsese. Griffin Dunne, Rosanna Arquette, and a fabulous supporting cast get mixed up in a night in SoHo that goes hilariously—and terrifyingly—wrong.

- *Dead End* (1937), directed by William Wyler, with a screenplay by Lillian Hellman. Humphrey Bogart, Sylvia Sidney, Joel McCrea, Claire Trevor, Wendy Barrie, and the Dead End Kids wow in this classic look at the poor versus the rich in far west Manhattan.

- *The Godfather* and *The Godfather II* (1972 and 1974), Francis Ford Coppola's triumphs—whoever thought he could trump the first *Godfather*?—tell us volumes about the history and soul of New York, especially immigrant life in the early 20th century.

- *I Am Legend* (2007), directed by Francis Lawrence. This is a grim view of post-apocalyptic New York, with Will Smith as possibly the last man on earth, vying with scary "Infecteds" who survived, sort of.

- *Manhattan* (1979), directed by Woody Allen. With the New York skyline opening and closing the film and music by George Gershwin, you can't get much more New York than this. In fact, you might as well add most of Allen's Manhattan-centric films to the list, especially *Hannah and Her Sisters* and *Annie Hall*.

- *Midnight Cowboy* (1969), directed by John Schlesinger. Ratso Rizzo slams his fist on the taxi hood, shouting, "I'm walkin' here! I'm walkin' here!" Many movies have been made about hicks who come to Manhattan in search of a dream—even a sordid one like that of would-be gigolo Joe Buck. But few express the struggle better than Dustin Hoffman and Jon Voight in this sad and edgy classic.

- ***Miracle on 34th Street*** (1947), directed by George Seaton. Young Natalie Wood is at her adorable best as the little girl who learns to believe in Santa Claus (Edmund Gwenn), despite the best efforts of her mother (Maureen O'Hara), who hires Santas for Macy's department store. This is the movie that introduced the Macy's Thanksgiving Day parade to the world.

- ***The Naked City*** (1948), directed by Jules Dassin. Some argue that this is *the* best movie ever made about New York. Two detectives follow a series of leads in the murder of a young model in her bathtub and incidentally take us on a wonderfully visual tour of Manhattan. Unlike many New York movies of the day, this one was shot entirely on location in the city.

- ***New York, New York*** (1977), directed by Martin Scorsese. You may have noticed that Mr. Scorsese's name also pops up a lot when you talk about Manhattan movies. In this ambitious musical, two young jazz musicians, Liza Minnelli and Robert De Niro, pursue their art, and romance, in post–World War II New York. Remember: If you can make it here, you can make it anywhere.

- ***On the Town*** (1949), directed by Stanley Donen and Gene Kelly. Frank Sinatra, Kelly, and Jules Munshin are three sailors on shore leave in search of all things Manhattan, especially girls. You'll be singing Leonard Bernstein's "New York, New York" for weeks.

- ***The Out-of-Towners*** (1970), directed by Arthur Hiller. This sour but hilarious Neil Simon masterpiece flings a hapless couple from Ohio into an NYC night that involves strikes, kidnappings, drenching storms, muggings, and other only-in-New-York mayhem. Jack Lemmon and Sandy Dennis are grand as the victimized pair.

- ***Sex and the City*** (2008), directed by Michael Patrick King. What happens when the quintessential Manhattan single girl decides to get married? At the New York Public Library, no less? Delicious chaos. All New Yorkers dream of the penthouse Carrie Bradshaw almost owned.

- ***Wall Street*** (1987), directed by Oliver Stone. An unscrupulous, money-mad financier (Michael Douglas) tutors a young broker (Charlie Sheen) in this look at the worst of NYC power and wealth, long before anyone ever heard of bailouts or Bernie Madoff.

Fast Facts

- How long did it take the New York Stock Exchange (founded in 1792) to admit a woman to membership? Almost two centuries! Muriel Siebert, a veteran investment professional, took her seat in December 1967.

- The idea for La Guardia Airport originated in 1934, when Mayor Fiorello La Guardia's ticket to New York landed him in Newark. He ordered the plane to Brooklyn, making the point that the city needed its own airport.

- On September 16, 1940, incensed Dodger fan Frank Germano leapt from the Ebbets grandstand and assaulted huge umpire George Magerkurth. Germano lost the scuffle but later admitted it was a diversion for a pickpocketing cohort.

- Ever wonder why the British didn't mess with NYC in the War of 1812? Thank Mayor DeWitt Clinton. In the prewar years, he had several solid forts built in New York Harbor.

- Back in the late 1960s, when Brooklyn's own Barry Manilow was struggling to make his mark, he did ad jingles. If you can't get "like a good neighbor, State Farm is there" out of your brain, thank Barry.

- As of the early 1960s, Teamsters delivering bagels in New York took part of their pay in bagels. Each union delivery person got two-dozen bagels a day.

- Slavery faded out gradually in New York. The end began on July 4, 1799; slaves' children born after that date were born free. By 1810, the city's free African American community was America's largest.

- The 47-acre Queens County Farm Museum (Glen Oaks) has operated since 1697, making it the city's oldest operating farm. Your small-town relatives probably won't believe you when you tell them you visited a corn maze or enjoyed a hayride in New York City.

Bragging Rights

Walk down a busy sidewalk or ride a crowded subway, and you're bound to hear them—words of myriad languages from all parts of the globe, spoken by tourists and New Yorkers alike. Contrary to some popular jokes, they're not all four-letter words, either.

New York City as a whole is comprised mostly of English speakers, but there are areas, such as the Sunset Park neighborhood in Brooklyn, where other languages and cultures dominate. No one can get an exact count, but some experts claim that as many as 800 different languages are spoken throughout the Big Apple. The city's public school system itself serves students speaking 176 languages. This leaves some linguists speechless.

The 109 square miles of Queens, New York City's most ethnically diverse and easternmost borough, are abuzz with more languages than any other part of the city. There were 138 different languages listed on its 2000 census forms! While 48.3 percent of Queens residents are foreign born, according to 2005-7 American Community Survey Estimates, 54.5 percent speak a language other than English at home.

People in Queens hang on to their culture, no matter how far they may be from the motherland. It's no wonder that foodies and travelers in-the-know go there for authentic ethnic food and cultural experiences. Want a real taste of Tibet, Malaysia, Greece, India, or any other place you can imagine? Take the 7 train.

Like rare animal species, languages can also become endangered and go extinct. Consider one man in Rego Park, Queens, who hasn't found anyone else in the city who speaks his native Mamuju, an Austronesian language spoken in the Indonesian province of West Sulawesi. When you can't find something in New York City, you know it's rare.

Daniel Kaufman, a linguistics professor at the City University of New York, started the Endangered Language Alliance to identify and record languages particularly vulnerable to extinction, including those from remote parts of the world that have no written component. One of his first sites to study? Queens, the original melting pot.

Broadway's Biggest Losers

♥ ♥ ♥ ♥

Broadway is known for producing some of the world's largest shows ever seen on stage. Still, they can't all be Cats. *Here are some of the biggest tankers in Broadway history.*

Probably the worst play on Broadway, the stinker that all subsequent bombs have been compared to, was Arthur Bicknell's *The Moose Murders.* The script included one character who tried to have sex with his mother; meanwhile another character, dressed in a moose costume, was kicked in the groin by a quadriplegic. *New York Times* theater critic Frank Rich called it "the worst play I've ever seen on a Broadway stage." It had one performance at the Eugene O'Neill Theatre on February 22, 1983, before it was closed down.

Quick Closers

Another early closer was the 1966 stage version of the movie classic *Breakfast at Tiffany's.* Although it had big-name star Mary Tyler Moore playing Holly Golightly, the musical, nearly four hours long, was constantly being revised. *Breakfast* had its first preview on December 12, but producer David Merrick shut it down four nights later, saying the show's closing was preferable "rather than subject the drama critics and the public to an excruciatingly boring evening."

Another movie adaptation to bomb big on Broadway was a 1988 musical version of Stephen King's horror novel, *Carrie,* which closed after a measly five performances. Actress Barbara Cook was actually nearly decapitated by a set prop, and lead actress Linzi Hateley's body microphone stopped working after the show's climactic blood-soaked scene. The $7 million show was the most expensive quick-to-close flop in Broadway history.

An older stinker on Broadway was *Portofino,* a confusing musical that combined an auto-racing storyline with witches, priests, and the devil. Opening on February 21, 1958, it seemed destined to bomb. It closed after only three shows. Famed theater critic Walter Kerr wrote, "I will not say that *Portofino* was the worst musical ever produced, because I've only been seeing musicals since 1919."

Battle for the Sky

♥ ♥ ♥ ♥

When auto magnate Walter Chrysler erected his stylish art deco skyscraper in 1928, he closely guarded its intended height, hoping to outdo others with equally lofty intentions. Thus began New York's skyscraper wars.

The prosperity of the 1920s encouraged a major trend among developers: Lacking horizontal space in which to grow their empires, New York builders looked to the sky. Here, in this untapped landscape of altitude, skyscrapers could offer not only vast amounts of commercial space, but breathtaking views to boot. A select few aspired for the top prize: World's Tallest Building. Only one building at a time could hold the coveted title, of course, but anybody who undertook that sort of costly construction might create enough excitement and publicity to offset—for everybody—the increased costs of gunning for the top. And for the ultimate winner, success would cement his name into the public psyche. Yes, big money and overstuffed egos were in collusion, and the results would be fabulous.

High Hopes

The auto baron Walter Chrysler decided to enter the skyscraper sweepstakes in 1928. Chrysler hinted that his namesake structure on Lexington Avenue would be a building of monumental proportions but declined to divulge its intended height. Walter was noted for being coy in public, and his caginess here suggested that he was indeed shooting for the world mark.

A former General Motors vice president, John Jakob Raskob, was an equally ambitious sort. On 34th Street in 1929, he began construction of a tower soon to be called the Empire State Building. When he hired the architectural firm of Shreve, Lamb & Harmon, Raskob asked, "How high can you make it so it won't fall down?"

Tit for Tat

As buildings grew progressively taller, developers grew more concerned. "We thought we would be the tallest at 80 stories," declared Hamilton Weber, the rental manager for the Empire State Building. "Then the Chrysler went higher, so we lifted the Empire State to 85 stories, but only four feet taller than the Chrysler."

Four feet was the slimmest of margins. Raskob wondered if Chrysler and his boys were planning some sort of trick. They could easily conceal a rod in the building's spire and then raise it at the last moment to claim the title (which they in fact did at a later date). In Raskob's view, the Empire State Building needed a revamped plan that would guarantee its preeminence over all other skyscrapers.

It Needs a Hat!

While looking at a scale model of the Empire State, particularly at its flat, featureless roof, Raskob found his answer. "It needs a hat!" he shouted. But this would be no ordinary bonnet. This addition would be a functional mooring mast built to accommodate airships—a form of transport then coming into vogue. The building's designers took Raskob's forward-thinking suggestion and ran with it. They couldn't know it at the time, but their new plan would not only secure for them the title of world's tallest building, it would positively trounce Chrysler's 'scraper in the process.

A Champ Emerges

On May 27, 1930, the Chrysler Building opened for business. At some 77 stories and 1,046 feet tall, it became the WTB, beating the former champion, 40 Wall Street (72 stories, 927 feet) by a considerable margin. However, the Chrysler Building's reign was short-lived. On May 1, 1931, the Empire State Building swung open its doors. At 1,250 feet and 102 stories, it made Walter Chrysler's effort appear almost puny in comparison.

Although Walter Chrysler's building didn't hold the world title for very long, it would be a mighty tall mistake to write the structure off. With art deco styling so exquisite it routinely wins design awards, the Chrysler Building is widely viewed as a marvel of architectural style. Not the world's tallest, but surely among the most beautiful!

NYC Timeline

(Continued from p. 116)

1800
New York's population nearly doubles from 1790 to 60,515 residents.

1801
Alexander Hamilton founds *The New York Evening Post.*

July 11, 1804
Alexander Hamilton is shot by Aaron Burr in a duel and dies the next day.

November 11, 1807
Author Washington Irving gives NYC the nickname "Gotham," an Anglo-Saxon word meaning "Goat's Town."

1808
The Erie Canal, a 363-mile waterway to run from Albany, on the Hudson River, to Buffalo, is proposed.

1811
The New York State legislature formulates the street grid for the development of Manhattan above Hudson Street.

July 4, 1811
The new City Hall building opens (but remains under construction for another year).

October 26, 1825
The Erie Canal opens for business.

July–October 1832
Across the city, 4,000 people, mostly Irish immigrants, die from cholera.

1835
New York becomes the most populous city in the United States.

December 16–17, 1835
The Great New York Fire destroys the New York Stock Exchange and most buildings on Manhattan's southeast tip.

1838
The Manhattan Detention Complex, aka "The Tombs," is built in Lower Manhattan. Erected on a marsh, it soon begins to sink.

September 23, 1845
The New York Knickerbockers Baseball organization is formed.

1850
The population of New York is over half a million.

1853
The New York legislature buys, for $5 million, a 700-acre parcel that will become Central Park.

July 13–16, 1863
The city is shaken by the Civil War Draft Riots.

September 24, 1869
Black Friday, when America's stock market collapses for the first time.

1870
French sculptor Frédéric Bartholdi creates a small terra-cotta model of the Statue of Liberty.

1872
The Metropolitan Museum of Art opens.

1879
The city's first telephone directory, a card listing 252 names, is published.

May 24, 1883
The Brooklyn Bridge opens.

October 28, 1886
The Statue of Liberty is dedicated.

May 5, 1891
Carnegie Hall opens with Pyotr Ilyich Tchaikovsky conducting.

(Continued on p. 233)

Ship of Honor!

♥ ♥ ♥ ♥

As a tribute to those who perished on 9/11, the USS New York contains more than seven tons of steel from the World Trade Center.

You could call it history that now lives on the sea: The USS *New York,* an amphibious transport dock ship, was commissioned on November 7, 2009, more than eight years after terrorist attacks that destroyed New York City's World Trade Center.

There's an important connection between the two events. The *New York*'s bow was constructed using seven and a half tons of steel salvaged from the skyscrapers' wreckage. Five days before it was officially commissioned, the *New York* paused across from the World Trade Center site, dipped its flag, and delivered a 21-gun salute before an assembled crowd that included members of the Fire Department of New York, the New York Police Department, Port Authority Police, and family members of those who perished in the 2001 attack.

Strong as Steel

In the months following the tragic events of 9/11, New York Governor George Pataki wrote the Department of the Navy to request that it revive the name USS *New York* in honor of those who died, and that steel from the Twin Towers be incorporated into the construction of the ship. "The significance of where the WTC steel is located on the 684-foot-long ship symbolizes the strength and resiliency of the citizens of New York as it sails forward around the world," observed Navy Commander Quentin King.

The *New York* isn't alone in honoring the victims of 9/11; two other amphibious assault ships were constructed using steel salvaged from terrorist attack sites. The bow of the USS *Arlington,* named for the Virginia county in which the Pentagon is located, was cast using metal from the Pentagon building's structural girders, and the bow of the USS *Somerset* contains steel from a crane used to excavate United Airlines Flight 93, a hijacked plane forced to crash by quick-thinking passengers before it could reach its intended target in Washington, D.C.

The Marx Brothers

♥　♥　♥　♥

*They were zany New Yorkers who started in vaudeville and made
anarchic comedy popular. Here are superlatives of the Marx boys:*

- **First Born:** Manfred (born 1886). Sadly, the earliest Marx son
  lived only seven months before dying of asthenia and flu.
  (Henceforth, let's let the little fellow rest in peace and consider
  only the five who lived to adulthood.)

- **Youngest:** Herbert ("Zeppo," born 1901). Eight years younger
  than Milton ("Gummo")

- **Shortest-lived:** Leonard ("Chico"), age 74

- **Longest-lived:** Julius ("Groucho"), age 86

- **First to pass on:** Chico (d. October 11, 1961)

- **Last survivor:** Zeppo (d. November 30, 1979)

- **Most movie credits:** Groucho, 21 (plus two uncredited roles)

- **Fewest movie credits:** Gummo, a big fat zero

- **Best instrumentalist:** probably Harpo, a self-taught harpist,
  though Chico played a mean piano

- **First to write a book:** Groucho, *Beds* (Farrar & Rinehart, 1930)

- **Most marriages:** Groucho, three (Ruth Johnson, 1920–42; Kay
  Marvis, 1945–51; Eden Hartford, 1954–69)

- **Fewest marriages:** tied at one—Harpo (to Susan Fleming) and
  Gummo (to Helen von Tilzer)

- **Most often mispronounced nickname:** Chico. It is actually
  CHICK-o, not CHEE-ko

- **First to go bald:** Harpo. His wig covered up near-total baldness,
  thus he was rarely recognized in public without it

- **Least movie lines:** Gummo, because he wasn't in any movies.
  Next to him, of course, the ever-silent Harpo. However, he did
  utter two words in the newsreel hyping the premiere of *The Great
  Ziegfield* (1936). He said, "Honk, honk!"

Quotables

"New York is the only city in the world where you can get deliberately run down on the sidewalk by a pedestrian."

—Russell Baker

"I remember how often some of us walked out of the darkness of the Lower East Side and into the brilliant sunlight of Washington Square."

—Harry Golden

"There's no room for amateurs, even in crossing the streets."

—George Segal

"The whole of New York is rebuilt about once in ten years."

—Philip Hone

"Skyscraper National Park."

—Kurt Vonnegut

"Sometimes, from beyond the skyscrapers, the cry of a tugboat finds you in your insomnia, and you remember that this desert of iron and cement is an island."

—Albert Camus

"There's something hypocritical about a city that keeps half of its population underground half of the time; you can start believing that there's much more space than there really is—to live, to work."

—Gloria Naylor

"Vehement silhouettes of Manhattan—that vertical city with unimaginable diamonds."

—Le Corbusier

"New York is Paris with the English language."

—Brendan Behan

"Movement in New York is vertical, horizontal, angular, never casual. In Versailles, you bow; in New York, you dodge cabs."

—Boris Aronson

Taste of New York

Perhaps the quintessential New York City "street" food is pizza, an oft-oily slice folded and gobbled on the run. True denizens are very particular about their pies (authentic pizzerias don't offer slices, and most street vendors only take cash). With few variations, New York pizza sauce derives from imported Italian San Marzano tomatoes, and the mozzarella is fresh and locally made. The crust is inevitably thin, with a blistery char and smoky flavor only found with the intense heat of coal-fired ovens that are no longer built under environmental laws but have been "grandfathered" in for decades-old restaurants. Some aficionados, however, insist the secret is in the hand-tossed high-gluten dough, made with New York tap water.

Arguments over who has "the best" can, and do, go on forever, but for brevity's sake, here are a few places that are consistently rhapsodized:

- Lombardi's, in Manhattan's NoLiTa, is America's oldest pizzeria, founded in 1905. If it was good enough for Joe DiMaggio and Marilyn Monroe, it ought to be fine by you.

- Grimaldi's, in the shadow of the Brooklyn Bridge in Dumbo, dates back to 1990 and counts actor John Turturro among its fans.

- Patsy's (since 1933) also has its proponents, but purists insist that, of the seven Manhattan Island locations using that name, only the East Harlem original offers the "real deal" (and you can get it by the slice).

- Likewise, those seeking the "real" Totonno's (opened in 1924) must travel to the Coney Island location, restored after a fire, rather than settle for its two Manhattan outlets. It's been named "Best Old-School Pie" and a "work of art" by *New York* magazine.

- If you're going to schlep, check out DiFara (opened 1964) in Brooklyn's Midwood nabe, recommended as the best by *New York* magazine food critic Adam Platt (brother of actor Oliver, who looks like he might also appreciate a good pie).

- And then there's John's, since 1929. Those in the know insist "the best pizza ever" is only available at the first incarnation on Bleecker Street.

Tales from Central Park: At the Center of It All

♥ ♥ ♥ ♥

A stroll through New York City's Central Park might lead you to believe that it is the one remaining slice of nature amid the towering skyscrapers of steel and glass that flank it. But, in fact, this urban park was almost entirely human-made. And even though Manhattan's northern half was laid out in the early 19th century, the park was not part of the Commissioners' Plan of 1811.

Between 1821 and 1855, the population of New York nearly quadrupled. This growth convinced city planners that a large, open-air space was required. Initial plans mimicked the large public grounds of London and Paris, but it was eventually decided that the space should evoke feelings of nature—complete with running water, dense wooded areas, and even rolling hills.

Planning the Park

The original park layout included the area stretching from 59th to 106th streets and also included land between Fifth and Eighth

avenues. The land itself cost about $5 million. This part of Manhattan featured an irregular terrain of swamps and bluffs and included rocky outcrops left from the last Ice Age 10,000 years earlier; it was deemed unsuitable for private development but was ideal for creating the park that leaders envisioned. However, the area was not uninhabited. It was home to about 1,600 poor residents, most of them Irish and German immigrants—though there was a thriving African Amer-ican community there as well.

Ultimately, these groups were resettled, and the park's boundaries were extended to 110th Street.

In the 1850s, the state of New York appointed a Central Park Commission to oversee the development of the green space. A landscape design contest was held in 1857, and writer and landscape architect Frederick Law Olmsted and architect Calvert Vaux won with their "Greensward Plan."

Olmsted and Vaux envisioned a park that would include "separate circulation systems" for its assorted users, including pedestrians and horseback riders. To accommodate crosstown traffic while still maintaining the sense of a continuous single park, the roads that traversed Central Park from east to west were sunken and screened with planted shrub belts. Likewise, the Greensward Plan called for three dozen bridges, all designed by Vaux, with no two alike. These included simple granite bridges as well as ornate neogothic conceptions made of cast iron. The southern portion of the park was designed to include the mall walk to Bethesda Terrace and Bethesda Fountain, which provided a view of the lake and woodland to the north.

Construction Begins

Central Park was one of the largest public works projects in New York during the 19th century, with some 20,000 workers on hand to reshape the topography of nearly 850 acres. Massive amounts of gunpowder (more, in fact, than was used in the Battle of Gettysburg) were used to blast the rocky ridges, and nearly three million cubic yards of soil were moved. At the same time, some 270,000 trees and shrubs were planted to replicate the feeling of nature.

Despite the massive scale of work involved, the park first opened for public use in 1858; by 1865, it was receiving more than seven million visitors a year. Strict rules on group picnics and certain activities kept some New York residents away, but by the 1880s, the park was as welcoming to the working class as it was to the wealthy.

Over time, the park took on a number of additions, including the famous carousel and zoo, and activities such as tennis and bike riding became part of the landscape. Today, Central Park plays host to concerts, Shakespeare plays, swimming, and ice-skating. It also features a bird sanctuary for watchers and their feathered friends alike and is a pleasant urban retreat for millions of New Yorkers.

Fresh Kills Landfill

♥ ♥ ♥ ♥

*The world's largest, stinkiest dumping ground is being turned
into a public park and ecologically friendly beauty spot.*

In its prime it was, arguably, the biggest human-made structure
on earth, larger in volume than the Great Wall of China, taller by
25 meters than the Statue of Liberty, capable of being seen with the
naked eye from outer space. However, this was no wonder of nature,
no miracle of human endeavor or ingenuity. Instead, it was just a pile
of garbage; rotting, stinking, and overrun by feral dogs and cat-size rats
that rummaged for their next meal in a veritable mountain of human
waste.

The Fresh Kills Landfill, so named because of its location alongside the Fresh Kills estuary on the western shore of Staten Island, was
New York City's—and the world's—largest refuse heap during the
second half of the 20th century. Yet, that wasn't the intention when the
place began operations on the rural, 4.6-square-mile parcel of land
back in 1948. Rather, the landfill was the result of city planner Robert
Moses's scheme to use garbage as a foundation beneath the approach
system to the double-decker Verrazano-Narrows Bridge that he
intended to build between Staten Island and Brooklyn. (Constructed
between 1959 and 1969, the suspension bridge would encourage a
large increase in Staten Island's population . . . and its trash.)

At the time of the plan's inception, the "temporary landfill" was
to last no longer than 20 years, after which the site would be converted into residential, recreational, and industrial areas. As things
turned out, the dreck-dumping continued long past 1968, all the way
to 2001. Years later the place is *still* in transition.

Toxic, Not Pretty

Just picture it: four 225-foot-high mounds of 50-plus years of decom-
posing trash—once transported there by a daily convoy of up to
20 barges, each carrying 650 tons of rubbish that 400-ton cranes
deposited into trucks—emitting noxious odors and toxic chemicals
into the air and nearby waterways. Yuck. However, this hasn't

deterred a wide assortment of birds from flying overhead as they migrate north and south each spring and fall, and it also hasn't prevented various birds of prey from populating the scenic surrounding region to keep the rodent community in check.

Future archaeologists who poke their way around mountains of cigarette butts, diapers, and empty food containers will get plenty of good info about New Yorkers' tastes and habits. However, Fresh Kills had certainly outlasted its own shelf life when, in 1992, a year after other landfill closures had turned it into the sole lucky recipient of the city's garbage, pressure from the United States Environmental Protection Agency (EPA), and local stench-assaulted residents, finally prompted city officials to instigate plans to close the oversized dump.

In 1996 Mayor Rudy Giuliani and Governor George Pataki set a December 31, 2001, deadline for Fresh Kills' closure, aware that it would cost the city around $1 billion to do what needed to be done: Cover and seal the rotting refuse; construct a network of pipes, wells, underground walls, and treatment stations to protect people from the daily emission of about 30 million cubic feet of foul gases and one million gallons of poisonous liquids; and adhere to federal law by administering and maintaining the site for the next 30 years. Furthermore, to export trash from the five boroughs to landfills in other cities would at least double the roughly $100 million a year that was already being spent to bury it at Fresh Kills.

Tragedy, and New Purpose

In the end, the dump closed nine months ahead of schedule, on March 22, 2001—only to temporarily reopen after the 9/11 attacks on the World Trade Center so that debris could be buried there on a restricted 40-acre site.

The 9/11 landfill comprised nearly 45 percent of the 2,200-acre site, which now also includes lowlands, wetlands, and open waterways. All of it is being converted into Freshkills Park, a five-section recreation/education/wildlife area that is nearly triple the size of Central Park. For what used to be garbage, that's not bad.

The Waldorf=Astoria

♥ ♥ ♥ ♥

*How a high-society family squabble resulted in the
celebrated union of two adjacent luxury hotels.*

They may have been blood relatives and next-door neighbors, but
(understatement alert) they weren't very close. Business executives
John Jacob Astor III and William Backhouse Astor Jr. were, as the
sons of William Backhouse Astor Sr., joint heirs to the Astor family
real estate fortune. In 1859, John Jacob built a home at 350 Fifth
Avenue, and by 1862 he was joined there by William Backhouse Jr.,
who built an adjacent townhouse and enjoyed the good life while
John ran the family business.

Money and Ego

The brothers really didn't get along at all,
and when they inherited about $50 million
after their father's death in 1875, the added
wealth mirrored the schism in their
relationship. The gulf grew wider after
John Jacob's wife Charlotte passed away in
1887. Intent on filling this void, William
Backhouse Jr.'s socialite wife, Caroline
Webster Schermerhorn Astor, shortened
her formal title from "Mrs. William Astor"
to "Mrs. Astor," infuriating John Jacob's
son, William Waldorf Astor. This honor,
William insisted, should be bestowed upon
his own spouse, Mary, since his dad was the
elder of the two brothers. However, Aunty

Caroline refused to back down, and the New York press enjoyed
stirring things up by referring to her as *"the* Mrs. Astor."

John Jacob's death in 1890 made William Waldorf Astor the
richest man in America and, in effect, the head of the Astor family.
Yet, Aunty Caroline still wouldn't budge on the "Mrs. Astor" issue.
In a pretty dramatic act of retaliation, William demolished his house

at 350 Fifth Avenue and sold the land to Prussian-born millionaire George Boldt, who erected a hotel just a few feet from the residence of William Astor's aunt and uncle. *Now* guess who was furious. William relocated to London with his wife, and after his uncle died in 1892, he left Caroline and her son, John Jacob Astor IV, to fume over the intrusion of the Waldorf Hotel, which was, Caroline asserted, just a "glorified tavern."

"You're a Waldorf Salad"

High society wouldn't dream of patronizing a tavern, but the 13-story Waldorf was no tavern. It opened in 1893 and quickly became a prestigious destination. What's more, its maître d'hôtel, Oscar Tschirky, helped create several signature dishes, including Veal Oscar, Eggs Benedict, and, most notably, the Waldorf salad. This concoction of apples, celery, mayonnaise, and lettuce, embellished with chopped walnuts, earned an honorable mention from Cole Porter in his song "You're the Top," and it also brought lasting fame to "Oscar of the Waldorf."

Aunty Caroline, meanwhile, was not a happy camper. After she moved into a new home on 65th Street with her son and his family, John Jacob Astor IV tore down their Fifth Avenue townhouse and built the Astoria Hotel, right next to the Waldorf. The Astoria opened in 1897, again under the auspices of George Boldt, and what had originally been conceived as two separate entities joined forces to become the Waldorf=Astoria, world's largest hotel. (The double hyphen is official.) The buildings were connected by a grand 300-foot-long corridor called Peacock Alley in recognition of the ceaseless procession of fashionably dressed, feather-hatted women who strutted up and down like peacocks between the Empire Room and the Palm Room.

In 1929 the Waldorf=Astoria was razed to make way for the Empire State Building, but the hotel was resurrected two years later within a grand, 47-story, Art Deco skyscraper at 301 Park Avenue. Boasting its own Grand Central Terminal railway platform (once used by generals Douglas MacArthur and John J. Pershing, and presidents Franklin D. Roosevelt and Harry S. Truman), the Waldorf=Astoria prospered. It was purchased by hotelier Conrad Hilton for $3 million in 1949 and remains a much-admired New York landmark.

Fast Facts

- *To look at Central Park today, you'd never imagine how nasty the area was before the park opened in 1858. It housed a pair of rag pickers' shantytowns, with goats and pigs roaming at random. Sanitation? You're joking, right?*

- *Manhattan's first Chinese population came east looking for work between 1870 and 1882, after being pushed out of railroad work by European immigrants. They settled in Mott Street, which remains the heart of Chinatown.*

- *New Year's 1907 in Times Square was an evening of pea-soup fog—until midnight. At almost exactly that time, the clouds opened to reveal a glorious near-full moon. No eyewitness could ever forget it.*

- *In 1956, Cleveland Browns coach Paul Brown experimented with signal calling via helmet radio. The New York Giants brought a sideline radio receiver to Cleveland to see what they could pick up. After three straight rounds of three-and-out, Radio Free Brown went off the air.*

- *The NYPD has its own museum, in Lower Manhattan near Wall Street. The place has one of the most eclectic collections of copanalia you could imagine. Most interesting: the "improvised weapons" display, which proves that people's imagination knows no limit when the desired outcome is mayhem.*

- *Cocky gangster actor James Cagney (born in Manhattan; 1899–1986) got his start dressed as a woman for a chorus line. A devoted son, he sent at least half his income to his mother while she lived.*

- *Henry Ward Beecher (1813–87) held "freedom auctions" in Brooklyn. Southern slave brokers would consign a slave to Beecher, who would transport the fortunate individual to Brooklyn. Beecher's congregation would chip in to emancipate the slave.*

What Used to Be Here?

♥ ♥ ♥ ♥

New York has been so intensely modified, shaped, demoed, burnt, rebuilt, filled, and drilled that there is a past city modern residents barely know.

Beekman's Swamp is a roughly 30-acre bog in Lower Manhattan just south of the modern Brooklyn Bridge. Beekman Street would border its south edge if Southbridge Towers wasn't built smack on the spot. The swamp was drained in 1734.

Collect Pond was a 48-acre lake in Lower Manhattan (modern Foley Square) until about 1800. It was fed by groundwater and drained to the Hudson. The Pond was the city's water supply until people literally trashed it. By 1811, it was filled in completely.

Eastern Park was home to the Brooklyn Grooms/Bridegrooms during 1891–97, and the spot where the Trolley Dodger name (later the "Dodgers") originated. The park stood between Pitkin and Sutter avenues and between Van Sinderen Avenue and Powell Street in East New York. The team left the Eastern in '97 for another, cheaper venue, and the park was demolished within a few years.

Ebbets Field was the Dodgers' last real home, and fewer and fewer fans are left who remember the Marble Rotunda in this fabled place at 55 Sullivan Place, Flatbush. Its team gone after the 1957 season, it succumbed to the wrecking ball in 1960, leaving only memories and some high-rise apartments.

Five Points resulted from a haphazard fill job on Manhattan's Collect Pond that left a smelly, miasmal area near modern Worth and Baxter streets. Five Points was the archetypical Victorian den of urban squalor and crime. Cleanup began in the 1890s, and today the area houses municipal buildings.

Fort Amsterdam was a square fortress in Lower Manhattan in modern Bowling Green Park. From above it would have looked like a square ninja-throwing star. Finished in 1625, it was dismantled in 1790—probably due to decrepitude.

Hilltop Park was where the first Yankees—who were called the Highlanders—played from 1903 to 1912. It stood in Washington Heights between 165th and 168th streets, between Fort Washington Avenue and Broadway. After the team departed, Hilltop was purchased by investors and was razed in 1914.

Lenape Villages stood near modern City Hall, east of Chinatown, on the Lower East Side and in Chelsea. These American Indian dwellings were extant when Dutch settlers arrived, with the biggest concentrations found in Inwood along the Harlem River and in Washington Heights near the I-95 bridge's west base.

Lower Manhattan Waterfront roughly followed Greenwich Street; the eastern followed Pearl Street. The southernmost tip was just south of Water and State Streets. The waterfront landfill process that erased LMW has taken centuries.

Pennsylvania Station was a magnificent neoclassical structure at the corner of West 34th Street and Eighth Avenue. Wait, you're thinking, you go into Penn Station at Seventh and 32nd. And you'd be right—but that's the new, unimproved Penn Station. The original was built in 1910 on the site of today's Madison Square Garden. Among its many grand features was a glass-and-steel vaulted ceiling that rose 150 feet above the tracks. It was demolished in 1963.

Polo Grounds I housed the Gothams/Giants between 1883 and '88. It stood between Fifth and Sixth avenues and 110th and 112th streets. In 1888, the city confiscated the land adjoining Central Park and tore down the Polo Grounds shortly thereafter. Today, 111th Street runs right through the old outfield.

Polo Grounds II/III/IV were "home" for many New York sports teams, and saw many great moments, from 1889 to 1963. These venues actually comprised two different Manhattan parks, both located between Edgecombe Avenue and the Harlem River, and 155th and 159th streets. They were flattened in 1964 to build apartments.

Shea Stadium opened in 1964 as the Mets' new home in Flushing, at 126th Street and Roosevelt Avenue; the Jets played here, as well, until 1983. The Mets stayed through the 2008 season, after which Shea was pulled down to provide parking for the new Citi Field.

Stadt Huys, Manhattan's first city hall, was also a tavern. It stood where 85 Broad Street is today, between South William and Pearl streets. Built in 1642, it was city hall for the Dutch until 1667 and continued as such for the English until 1699. During its glory years, it was fronted by stocks that provided public punishments to wrong-doers. Stadt Huys evidently fell apart around 1700.

Wall Street Bastions was the original Dutch wall along "Het Cingle" (now Wall Street). It had two north-extending stone bastions, one just east of Broadway, the other just west of the American International Building. The bastions and the entire wall came down in 1699.

Washington Park I/II/III were early homes of the Brooklyn Atlantics and the Trolley Dodgers, 1884–1912, and then housed the Federal League's Brooklyn Tip-Tops. The venue was comprised of two different parks in adjoining lots, both between First and Fifth streets and Third and Fifth avenues. Remnants of the final park can still be seen today on Third Avenue between First and Third streets. The wall of the Con Edison yard is part of the old clubhouse wall.

The World Trade Center, actually multiple buildings in Lower Manhattan dominated by a pair of enormous, peg-like skyscrapers, was in Lower Manhattan. Construction wrapped in 1973. Until both towers were brought down by the terrorist attack of September 11, 2001, the so-called Twin Towers were iconic parts of the newer NYC skyline. The WTC will eventually rise again, on the original location between Liberty and Vesey streets. A memorial to the dead has been planned as part of the new development.

Yankee Stadium I/II was "The House That Ruth Built," opening during the glory year of 1923, just south of the current incarnation at East 161st Street and River Avenue in the Bronx. The park was closed for renovation following the 1973 season and opened for the '76 campaign. Yankee Stadium closed for good at the end of the Yankees' 2008 season. Why replace one of baseball's most historic structures? Stripped of business doublespeak, the answer is: to make more money.

More Famous People from Manhattan

♥ ♥ ♥ ♥

Oscar Hijuelos (1951–) Morningside Heights native; Pulitzer Prize–winning novelist on Hispanic American themes.

Washington Irving (1783–1859) Native; best-selling author specializing in short stories, biographies, and essays.

Rabbi Mordecai Kaplan (1881–1983) Immigrant to Manhattan; maverick Jewish thinker who held the first Bat Mitzvah when he summoned his daughter to read Haftarah.

John F. Kennedy Jr. (1960–99) Studied and worked in the borough; remembered for saluting the coffin of his dad, JFK, as a toddler, and for his own untimely death in a plane crash off Martha's Vineyard.

Alicia Keys (1981–) Hell's Kitchen daughter; R&B singer and pianist who may need an extra room if she wins any more Grammys.

Alan King (1927–2004) Spent his early years on the Lower East Side; Borscht Belt comic fixture and actor.

Fiorello La Guardia (1882–1947) Village native; one of the city's most famous (and progressive) mayors, and a scourge of the Mob.

Emma Lazarus (1849–87) Lifelong resident; her poetry adorns the base of the Statue of Liberty.

Deborah Lipstadt (1947–) Native; highly regarded historian of anti-Semitism and the Holocaust.

Lena "Lane" Himmelstein Bryant Malsin (1877–1951) Clothier who lived much of her life in Manhattan; founded Lane Bryant women's plus-size clothing chain.

Henry "Billy the Kid" McCarty (1859–81) Born in Manhattan; a punk who perhaps grew more infamous as an outlaw than he deserves, but nevertheless an iconic figure of the Old West.

Herman Melville (1819–91) Native and author of, among many other things, *Moby-Dick*.

Eugene O'Neill (1888–1953) Actual native of Times Square; as a playwright he became a Nobel Laureate.

Manny Ramirez (1972–) Controversial 12-time major league baseball All-Star; raised in Washington Heights.

Christopher Reeve (1952–2004) Born and spent his early years in Manhattan; starred as *Superman* (1978), broke his neck riding a horse (1995), and became even more admired as activist for the paralyzed.

Jacob Riis (1849–1914) Danish immigrant who used his camera to show America how the Lower East Side lived; without him, social welfare would surely have moved more slowly.

Norman Rockwell (1894–1978) Native who became a hugely popular portrayer of Americana on canvas.

Alex Rodriguez (1975–) Born in Washington Heights; massively paid but high-achieving Yankee and likely future Hall of Famer.

J. D. Salinger (1919–2010) Native author of *The Catcher in the Rye* (1951); spent most of the rest of his life as a recluse.

Jonas Salk (1914–95) Son of immigrants to East Harlem; developed polio vaccine to whom countless owe their mobility—and their lives.

Tupac Shakur (1971–96) East Harlem native who was one of the most visible rappers of his day; his murder in Las Vegas remains unsolved.

Ben Silverman (1970–) Raised in Manhattan; Emmy-winning TV producer and TV network executive.

Ben Stiller (1965–) Manhattan native whose films include *There's Something About Mary* (1998) and *Tropic Thunder* (2008).

Tiny Tim (1932–96) Washington Heights native who had a long musical career that featured a ukulele and a remarkable falsetto.

Garry Trudeau (1948–) Native creator of the long-running political cartoon strip *Doonesbury*.

Sigourney Weaver (1949–) Native actress whose most famous role is as the heroine of the *Alien* science-fiction franchise.

Billy Dee Williams (1937–) Harlem native who earned his chops as an actor on Broadway before making his mark in film.

The Boroughs and Their Bragging Rights

Okay, Brooklyn, the Bronx, Manhattan, Queens, and Staten Island.
Line up, and let's see what you've got going as of the 2000 census.

- **Largest physical area:** Queens, 109.2 square miles (land area alone). Next largest, Brooklyn, which isn't quite three-quarters the size of Queens.

- **Smallest physical area:** Manhattan, 23 square miles, just over half the size of the Bronx.

- **Most people:** Brooklyn, 2.47 million, which just nudges out Queens.

- **Fewest people:** Staten Island, by far the least populated, with 444,000 people.

- **Most elderly people:** Queens (12.7 percent age 65 or older).

- **Fewest elderly people:** The Bronx (10.1 percent 65 or older).

- **Most young people:** The Bronx (29.8 percent under age 18). Staten Island and Brooklyn aren't far behind, at about 26 percent apiece.

- **Fewest young people:** Manhattan (16.8 percent younger than 18). Queens is well behind, at about 23 percent.

- **Most densely populated:** Manhattan, with about 66,900 per square mile. That's nearly double the figure of second-place Brooklyn.

- **Least densely populated:** Staten Island, about 7,600 per square mile, about a third as dense as Queens.

- **Most male:** Staten Island, 48.3 percent. Queens is very close.

- **Most female:** The Bronx, 53.5 percent. Nudges out Brooklyn.

- **Whitest:** Staten Island, 77.6 percent, which is considerably whiter than Manhattan (54.4 percent)

- **Least white:** The Bronx, 29.9 percent white. Next is Brooklyn, at 41.2 percent.

- **Most Hispanic (any nation of origin):** The Bronx, 48.4 percent. That figure is not quite double that of Queens or Manhattan.

- **Least Hispanic (any nation of origin):** Staten Island, 12.1 percent. Next least: Brooklyn, 19.8 percent.

- **Most African American:** Brooklyn, 36.4 percent, which just edges out the Bronx.

- **Least African American:** Staten Island, 9.7 percent, about half that of Queens or Manhattan.

- **Most Asian:** Queens, 17.6 percent, nearly double the percentage of Manhattan.

- **Least Asian:** The Bronx, 3 percent, barely half of Staten Island's ratio.

- **Most foreign born:** Queens, 46.1 percent. Next is Brooklyn, at 37.8 percent.

- **Least foreign born:** Staten Island, 16.4 percent. No other borough is even close.

- **Highest 1999 income per capita:** Manhattan, $42,922, nearly double Staten Island's.

- **Lowest 1999 income per capita:** The Bronx, $13,959. Brooklyn's is $16,775.

- **Least poverty (families):** Staten Island, 7.9 percent. Queens is next at 11.9 percent.

- **Most poverty (families):** The Bronx, 28 percent. Brooklyn is a fairly long second.

- **Longest average commute:** Staten Island, 43.9 minutes. The other boroughs, except Manhattan, are in the same ballpark.

- **Shortest average commute:** Manhattan, 30.5 minutes.

- **First permanent European settlement:** Manhattan, 1620.

- **Last to be permanently settled:** Staten Island, 1661.

New York City's Worst Catastrophes

♥ ♥ ♥ ♥

The city presents itself like Rocky: It can take a punch and keep swinging. Given that New York remains standing after the following haymakers, the image is deserved.

- **The Peach Tree War:** In September 1655, New Amsterdam governor Peter Stuyvesant marshaled troops to attack New Sweden (in modern Delaware). Furious Native Americans promptly raided New Amsterdam, Hoboken, and Staten Island. The burning and looting that followed left about 100 colonists dead, and 100 or more were taken hostage.

- **Yellow Fever Epidemics:** The city was struck by the mosquito-borne virus in 1668, 1702, 1794–95, 1798, 1803, 1819, and 1822. Some of the outbreaks killed hundreds; others killed thousands. The outbreak of 1798, with more than 2,000 deaths, was the worst.

- **Great Fire of New York:** This conflagration that consumed the west side of southern Manhattan started on September 21, 1776, probably in a waterfront tavern, during the colonial defense of the city against the British. Some 400 to 500 buildings were destroyed.

- **Chatham Street Fire:** On May 19, 1811, high winds gusting to gale force turned a factory blaze into a pyre for 100 buildings. A general shortage of water available to firefighters was an early wake-up call about the city's future needs.

- **Long Island Hurricane:** The only major hurricane in the city's history hit at Jamaica Bay on September 3, 1821. The 13-foot storm surge flooded Battery Park and lower Manhattan as far as Canal Street. While damaging, the flood caused few deaths.

- **Cholera Epidemics:** In 1832, 1848–49, and 1866, cholera outbreaks killed thousands at a time. Indelicately put, the ailment killed with diarrhea that led to irreversible fluid loss. Early treatments included opium suppositories and tobacco enemas—neither of which is recommended for home treatment today!

- **Great Financial District Fire:** On December 16–17, 1835, city firefighters discovered that water is very hard to pump when the air temperature is -17 degrees Fahrenheit. This largely unchecked blaze incinerated 500 buildings around Wall Street, including most of the few remaining Dutch-era structures.

- **Civil War Draft Riots:** Resentment over Civil War conscription became a pretext for 1863 rioting against war profiteers and African Americans. During July 13–16, at least 119 people died (many at the hands of murderers), and thousands were injured. Property damage was extensive.

- ***Westfield II* Ferry Explosion:** The boiler of this Staten Island steamer blew up at Manhattan dockside on July 30, 1871, killing 125 and injuring about 140.

- **Brooklyn Theatre Fire:** On December 5, 1876, theatergoers who had gathered to see a popular French melodrama, *The Two Orphans*, were sent into panic when fire broke out at the Brooklyn Theatre. Many of the 278 dead were children in the cheap seats, where fire-escape provisions were inadequate.

- **Great Blizzard of 1888:** New York tried to absorb snowdrifts of 20 feet or more and winds in excess of 45 mph, when a late-winter storm slammed the Atlantic coast from Maryland to Maine. Two hundred of the storm's 400 deaths occurred in New York City.

- **Heat Wave of 1896:** During the long span of August 5–13, sustained temperatures above 90 degrees Fahrenheit scorched people in tenements, sometimes lethally. In the end, 420 or more people died, mostly in the overcrowded squalor of the Lower East Side.

- ***General Slocum* Disaster:** Until 9/11, June 15, 1904, was New York's deadliest day. During a church picnic aboard a chartered steamboat in the East River, more than 1,000 people, most of them German-American women and children, died when the triple-deck, wooden ship caught fire.

- **Triangle Shirtwaist Fire:** On March 25, 1911, a carelessly tossed match or cigarette started a fast-spreading fire inside Max Blanck and Isaac Harris's shirtwaist (blouse) sweatshop, which occupied the eighth, ninth, and tenth floors of Manhattan's Asch Building. Grossly inadequate fire exit provisions, plus locked inner doors, spelled disaster. Most of the 146 dead were immigrant women, mainly Jewish. Those that did not burn to death died of smoke inhalation or from injuries sustained when they leapt from windows.

- **Wall Street Bombing:** Was it a car bomb that exploded in the financial district on September 16, 1920? No, it was a horse-drawn wagon bomb carrying 100 pounds of dynamite and hundreds of pounds of iron that went up in front of 23 Wall Street. The massive explosion killed 38 people and wounded more than 300. No perpetrator was ever found, but authorities unofficially blamed two popular bogeymen of the day: anarchists and Communists.

- **1943 Harlem Riots:** When a black G.I. who tried to prevent a white police officer from manhandling a black woman was shot, simmering racial tensions ignited. It was August 1, 1943, and throughout the night and into the following day, rioters destroyed property across Harlem. Six African Americans died, and hundreds of people (including 40 cops) were injured. At least 500 people were arrested.

- **Holland Tunnel Fire:** New York City officials have good reasons for banning highly explosive carbon disulfide from being driven through the Holland Tunnel. On Friday, May 13, 1949, a 55-gallon drum of the solvent fell off a truck and caught fire. The blaze spread quickly, engulfing many of the 125 vehicles that were in the tunnel at the time, and ravaging the structure's ceiling and walls. An FDNY battalion chief was felled by smoke and died four months later. Sixty-six people were injured.

- **TWA Flight 266/United Flight 826:** Snow, rain, and fog, plus pilot error, precipitated the December 16, 1960, midair collision of a TWA Constellation and a United DC-8 some 5,200 feet above the city. United Flight 826 had been badly off course. The DC-8 fell onto Brooklyn's Park Slope neighborhood, killing six people on the ground. The Constellation disintegrated on impact and crashed at Miller Field on Staten Island. All 128 people on the two planes perished, although an 11-year-old boy aboard the DC-8 survived long enough to describe the crash to authorities.

- **Eastern Airlines Flight 66:** June 24, 1975, a Boeing 727 attempting to land at JFK International Airport was knocked to earth short of the runway by freak wind shear caused by a thunderstorm. Seven passengers and two flight attendants survived; the other 115 passengers and crew did not.

- **1977 Blackout:** Except for south Queens, all of NYC lost power on July 13–14, 1977, when a lightning strike sent electrical grids into a tizzy. Unlike the famed 1965 blackout, which was notable for its peaceful nature, this one encouraged widespread looting, arson, and vandalism. More than 3,700 people were arrested, and hundreds of police were injured.

- **World Trade Center Garage Bombing:** On February 26, 1993, Islamic terrorists detonated 1,500 pounds of explosives in a lower-level garage, killing six people. Over 1,000 were injured, mostly during the towers' frantic evacuation.

- **TWA Flight 800:** A Boeing 747 out of JFK Airport with 230 people aboard blew up south of Long Island on July 17, 1996. There were no survivors, but numerous conspiracy theories made the rounds. The FBI found no evidence of a criminal act, and the NTSB attributed the crash to an electrical spark that ignited fuel vapors in a wing tank.

- **World Trade Center Attacks:** September 11, 2001, will live in infamy as the nation's worst terrorist attack. Two airliners hijacked by Islamic extremists were flown into Manhattan, where each of the planes struck one of the twin towers of the World Trade Center, which ultimately collapsed. A total of 2,751 died, and over 6,000 were injured—many of the casualties were police and firefighters. (On the same morning, another hijacked airliner crashed into the Pentagon, and a fourth crashed in rural Pennsylvania.)

- **American Flight 587:** Freak physics and some operator over-reaction were the causes of the November 12, 2001, crash of an Airbus A300 just minutes out of JFK International Airport. The American Airlines flight took off in a wake of intense turbulence left by a larger 747. The pilots' struggle with the rudder led to catastrophic structural failure: The vertical stabilizer sheared off, followed by both engines. What remained of the plane went down in the Belle Harbor neighborhood of Queens, demolishing houses and killing five people. In all, 265 people lost their lives.

Local Legends

The myth that albino alligators sightlessly prowl the New York City sewer system has its roots in an alleged decades-old fad. Some say vacationers brought the infant 'gators home from Florida, while others insist that New York pet shops enjoyed a thriving trade in such babies (the reptiles sometimes sold in stores today are actually caimans, crocodilians from South America). When these 'gator tots grew too large for apartment dwelling, they were supposedly dispatched by flushing down the toilet—a trip these hardy creatures survived all the way down to the sewers, where, it was claimed, they evolved over the years, adapting to their new environment by becoming blind and losing their pigmentation. The legend grew legs, as it were, when an alleged eyewitness—a retired sewer official who swore he'd seen a colony of the things back in the 1930s—was quoted in a 1959 book entitled *The World Beneath the City*. Thomas Pynchon also wrote of them in his 1963 novel *V.*

Reports of regular alligators in New York City might be a little bit more believable. In 1932, "swarms" of alligators were reportedly spotted in the Bronx River, and on February 10, 1935, the *New York Times* wrote that several urban teens had pulled a seven-footer from an open manhole while clearing snow—and had beaten the beast to death after it snapped at them. The paper suggested that perhaps the animal had escaped from a ship "from the mysterious Everglades." Even before this—a full century earlier in 1831—a little-known paper called *The Planet* noted a 'gator sighting in the East River.

However, any herpetologist worth his or her scales will tell you that it's impossible for the tropical-thriving 'gator to get through a New York City winter, in polluted waters, no less. One explained that alligators can't digest food when they're cold. Plus, living without sun destroys their ability to utilize calcium, which would result in too soft of a skeletal structure for the creature to survive. As one spokesperson for the city's Department of Environmental Protection, who has been denying the rumors for 30 years, wearily sighed: "Sewers simply are not a prime environment for alligators."

But you're still going to check before you sit down, though—right?

Colleges and Universities of New York

♥   ♥   ♥   ♥

These aren't even all of them! Schools marked with an asterisk are part of the City University of New York system.

- **Barnard College** (1889, Morningside Heights, Manhattan)
- **Baruch College** (1919, Gramercy Park, Manhattan)*
- **Berkeley College** (1931, Midtown Manhattan)
- **Brooklyn College** (1930, Midwood, Brooklyn)*
- **City College of New York** (1847, Manhattanville, Manhattan)*
- **College of Staten Island** (1976, Willowbrook, Staten Island)*
- **Columbia University** (1754, Morningside Heights, Manhattan)
- **Fordham University** (1841, Rose Hill, the Bronx)
- **Hunter College** (1870, Upper East Side, Manhattan)*
- **Jewish Theological Seminary** (1886, Morningside Heights, Manhattan)
- **Juilliard School** (1905, Lincoln Square, Manhattan)
- **Marymount Manhattan College** (1936, Upper East Side, Manhattan)
- **New York Institute of Technology** (Manhattan campus; 1955, Lincoln Square)
- **New York University** (1831, Greenwich Village, Manhattan)
- **Pace University** (1906, Lower Manhattan)
- **Polytechnic Institute of New York City** (1854, Brooklyn and Manhattan)
- **Queens College** (1937, Flushing, Queens)*
- **Rockefeller University** (1901, Upper East Side, Manhattan)
- **St. Johns University** (1870, Jamaica, Queens)
- **Yeshiva University** (1886, various locations, Bronx and Manhattan)
- **York College** (1966, Jamaica, Queens)*

Super Speakeasy: '21'

♥ ♥ ♥ ♥

Prohibition didn't inhibit the alcohol consumption of habitués of New York's most famous watering hole.

In January 1920, the United States government attempted to banish public consumption of alcohol by instituting Prohibition. (Previous "temperance" movements, led by religious groups and fed-up women, had been confined to the state level.) The manufacture or distribution of liquor was prohibited, nationwide. Americans could possess alcohol, but it was only to be consumed at home, indoors, with family and guests.

As everybody with half a brain predicted, the law failed miserably and spawned an underground Jazz Age society that delighted in thumbing its collective nose at the law. The government's wet blanket was going to be wetter than the "drys" could ever have imagined.

The City That Never Sleeps Also Likes Its Drink

New Yorkers in particular have never appreciated being told what to do, and the city's eating and drinking establishments had no intention of folding just because the Constitution said so. Thus was born the "speakeasy" (as in, keep your voice down): Food might be served as a cover, but booze was the *raison d'être*.

At the height of Prohibition, New York had an estimated 100,000 downstairs dives, uptown haunts, and midtown hoocheries. Would-be patrons needed to know the guard at the door and/or a special password. This was risky business. There was money to be made, but first people had to be paid off. In an atmosphere in which respectable businessmen mingled with bootleggers, many police and others in positions of authority were known to be "on the take."

Take Us to the '21' Club

Named after its address on West 52nd Street between Fifth and Sixth avenues (the block's generous number of saloons earned it the nickname "Swing Street"), '21' was the classiest gin joint in Manhattan. The food was reliably delicious, the place's genteel clientele ad-

hered to a strict dress code, and an alert doorman kept out gangsters and other undesirables—including the Feds. Owned by cousins Jack Kriendler and Charlie Berns and operating out of an 1872 town-house that had previously been home to a bordello, '21' opened on New Year's Eve 1929. Later that year, the club's alleged and inexplicable ban of all-powerful newspaper and radio gossip Walter Winchell sparked a vengeful column wondering why '21' hadn't yet been raided. The police, predictably, arrived the next night.

The Secret Wine Cellar

Kriendler and Berns promptly hired architects and engineers to redesign '21.' Four alarm buttons were installed in the vestibule; if the doorman pressed any one, stashes of booze were locked behind secret doors by switches designed to automatically short-circuit. Bar shelves were rigged to collapse and ditch bottles down a brick-lined chute, where they would shatter and their contents drain directly into the sewer. And in the basement, behind smoked hams hanging from the ceiling and a shelf of canned goods, stood a cement wall camouflaging an airtight door weighing 2.5 tons, which opened only when a meat skewer was inserted into the appropriate crack. The doorway led into a basement located next door at 19 West 52nd, where the comfortably appointed wine cellar housed 2,000 cases of wine—and frequently, New York Mayor Jimmy Walker, who sipped in seclusion while his police department searched in vain above.

Eat, Drink, and Be Merry

On December 5, 1933, the 21st Amendment repealed Prohibition, and people drank openly once more. Still standing at its original location, the '21' Club invokes its past with "Speakeasy" Steak Tartare. Patrons can't help but remember that this is where Bogart and Bacall once billed and cooed, where presidents and moguls made deals and policy, where Groucho Marx ordered and returned a single bean ("Undercooked!") to the kitchen.

As for the wine cellar, it's now a meticulously restored private dining room that can hold up to 22 free-spenders who come for costly three-course lunches or seven-course dinners. If you ask nicely, they may even show you Mayor Walker's favorite corner.

Fast Facts

- *The saga of 1800s retail mogul A. T. Stewart didn't end with his 1876 death. Tomb raiders dug him up in 1878, and sordid negotiations began. For $20,000 his widow got her husband's body back in a late-night swap.*

- *When the city dedicated the Statue of Liberty in 1886, women weren't on the invitation list (officials worried they would be crushed in the crowd). Not to be left out, the New York Woman Suffrage Association invited itself by sea on a chartered boat.*

- *Under the Dutch, New York had two Burgomasters (chief executives), five Schepens (magistrate), and a Schout-Fiscal (public safety official). When the English took over in 1665, these officials became mayor, aldermen, and sheriff, respectively.*

- *Most football fans know of the 1968 "Heidi Bowl," when NBC shifted coverage from a great Jets-Raiders contest (that still had more than a minute to play!) to a made-for-TV movie of the children's classic* Heidi *at 7:00 P.M. Irate New York callers actually blew fuses on the switchboard at the local NBC station. When they couldn't get through to the network anymore, they called the police. To make things worse, the Jets, who had the lead when the broadcast was terminated, managed to lose when the Raiders scored twice in that final minute!*

- *The F, A, and O in FAO Schwarz, the iconic toy store that's a must-see New York destination for kids and adults alike, stand for Frederick August Otto, the given names of the store's founder. Frederick Schwarz established his first toy store in Baltimore in 1862 and moved to Manhattan in 1870.*

- *Teddy Roosevelt (1858–1919), born at 28 East 20th Street in Gramercy is the only native New Yorker to become president. Unfortunately, the original brownstone was demolished in 1916.*

- *In 1937, a Manhattan native became Ireland's first Taoiseach (prime minister) under the newly enacted Bunreacht (Constitution). Eamon de Valera would lead the Republic until 1948, steering it neutrally through World War II.*

L.I.N.G.O. ("Language in New York Gets Outrageous!")

♥ ♥ ♥ ♥

If you really want to assimilate in New York City, you gotta know the lingo. Here are some words and terms you should brush up on before taking a trip to Gotham. Many refer to places in New York, but others are widely familiar slang terms that have their roots in the city that never sleeps.

Dumbo—This acronym is a name for the Brooklyn neighborhood found "Down Under the Manhattan Bridge Overpass."

Breadline—New York City baker Louis Flieshmann began handing out free bread to the poor and hungry in 1876, often giving away 500 loaves a night. "Breadline" was soon used to describe any line made up of those in need of charity.

SoHo—This is just a shortened way to say "South of Houston," referring to the now ubertrendy neighborhood below Houston Street in lower Manhattan.

10–85—This term comes via the NYPD, who use it to describe a nonemergency situation, as in, "10–85 me a cup of coffee, would'ja?"

Alphabet City—This refers to a particular neighborhood within a neighborhood. The avenues of A, B, C, and D can be found in Manhattan's East Village, the only streets in NYC with single-letter names.

Rubbernecking—A reference to the activity of craning one's neck around to look at something. New Yorkers in the late 19th century used a derogatory variation, rubberneckers, to describe the tourists who slowed everyone down while they gaped at the city.

The Great White Way—This is the nickname given to the Theater District area found on Broadway at Times Square. The "white" is a reference to the light from the millions of marquee lights found there.

TriBeCa—This mash-up of a word refers to the neighborhood created by the "Triangle Below Canal Street," or "TriBeCa."

"Ford to City: 'Drop Dead'"

♥　♥　♥　♥

Two words may have killed a U.S. president's reelection chances—but did he really say them?

When a request for help is met with a nasty refusal, it's hard to take, especially if it's from a good friend or a close relative. However, when that dose of tough love is doled out by the president of the United States, it can be an even more bitter pill to swallow.

In 1975, New York City was broke. Following years of fiscal mismanagement, a downturn in the national economy pushed the Big Apple to the brink of disaster. While its lawyers filed a bankruptcy petition in the State Supreme Court, Mayor Abraham Beame was forced to beg the White House for a bailout. On October 29, in a speech before the National Press Club, President Gerald R. Ford likened the city's profligate spending to "an insidious disease" and asserted that he was "prepared to veto any bill that has as its purpose a federal bailout of New York City to prevent a default."

Hooked on Heroin?

Meanwhile, Ford's press secretary, Ron Nessen, compared the city to "a wayward daughter hooked on heroin. You don't give her $100 a day to support her habit." None of this sat well with Mayor Beame, who accused the President of "writing off New York City in one speech." The next day, a banner headline on the front page of New York's *Daily News* announced: "FORD TO CITY: 'DROP DEAD.'"

Those two words, although never uttered by the President, did capture the essence of his remarks—at least, as perceived by many New Yorkers. Yet, even the President did an about-face just two months later, signing legislation for federal loans. But the damage had been done, and Ford later acknowledged that the *Daily News* interpretation of his thoughts probably cost him the 1976 election, when Jimmy Carter narrowly carried New York State. Galvanized by the President's speech, a defiant New York City never did drop dead.

Murder, Inc.

♥ ♥ ♥ ♥

*A gun; an ice pick; a rope; these were some of the favorite
tools of Albert Anastasia, notorious mob assassin. When
he wasn't pulling the trigger himself, this head of Murder,
Inc.—the enforcement arm of New York's Five Families
Mafia—was giving the orders to kill, beat, extort, and rob on
the mob-controlled waterfronts of Brooklyn and Manhattan.*

Born in Italy in 1902 as Umberto Anastasio, Anastasia worked as a deck
hand before jumping ship in New York, where he built a power base in
the longshoremen's union. Murder was his tool to consolidate power.
Arrested several times in the 1920s, his trials were often dismissed
when witnesses would go missing. It wasn't long before he attracted
the attention of mob "brain" Lucky Luciano and subsequently helped
whack Joe "the Boss" Masseria in 1931, an act that opened the way for
Luciano to achieve national prominence within the organization.

Luciano put Anastasia, Bugsy Siegel, and Meyer Lanksy in
charge of what became known as Murder, Inc., the lethal button
men of the Brooklyn Mafia. With his quick temper and brutal dis-
position, Anastasia earned the nickname "Lord High Executioner."

A psychopathic assassin named Abe "Kid Twist" Reles was a key
man of Murder, Inc., but turned prosecution witness when he was
arrested in 1940. Reles fingered Anastasia, only to mysteriously "fall"
from his hotel room while under police protective custody.

A History of Violence

Anastasia climbed the next rung in the mob ladder by ordering the
violent 1951 deaths of the Mangano brothers and ultimately taking
over the Mangano family. Eventually, however, he alienated two
powerful rivals, Vito Genovese and Meyer Lansky. On October 25,
1957, as Albert Anastasia dozed in a barber's chair at New York's
Park Sheraton Hotel, he was riddled by two masked gunmen (possibly Larry and Joe Gallo), who acted on orders from Genovese.

Anastasia had evaded justice for decades, but he couldn't escape
the violence he himself cultivated in organized crime.

Quotables

Cogent observations about the Yankees.

"You don't save a pitcher for tomorrow. Tomorrow it may rain."

—Leo Durocher

"I will never have a heart attack. I give them."

—George Steinbrenner

"Everybody says we hated the Yankees. We didn't hate the Yankees. We just hated the way they beat us."

—Al Lopez, opposing catcher and manager

"Hating the New York Yankees is as American as apple pie, unwed mothers and cheating on your income tax."

—Mike Royko

"The Yankees don't pay me to win every day, just two out of three."

—Casey Stengel

"Rooting for the Yankees is like rooting for the house in blackjack."

—Adam Morrow

"A ball player's got to be kept hungry to become a big-leaguer. That's why no boy from a rich family ever made the big leagues."

—Joe DiMaggio

"Owning the Yankees is like owning the Mona Lisa."

—George Steinbrenner

"I would rather beat the Yankees regularly than pitch a no-hit game."

—Bob Feller

"Like those special afternoons in summer when you go to Yankee Stadium at two o'clock in the afternoon for an eight o'clock game. It's so big, so empty and so silent that you can almost hear the sounds that aren't there."

—Ray Miller, Baltimore Orioles pitching coach

Bits of Broadway

♥ ♥ ♥ ♥

Singers, actors, and dancers all share the limelight on Broadway,
but New York's legitimate theaters have their own stories to tell.

Few things say "New York" as resoundingly as Broadway shows, the
apex of American theatrical arts. New York theaters have been
packing them in since the early 19th century, creating a wealth of
stars, legends, and myths along the way. Ghosts, unfortunate acci-
dents, great opening nights, read-'em-and-weep reviews—all have
contributed to the lore of The Great White Way.

Night Lights, Cigars, and Flirts

Ghosts, especially, play a time-honored role in the New York theater.
So much so that all theaters leave a single light burning at night after
the house has emptied, called the ghost light. Whether it is to light
the way for cranky theater ghosts who hate a dark stage or for safety in
case of fire or other trouble is unclear. But the tradition is hallowed.

One figure who might make use of the ghost light is colorful producer David Belasco, who famously haunts the theater he built in
1907 and that is named for him. Belasco, who lived in an apartment
above the theater, was called the Bishop of Broadway for the clerical-
style garb he wore. Though he died in 1931, it is said that he has made
appearances since then. He talks to performers, his cigar smoke occasionally wafts through the house, and his footsteps are often heard.

Perhaps the most famous Broadway ghost is also the saddest.
Olive Thomas was the darling of the 1915 Ziegfeld Follies, a celebrated beauty who was painted by the leading artists of her day,
including Alberto Vargas, who did a nude portrait for the New
Amsterdam Theatre, home to the Follies. Olive Thomas was married
to Jack Pickford, the brother of film star Mary Pickford. Legend has
it that when Thomas discovered that her young husband was being
treated for syphilis, she grabbed the pills he was taking and downed
them all, killing herself. She has been a fixture at the theater ever
since, flirting with men and causing mischief of various sorts. She
apparently regrets having died young.

The Actor Who Wasn't

Speaking of the mysterious, one wildly prolific Broadway actor never existed at all. The particulars of George Spelvin's birth late in the 19th century remain a mystery, but we know that he's one of the most widely seen actors in history. In a single night, the legend goes, he appeared at nine theaters in 11 different roles. "George Spelvin," of course, is the name used when an actor plays more than one part, or when the actor's true identity would give away the plot. George Spelvin has done literally thousands of performances on Broadway and has had luck in the movies as well. His daughter, Georgette, sometimes called Georgina, followed her father into the theater.

Triumphs and Disasters

Acting dynasties are rare but far from unheard of. Judy Garland made legendary appearances at the famed Palace Theatre in 1951, 1956, and 1967, and daughter Liza Minnelli triumphed at the same venue in 1999 and 2008. When the famous Carradine family played the Palace, the results were inconsistent: Patriarch John Carradine bombed in *Frankenstein* in 1981, but ten years later his son Keith wowed Palace audiences in the smash hit musical, *The Will Rogers Follies.* Success of that sort is especially impressive at the Palace, which began life as a vaudeville stage and became a movie theater before finally becoming a legit theater in the 1960s.

Only three of Broadway's 39 theaters are actually on Broadway: the Marquis between 45th and 46th streets, the Palace at 47th Street, and the Broadway at 53rd Street. The Richard Rodgers Theatre has been home to the greatest number of productions that won the Tony for Best Play or Best Musical—ten, from 1951 to 2008. The Lyceum is the oldest continuously operating theater on Broadway. It opened in 1903 and has hosted a staggering number of hit plays, such as *Born Yesterday, The Country Girl, Master Harold . . . and the Boys, I Am My Own Wife,* and Neil LaBute's *reasons to be pretty.*

Finally, the Martin Beck Theatre was home to the most famously reviewed performance in theater history. Dorothy Parker, in reviewing Katharine Hepburn in *The Lake* in 1933, wrote the oft-quoted line: "Go to the Martin Beck Theatre and watch Katharine Hepburn run the gamut of emotion from A to B."

DeWitt Clinton High School:
The Moatless Castle

♥ ♥ ♥ ♥

"The Castle," founded in 1897, lives by its motto: Sine Labore
Nihil *(Without Work, Nothing Is Accomplished). It represents
a remarkable educational experiment that has evolved and
endured, producing an astonishing fraternity of alumni.*

Boys High School, which would become DeWitt Clinton High
School, opened in Greenwich Village as the 19th century wound
down. Its original location (60 West 13th Street in Manhattan) was in
"The Ladies' Mile," an area of town heavy with shopping options
such as R. H. Macy, Lord and Taylor, and Altman's.

Soon renamed for early state governor DeWitt Clinton, in
1906 the school moved to an iconic H-shaped building in Hell's
Kitchen. It has never had an entrance exam. From the beginning,
immigrant and inner-city kids formed the bulk of the student body.

Just as the stock market began to plummet in 1929, DeWitt
Clinton opened a huge, costly new Bedford Park campus next to an
abandoned reservoir project. Mayor James Walker (who was probably preoccupied with his investment portfolio by that time) was
keynote speaker at the opening. A selection of his words: "This
temple of education will repay us even after we are gone, by training
future generations to be good citizens."

That may sound like simple boilerplate, but Mr. Mayor couldn't
know how prophetic he would be. Today, you may not be able to get
through a day in the city without encountering a Clinton alum. Researchers estimate that 200,000 students (until 1983, all male) have
attended the school, the world's largest at its peak enrollment (12,000)
in the 1930s. Twelve thousand teenage boys? A woman passing through
might have grown chest hair just from huffing the testosterone.

The School Today

While DeWitt Clinton followed the trend of American public school
decline during the latter half of the 20th century, the institution has

enjoyed a strong rebound since becoming NYC's last public high school to integrate the genders. Clinton's first female contingent was small (10 percent of the student body) and created a fresh dilemma: girls' bathrooms! At first, the school assigned just one bathroom to the girls and covered the urinals in plastic. Plumbers needed a while to catch up to Clinton's altered demographics.

Modern enrollment is still large: just over 4,000. Of those students, 56 percent are female. Ethnically, Clinton is 66 percent Hispanic, 25 percent African American, 6 percent Asian/Pacific Islander, and 2 percent non-Hispanic Caucasian.

The original Clinton philosophy involved admitting any boy who wanted in, regardless of academic ability, to a generalized vocational environment much like that of a rural school. Clinton recruited excellent teachers and offered them considerable academic freedom. If the surprising number of famous alumni, and the cohesion of the alumni association, is any indication, this combination worked. (Clinton's alumni association is larger than that of numerous colleges.) There may be few high schools that can boast as many past students who are eager to recall their secondary educations with such affection.

Over the years, Clinton has evolved and refined its philosophy of learning. The school instituted SLCs (small learning communities), one of modern Clinton's key attractions. These include Business Enterprise, Future Teachers, Health Professions, the storied Macy Honors Gifted Program, Public Service, and Animal Professions. All have subcommunities that specialize further. For example, the best of the Macy Honors students have qualified for the very competitive Einstein program, which to date has embraced about 200 students.

Athletics in the Mix

Sports have certainly been a part of the program, as well. Clinton's football team is the Governors, but over the years some have dubbed them the Vagabonds because the team didn't get its own home field until 1966. Venues at which the Governors sometimes played football before that include Yankee Stadium, Ebbets Field, and the Polo Grounds. But in addition to football and other high school standbys such as basketball, soccer, and track and field, Clinton has offered an unexpected variety of sporting opportunities for its students, such as fencing, riflery, and handball. A recent influx of

students of Indian and Pakistani backgrounds has even inspired the school to field a cricket team.

Some Famous Alums

The list is immense, so we'll focus on a few that may be familiar:

- **Burt Lancaster** (Class of 1930): Starred in sports at Clinton and became one of Hollywood's most successful actors. Credits include *The Killers* (1946); *From Here to Eternity* (1953); *Run Silent, Run Deep* (1958); *Elmer Gantry* (1960); *The Birdman of Alcatraz* (1962); *Atlantic City* (1980); *Local Hero* (1983); and *Field of Dreams* (1989).

- **Daniel Schorr** (1933): Cultivated a love of investigative journalism at Clinton and gained fame pursuing that career for CBS. An Edward R. Murrow teammate, Schorr won three Emmys and a Golden Baton award. He so annoyed the Nixon administration that he ended up on its infamous "Enemies List."

- **Ed Lopat** (1935): Left-handed pitcher who won 166 major league games, primarily with the Yankees.

- **"Paddy" (Sidney) Chayefsky** (1939): Legendary screen and television writer with three solo Academy Awards. Works include *Marty* (1955), *The Bachelor Party* (1957), *The Goddess* (1958), *Middle of the Night* (1959), *The Hospital* (1971), and *Network* (1976).

- **Neil Simon** (1944): One of the 20th century's most successful and well-liked playwrights, with a long list of glittering credits, such as *The Odd Couple* (1965), *The Sunshine Boys* (1972), *Brighton Beach Memoirs* (1983), *Biloxi Blues* (1985), and *Lost in Yonkers* (1991).

- NBA Hall of Famers **Barney Sedran** (1907), **Dolph Schayes** (1945), and **Nate Archibald** (1966).

- **Garry Marshall** (1952): One of Hollywood's greatest sitcom producers. His legacy includes classics such as *The Odd Couple, Happy Days, Laverne & Shirley*, and *Mork & Mindy*, plus movies such as *Beaches* (1988), *Pretty Woman* (1990), *Runaway Bride* (1999), and *The Princess Diaries I* and *II* (2001, 2004).

- **Tracy Morgan** (Honorary diploma, 2002): Gained fame on *Saturday Night Live* and *30 Rock* and as a stand-up comic. He dropped out of the class of '87 but was later awarded an honorary diploma.

Fast Facts

- *The modern perception of the 1929 market crash is that it all happened in one day. The reality was more tortuous; several days of big losses in October 1929 precipitated a general slide through 1932.*

- *Kleindeutschland, New York's German community, thrived on the Lower East Side in the second half of the 1800s. The neighborhood began to fade around 1870, when the German population began moving north. They were replaced by immigrant Ashkenazi Jews.*

- *Many people assumed Ethel Merman (born 1908, Astoria, Queens) was Jewish. Why? She was born Ethel Agnes Zimmermann, and she came from New York. In reality, she was raised Protestant.*

- *New York City gave the world the Oreo. An 1898 merger created Nabisco, located in West Chelsea. The first Oreos, invented in 1912, came in lemon meringue and cream flavors.*

- *So you think Reggie Jackson was the ultimate hot dog and braggart? When he belted five dingers in the '77 Series, he respected the Old School by saying: "Babe Ruth was great. I'm just lucky."*

- *What might be most amazing about Harlem native Sammy Davis Jr. (1925–90) was his enduring good humor despite the racist brutality he experienced in the Army as a five foot five African American soldier.*

- *In the 1970s, philanthropist Brooke Astor decided to focus her considerable fortune on the New York Public Library. Other wealthy New Yorkers followed her example, completely rejuvenating the city's library system.*

- *To see what most of Manhattan would look like if it weren't for DeWitt Clinton's orderly street grid, visit Greenwich Village. The city would be quirkier, but the sight lines wouldn't extend nearly as far.*

Subway Vigilante!

♥　♥　♥　♥

Bernhard Goetz shot four young men he said tried to rob him. The result was a national debate on vigilantism that still rages today.

It was like a scene out of the Charles Bronson thriller *Death Wish*. Three days before Christmas in 1984, Bernhard Goetz, a mild-mannered, white electronics expert, shot four youths he claimed tried to rob him on a crowded Manhattan subway car. He then fled the scene, eventually turning himself into police in New Hampshire.

The incident was headline news for weeks. Some hailed Goetz as a hero and commended him for standing up to thugs; others considered him just as bad as the young men he said tried to rob him.

Instinct or Malice?

According to accounts, it all went down quickly. The youths—Barry Allen, 18; Troy Canty, 19; James Ramseur, 19; and Darrell Cabey, 19—told police they were just panhandling money to play video games. Goetz, who had been mugged previously, claimed he felt threatened and believed the youths, all of whom were black, were going to rob him. When Canty demanded five dollars, Goetz rose, pulled a gun from beneath his windbreaker, and quickly fired five shots, striking each of his alleged assailants. All survived, though Cabey was left paralyzed and brain damaged when a bullet severed his spinal cord.

In the aftermath of the shooting, Goetz found himself a reluctant public figure. He gave only one interview, to the *New York Post*, in which he said, "I'm amazed at this celebrity status. I want to remain anonymous." But that was not to be.

In 1987, Goetz was acquitted of attempted murder and assault but found guilty of criminal possession of an unlicensed weapon. He spent 250 days in jail. Nine years later, Cabey and his family won a $43 million civil-court judgment against Goetz, who declared bankruptcy.

Old School Gaming with Strat-O-Matic Baseball

♥ ♥ ♥ ♥

It's been around since 1961, a tabletop baseball game that includes a detailed stats card for every real-life player. Today, people still spend obsessive amounts of time replaying vintage games, recording statistics, and communicating on message boards. Strat-O-Matic is one other thing: a product with deep roots in Queens.

On a given day each February, dozens of men converge on Glen Head in Long Island, New York. Many come from the Tri-State area, but some may come from Alberta or Texas or Michigan. They stand bundled up in line before a cinderblock building, talking baseball, sharing coffee from thermoses, brimming with excitement. A few camped out the night before, like Deadheads hoping to score concert tickets. But these guys are on Long Island to pick up the new-season cards for a tabletop baseball game.

No, really. Shortly after "Opening Day," thousands more fans across the continent watch for the UPS or mail delivery like eager children. These are stockbrokers, accountants, store managers, janitors—the gamut of life. Most started playing this game as boys.

The Game in Brief

In Strat (as most enthusiasts call it), each Major League Baseball player has a batting or pitching card. Half the time (at random) the result of an at-bat comes from the hitter's card, and half the time from the pitcher's. The result is great statistical clarity, with players rated for fielding range, pitching endurance, clutch hitting, bunting, leading off base, and so on. People take Strat's fielding ratings so seriously that big league ballplayers phone owner Hal Richman to complain about the ratings on their own Strat cards. Fans even heckle players at games: "You're a 5, Jones!" (In Strat, 5 is the worst fielding range rating; players not only get the reference, they resent it.) Strat-O-Matic Game Co., Inc., also makes football, basketball, and hockey games, but baseball remains the core product.

Deep Hal

Strat is the brainchild and life achievement of entrepreneur Hal Richman. Born in 1936 to a domineering insurance salesman from the Lower East Side, the cerebral, introverted Hal had a difficult childhood in Kew Gardens. Whether he was bullied for being Jewish, or just for shyness, young Hal retreated into baseball—simulated baseball. At 11, the gifted young mathematician began finding flaws in spinner-based baseball games. Over the next 15 years, he evolved what would become Strat-O-Matic Baseball.

With only selected players and/or teams, the game's first release was a sales flop. Only when Richman began to include all teams and all significant players did Strat start to sell. John F. Kennedy was president when Hal made that decision—and Hal is still in business.

Very Old School

Strat doesn't even take baseball's word for its own statistics—it compiles them from old box scores. Strat still calls its computer version "CD-ROM Baseball." The company has been in the same building since 1975, slow to change anything. Sometimes lack of change is good, though; gamers have long respected Strat for its scrupulously honest reputation. Hal Richman personally reads and acts upon his mail, ensuring that customers receive fair value.

Well he should, because Strat is boy-howdy expensive, especially for a text-based game. But it's not just average Joes playing. Many big league ballplayers grew up playing Strat, and some still do. Mets great Keith Hernandez has played it since childhood. Spike Lee still loves the game. Trip Hawkins, founder of Strat semicompetitor Electronic Arts, is still rolling the dice. (The baseball game from EA has graphics, costs less, and includes the current season, not last season. Strat junkies remain indifferent to EA.)

Strat Today

It hasn't been easy for Strat, of course. The rights to use player names, the imbroglios created by baseball strikes, an aging customer base, and graphics-based games pose big challenges. But like the single-minded Jewish kid from Queens who borrowed money from a grumpy dad to start his company, Strat-O-Matic is a survivor.

Noteworthy Brooklynites

♥ ♥ ♥ ♥

Lots of interesting people come from Brooklyn!

Aaliyah (1979–2001) Native Brooklynite who achieved swift fame as an R&B singer and actress before her untimely death in a plane crash.

Carmelo Anthony (1984–) Dominant, high-scoring NBA star, raised in the Red Hook housing projects.

Woody Allen (1935–)° Born in Brooklyn, raised in Midwood, this professionally neurotic genius has seemingly mastered every role in entertainment but singer and dancer: actor, director, writer, comic, and jazz clarinetist.

Pat Benatar (1953–) Diminutive big-voiced pop star of the 1980s, born in Greenpoint; won four Grammys singing about bad love.

Riddick Bowe (1967–) Heavyweight boxer from Brownsville, one of 13 children; in a fractured heavyweight division, Bowe won championships in 1992 and 1995.

Shannon "The Cannon" Briggs (1971–) Another heavyweight boxer, WBO champ 2006–7, from Brownsville; once knocked an opponent completely out of the ring.

Mel Brooks (1926–)° Born in Brooklyn and attended Eastern District High School; irreverent, cheerfully vulgar comic genius who has won one Oscar, three Tonys, two Emmys, and three Grammys over a career of more than half a century.

Al Capone (1899–1947) Native of Brooklyn kicked out of P.S. 133 at age 14; joined local gangs, made his bones, and eventually looked westward, turning himself into New York's love letter to Chicago.

Ruthe B. Mandell Cowl (1912–2008) Native Brooklynite, this businesswoman is revered in her adopted hometown of Laredo, Texas, for her many years of selfless philanthropy.

Vincent D'Onofrio (1959–) Actor from Bensonhurst, known as quirky Detective Goren on TV's *Law & Order: Criminal Intent.*

Ruth Bader Ginsburg (1933–) A Brooklyn native who grew up in Midwood, she's been an associate justice of the Supreme Court of the United States since 1993.

Susan Hayward (1917–75)* Born in Flatbush, she became a whirlwind in Hollywood as a flame-haired temptress; during a career that spanned five decades, Hayward was acclaimed for her talent and good looks and won an Oscar.

Shemp (Samuel), Moe (Moses), and Curly (Jerome) Howard (1895–1955, 1897–1975, 1903–52, respectively) The Horwitz brothers of Brownsville were the original Three Stooges; few today may remember Shemp's early days with the group, but he won fans after replacing Curly in the Stooges in 1947.

Michael Jordan (1963–) Brooklyn native and Chicago Bulls NBA star, likely the greatest basketball player of all time; Jordan's contribution to the Windy City probably makes up for Al Capone's time there.

Danny Kaye (1913–87)* Brooklyn-born movie actor, a product of P.S. 149 in East New York; excelled at comedy and light musicals while a major box-office draw in the 1940s and '50s.

Larry King (1933–)* Born in Brooklyn to immigrant parents, he became a successful overnight radio broadcaster and, later, a highly visible CNN TV interviewer.

Sandy Koufax (1935–)* A native, raised in Borough Park; first-ballot Baseball Hall of Fame pitcher, Brooklyn/L.A. Dodgers, perhaps history's greatest Jewish sports hero.

Vince Lombardi (1913–70)* Iconic, hardheaded football coach who grew up in Sheepshead Bay.

Norman Mailer (1923–2007)* Raised in Brooklyn, he went on to cofound the *Village Voice;* is revered as one of America's leading novelists, biographers, memoirists, and provocative controversialists; famously ran for mayor of NYC in 1969.

Mos Def (1973–) Born Dante Smith in Bed-Stuy, he was a child actor at 14, and later found success in films and on Broadway; well known to the general public as a hip-hop recording artist, Mos has riled many in NYC with his vocal defense of Al-Qaeda and his criticism of American political doctrine.

Ol' Dirty Bastard (1968–2004) Called "ODB" when talking to your grandma, the rapper was born in East New York and helped found hardcore hip-hop group Wu-Tang Clan.

Joe Paterno (1926–) A borough native who went to Brooklyn Prep and who's coached Penn State football for 60 years, compiling a 393–129–3 record.

Joan Rivers (1933–)* Born and raised in Brooklyn; talented actress, acerbic comedian, and poster child for what too much Botox and plastic surgery can do.

Phil Rizzuto (1917–2007) Hall of Fame Yankee shortstop, born in Brooklyn; a much-loved finesse player and later a successful broadcaster and product pitchman.

Carl Sagan (1934–96) Born in Brooklyn and lived there in his early years; a celebrated astronomer, author, Cornell professor, adviser to NASA, television personality, and extraterrestrial life theorist.

Judith Blum Sheindlin (1942–)* Snappy-comeback "Judge Judy" of TV fame; she's a Brooklyn native who went to James Madison High.

Barbra Streisand (1942–)* Born in Brooklyn, where she grew up poor, now she's a megawatt actress, director, and pop singer with 51 gold albums—that isn't a typo.

Marisa Tomei (1964–)* Saucy, doe-eyed Brooklynite who grew up in Midwood; 1992 Academy Award for *My Cousin Vinny* with repeat nominations for *In the Bedroom* (2001) and *The Wrestler* (2008).

Joe Torre (1940–)* This Brooklyn native is so well known for his 30-year baseball managerial career that people forget his lifetime .297 batting average.

Mae West (1893–1980)* Longtime stage and screen actress and sex symbol, who smartly pushed the boundaries of what was appropriate in popular entertainment; she was born in Bushwick.

Robert Anton Wilson (1932–2007) Provocatively skeptical, quasi-mystical author and philosopher who grew up in Flatbush.

* Honored on Celebrity Path in the Botanic Gardens.

He Calls Himself Crash

♥   ♥   ♥   ♥

*Not many people refer to John Matos by his given name.
Instead, he's known as Crash, a guy who jumped the tracks
from Bronx "graff guy" to professional artist. Along the way,
he linked underground art to aboveground painting.*

Crash was born to a South Bronx Puerto Rican family in 1961. He
began his artistic career at 13, with spray paint, using subway cars
and rundown buildings as canvases. Why "Crash"? As a kid, he
wanted to be a computer programmer. What do computers often do?

Unlike some taggers, Crash didn't just mark gang turf; he
created amazing murals, expressing himself in a very visible way. He
tried formal art studies but dropped out in disdain. At 19, Crash got
his first invitation to exhibit a mural, and his career exploded. Today
his work is mainstream art, exhibited worldwide.

Themes

Crash combines comic-book style with vivid color and imagery to
describe city life's constant state of change. His characters' eyes are
especially expressive, often riveting. The anger, despair, and gritty
violence of the street steadily radiate from Crash's paintings but
never in a gratuitous or immature way. Instead, those qualities are
like a lens into his world. The pain that tough urban environments
can inflict upon girls and women is a frequent subject of his work.

Since 1981, Crash has exhibited his work at galleries small and
large in places as diverse as Detroit, Rotterdam, Vancouver, Paris,
Des Moines, and Los Angeles. Not bad for the kid who once had to
look over his shoulder as he expressed his creativity!

Crashocasters

Crash met Eric Clapton when a mutual friend suggested Crash as
someone who could show the famed guitarist the streets. Clapton
liked Crash's art and floated the idea of putting some of it on a guitar.
Eventually, Crash ordered an unfinished Stratocaster, tagged it up,
and sent it to Clapton, who's since used it on stage.

You Can Thank New York

Every guy looks good in a tuxedo—and we have New Yorker (and wealthy tobacco magnate) Pierre Lorillard IV to thank for it.

This formal suit has been the epitome of male fashion finery for generations, and yet most people don't realize that it originated in the appropriately named Tuxedo Park region, a haven for the rich and famous located just outside New York City.

In October 1886, the story goes, Lorillard commissioned a new type of formal wear, which he had designed and intended to wear to the Tuxedo Club's Autumn Ball. The outfit, which Lorillard himself named after the tony area in which he lived, was most notable for its tailless black jacket—a dramatic departure from the era's traditional long tailcoat and white tie.

But for reasons unknown, Lorillard did not wear his new design to the ball—instead, his son, Griswold, and a handful of Griswold's buddies, did. It was a bold fashion statement, completely out of character for the times but one that was met with glowing approval by others in attendance. In short, the tuxedo was a hit.

But from where did the elder Lorillard receive his fashion inspiration? Some believe the tuxedo was modeled after a special dinner jacket designed by Henry Poole & Company of London's famed Savile Row, whose high-society clients included the Prince of Wales, later to become King Edward VII. Others believe Lorillard was inspired by the shorter red jackets often worn during fox hunts.

Regardless of its source, the tuxedo quickly found its way into the closet of every man who wanted to look dashing at a formal event, be it a wedding, a high school prom, or a high-society fund-raiser. To wear anything else was to look like a slob.

So the next time you find yourself stuffed into what is also sometimes called a penguin suit, take a moment to thank (or blame) Pierre Lorillard, the New York fashion plate who made it all possible.

The Real Gangs of New York

♥　♥　♥　♥

New York's gang history reflects the city's global diversity.

- **Amberg Gang** (Jewish, Brooklyn, ca. 1920–35). Run by Joseph, Hyman, and Louis "Pretty" Amberg. Was mostly involved in labor/protection racketeering in Brooklyn.

- **Bonanno Family** (Italian, all boroughs, 1931–present). Born from the post-Castellammarese War truce of 1931. The only Family still bearing its original name. Diverse criminal activity.

- **Bowery Boys** (Anglo-Saxon, Manhattan, ca. 1850–63). Mostly political in nature, specifically anti-Irish Catholic, plus other ethnic violence and petty crime.

- **Broadway Mob** (Sicilian, Manhattan and Brooklyn, ca. 1921–33). A Joe "Adonis" Doto, "Lucky" Luciano, and Frank Costello operation, precursor to the Five Families. Created to violate Prohibition.

- **Brownsville Boys** (Italian/Jewish, Brooklyn, ca. 1927–57). Tagged by media as "Murder, Inc." Mainly enforcement and murder for hire.

- **Bug & Meyer Mob** (Jewish, various boroughs, ca. 1920–35). Benjamin "Bugsy" Siegel and Meyer Lansky, sometimes called the "La Kosher Nostra;" gambling, bootlegging, and murder for hire.

- **Colombo Family** (Italian, mainly Brooklyn, 1931–present—in diluted form). They began as the Profaci Family after the Castellammarese War truce; diverse criminal activity.

- **Dead Rabbits** (Irish, Manhattan, 1850s). Partly political in focus, they were the Bowery Boys' rivals (especially during the famed 1857 riot). Mostly petty crime.

- **East Harlem Purple Gang** (Mostly Italian, Manhattan, 1970s). Including some very famous names, later amalgamated into the Mafia families. Drugs and murder for hire.

- **Five Percenters** (African American, Manhattan/Brooklyn, 1963–present). An offshoot of the Nation of Islam that smokes and drinks. On the cusp between street gang and church.

- **Five Points Gang** (Italian, Manhattan, ca. 1890–1910s). Prep school for Johnny Torrio and Al Capone centered on the famously poor Victorian district. Diverse petty crime: strong-arming, loansharking, and robbery.

- **Gambino Family** (Italian, all boroughs, 1920s–present). Began as the Mangano Family after the Castellammarese War truce. Led by Albert Anastasia, later John Gotti. Diverse criminal activity.

- **Genovese Family** (Italian, all boroughs, ca. 1900–present). Started as the Luciano Family under "Lucky" Luciano after the Castellammarese War truce. Perhaps the most powerful Family today; diverse criminal activity.

- **Hip Sing Tong** (Chinese, Manhattan, 1890s–present). Fought the On Leong for control of Chinatown in the early 1900s. Some legit activities plus gambling, loansharking, and drugs.

- **Jolly Stompers** (African American, Bronx/Brooklyn, ca. 1960s–1970s). Recruited a young Mike Tyson into their ranks. Very violent, mostly into robbery.

- **Latin Kings** (Hispanic, various boroughs, 1986–present). Came from Chicago. Strong in hierarchy and philosophy but also strong in arson, theft, drugs, and murder.

- **Lucchese Family** (Italian, various boroughs, ca. 1917–present). Grew out of the Reina gang after the Castellammarese truce. Diverse criminal activity.

- **Mau Maus** (Mostly Puerto Rican, Brooklyn, 1954–62). A particularly ruthless gang, they engaged in some petty crime and drug dealing but mostly violence for its own sake.

- **Monk Eastman Gang** (Mainly Jewish, Manhattan, ca. 1890s–1917). Fierce rival to the Five Points Gang. Pimping, political violence at Tammany's behest, petty crime.

- **On Leong Tong** (Chinese, Manhattan, 1893–present). Fought the early 1900s Tong Wars. Many legitimate endeavors; have also dealt in racketeering, drugs, gambling, and human trafficking.

- **Whyos** (Irish, Manhattan, 1860s–90s). Dominated Manhattan underworld until crushed by the Monk Eastman Gang. Extortion, prostitution, intimidation for hire.

Nick Fotiu: Pride of New Dorp

♥ ♥ ♥ ♥

He wasn't huge, and he wasn't flashy. But Nick Fotiu was surely the toughest NHL player to come from Staten Island.

Young Nick Fotiu (pronounced: fa-TEE-u), a Greek-Italian Staten Island construction worker, loved hockey enough to ride subways and buses from New Dorp all the way to New Hyde Park. Why there? The Rangers sometimes practiced there; also, if Nick came between 5 and 7 A.M., he could get ice time. While carrying their sticks, he told Ranger players that someday he'd be one of them. They probably didn't take the boast seriously. Had they seen him fight, however, they might have reconsidered, because Nicholas Evlampios Fotiu was a Police Athletic League boxing champ.

The WHA

Nick showed enough toughness during play in New Hyde Park that Cape Cod's minor league team signed him for the 1973–74 season. He compiled 12 goals, 24 assists, and 371 penalties in minutes (PIM). Short interpretation: A 12-goal minor leaguer is probably a two-goal NHLer, but 371 PIM is good enough to earn the guy some serious frequent-fighter miles. The New England Whalers of the World Hockey Association, the NHL's rival, brought Nick up. He quickly proved that he could handle the WHA's thugs—a good thing, because the league was full of stick-swingers and sluggers.

Madison Square Garden

The Rangers signed Nick in 1976, and except for two years with his old team (by now the Hartford Whalers, merged into the NHL), Nick was a Ranger through 1985. The Garden fans loved the hometown boy who'd made good. Nick didn't compile huge NHL PIM totals because he didn't need to; few players wanted a piece of him. Remembering how he used to camp out for Rangers tickets to sit in the cheap seats, he often threw pucks way up there during pregame warmups. In New York, the athlete that reaches out to the people is a deity. Nick Fotiu not only reached out, he was one of them.

"Gentleman" Jimmy Walker

♥ ♥ ♥ ♥

*The 1920s, a time of easy money, easy virtue, and
even easier vice, established a corrupt but colorful
mayor as the "Beau James" of the Jazz Age.*

American mayors hold one of the most important political executive
offices in the nation. While the best of all time in New York City was
arguably Fiorello H. La Guardia, the Republican "fusionist" reformer who fought the Mob and read children the funnies over the
radio during a newspaper strike, Gotham has also had more than its
fair share of mayoral villains.

These include Fernando Wood, whose vote rigging and criminal
affiliations made him the standard bearer for 19th-century institutionalized corruption, and Abraham Oakey Hall, known as "Boss
Tweed's mayor" because of the role he played in defrauding tax-
payers out of between $40 million and $200 million during his
1868–72 tenure. But these crooks and scam artists aside, New York's
worst mayor has to be Jimmy Walker, a skirt-chasing, former Tin Pan
Alley composer. His affairs with chorus girls and official lack of
interest in around 32,000 Prohibition speakeasies (some of which he
owned) endeared him to many voters, but his involvement with
kickbacks and public extortion led to his downfall.

A Large and Crooked Role

Like Wood and Hall, James John Walker was a product of the
Tammany Hall Democratic machine that, concurrent with the
political rise of Irish-Americans, played a large and often crooked
role in New York City politics from the late 18th century to the early
1960s. The son of an Irish-born assemblyman and alderman from
Greenwich Village, Walker, too, was a member of the New York state
assembly, as well as the New York state senate, before defeating the
incumbent John Hylan in 1925 to become mayor in 1926. His elec-
toral platform ballyhooed legalized beer and a five-cent subway fare,
as well as legalized Sunday boxing, baseball, and movies. You could
safely say that Walker was going for the "common-person" vote.

Hoping, as he said during his inauguration speech, that "the people of this city would not look upon their public servants as antagonistic, but . . . as their servants and friends," Walker quickly befriended plenty of females at the clubs he frequented. This allowed him to add the sobriquets of "Beau James" and the "Night Mayor" to that of "Gentleman Jimmy," which had come courtesy of his dandified demeanor and custom-made clothes.

Jimmy got off to a flying start during his first two years in office, spending 143 days *out* of the office for vacation trips to Palm Beach, Palm Springs, Europe, and the Caribbean. Then, when he was publicly brought to task for giving himself a pay raise from $25,000 annually to $40,000, he characteristically quipped, "Why, that's cheap. Think what it would cost if I worked full-time."

A Little Fireside Chat

Walker continually laughed off accusations of corruption. He won reelection easily in 1929, defeating the highly ethical La Guardia, but his dismissive attitude toward his troubles became more difficult to maintain after the onset of the Great Depression. In 1931, the New York state legislature commenced an investigation into his administration's misdeeds, including the extortion of money from innocent citizens who had been accused of bogus crimes. Just a year later, Walker was charged with extorting and accepting several hundred thousand dollars in kickbacks from business executives who had been handed sweet city contracts. At that point, Governor Franklin Roosevelt suggested he and Jimmy have a little fireside chat. Governor Roosevelt was not a man to be trifled with, and on September 1, 1932, Walker resigned as mayor and absconded to France, where he married his longtime mistress, the English actress Betty Compton, after divorcing his former-chorus-girl wife.

The Walkers returned to New York City in 1935. Jimmy became the head of Majestic Records, and in 1940, just before he and Betty received their own divorce, the irrepressible "Beau James" bounced back from his public disgrace with an appointment as municipal arbiter to the garment industry. Mayor La Guardia made the appointment.

Jimmy Walker passed from this realm of pleasure on November 18, 1946, at the age of 65.

Monsters Amok!

♥ ♥ ♥ ♥

New York City has been a playground for some of cinema's most destructive behemoths, not to mention a slew of smaller beasties.

In 1933, King Kong demonstrated his displeasure at being taken from Skull Island against his will by giving New York a monster-size beat-down before being shot from atop the Empire State Building. Since then, beasts large and small have had their way with the Big Apple.

The Beast from 20,000 Fathoms (1953). Awakened from a 100-million-year sleep by an experimental nuclear blast near the Arctic Circle, a huge "rhedosaurus" makes its way to the streets of New York City. There, it eats a cop, smashes buildings, and makes a general nuisance of itself before finally being killed with a deadly radioactive isotope shot from atop the Coney Island roller coaster.

The Deadly Mantis (1957). A prehistoric praying mantis the size of a large jet is freed from its icy confines in the Antarctic (sound familiar?) and carves a swath of destruction before landing in New York, where it is exterminated with gas inside the Holland Tunnel.

Wolfen (1981). Police Detective Dewey Wilson (Albert Finney) is assigned to solve a series of bizarre murders in the decaying South Bronx that appear to have been committed by wild animals. During his investigation, Wilson is told of a Native American legend regarding shapeshifters that can transform themselves into wolflike creatures. Could one of them be responsible for the horrendous deaths?

C.H.U.D. (1984). Exposure to illegally stored radioactive waste turns homeless people living in New York's cavernous sewer system into "cannibalistic humanoid underground dwellers." When their initial food source (other homeless people) becomes scarce, the C.H.U.D. start dining above ground, with gruesome results.

Cloverfield (2008). The nightly routine of young singles in Manhattan is thrown into disarray when an enormous monster attacks the city. *Cloverfield* was filmed on digital video, in a handheld style to suggest that the footage was shot by several of the film's characters. New York really takes it on the chin in this one—literally—as the Statue of Liberty's head goes crashing and rolling down the street.

Quotables

Even the most devoted lovers quarrel occasionally.

"New York had all the iridescence of the beginning of the world."

—F. Scott Fitzgerald

"It is a miracle that New York works at all. The whole thing is implausible."

—E. B. White

"I was in love with New York. I do not mean 'love' in any colloquial way, I mean that I was in love with the city, the way you love the first person who ever touches you and never love anyone quite that way again."

—Joan Didion

"I . . . wonder what it is in the New York air that enables me to sit up till all hours of the night in an atmosphere which in London would make a horse dizzy, but here merely clears the brain."

—James Agate

"New York is the only real city-city."

—Truman Capote

"There is something in the New York air that makes sleep useless."

—Simone de Beauvoir

"A hundred times have I thought New York is a catastrophe, and fifty times: It is a beautiful catastrophe."

—Le Corbusier

"New York is the dirtiest, largest, ugliest, broken-down city in the world—but it's the only one."

—Isaac Stern

"It is an ugly city, a dirty city. Its climate is a scandal. Its politics are used to frighten children. Its traffic is madness. Its competition is murderous. But there is one thing about it—once you have lived in New York and it has become your home, no other place is good enough."

—John Steinbeck

St. Mark's Church in-the-Bowery

♥ ♥ ♥ ♥

"Here [Peter Stuyvesant] built a manor and chapel. Here he would live out his life and be buried, and here, over the parade of centuries, flappers, shtetl refugees, hippies and punks—an aggregate of local residents running from Trotsky to Auden to Charlie Parker to Joey Ramone—would shuffle past his tomb."

—Russell Shorto, from *The Island at the Center of the World*

Originally built in 1799, twice restored after disastrous fires, St. Mark's Church in-the-Bowery is the oldest site of continuous worship in New York City. Since the 19th century, it's also been a treasured ongoing resource for arts and culture in a resolutely liberal neighborhood.

Uh ... This Isn't the Bowery

Don't be confused by its location at the intersection of 10th and Stuyvesant streets and Second Avenue: The Bowery itself, an avenue once dominated by the down-and-out (and home to famed rock haven CBGB's), runs diagonally from Chinatown's Chatham Square to Eighth Street in the Village, where it becomes Fourth Avenue. "Bouwerie" was the Dutch word for "farm," so this is where Petrus (aka Peter) Stuyvesant, governor-general of 17th-century New Amsterdam, located his in 1651. After his death in 1672, Stuyvesant was entombed beneath the church.

The son of a Calvinist minister (although Stuyvesant's great-grandchildren became Episcopalian, the church's denomination today), Stuyvesant was noted for his wooden leg (having had his right one amputated) and ill temper. There have been nearly a dozen re-ports of his restless spirit's manifestations in and around the church—visual sightings, earwitness accounts of the distinctive stomping of a peg leg—and, supposedly, a man's voice defiantly singing Calvinist hymns in Dutch during an Episcopalian service in English.

Home for the Arts

The Danspace Project, whose alumni include composer and chore-ographer Meredith Monk, was established here over 35 years ago;

regular performances take place on the same stage where the revered Martha Graham and Isadora Duncan exhibited new iterations of dance in the 1920s and '30s. Khalil Gibran was appointed to the parish arts committee in 1919, four years before the publication of *The Prophet,* which eventually made him the third best-selling poet of all time. Iconic American playwright Sam Shepard's career began here in 1964 when Theatre Genesis produced two of his one-act plays, *Cowboys* and *The Rock Garden.* Andy Warhol reportedly screened his earliest films here. Participants at various activities at the church have included poets Carl Sandburg and William Carlos Williams, writer Edna St. Vincent Millay, and illusionist-escape artist Harry Houdini.

Allen Ginsberg was involved with the church's decades-old Poetry Project, which continues its traditional annual New Year's Day 11-hour poetry marathon that has featured such luminaries as the late Jim Carroll, Yoko Ono, Alice Walker *(The Color Purple)*, John Cage, Amiri Baraka (aka Leroi Jones), Philip Glass, and Patti Smith. This is where playwright-director-designer Richard Foreman—author of more than 50 plays, winner of five OBIE (Off-Broadway) awards for best play, and recipient of a MacArthur Genius Grant—established the headquarters of his Ontological-Hysteric Theater, which puts on annual productions.

Power to the People

Originally serving an elite congregation, St. Mark's has evolved into a church of and for the people. It was an early supporter of immigrant, unions, and civil rights; hosted meetings of the Black Panthers and the Young Lords; and opened the first Manhattan clinic specializing in lesbian health issues. In 2009, St. Mark's appointed a 37-year-old East Indian lesbian as its rector. It continues its affiliation with the AIDS community by participating in the annual AIDS Walk and in Day With(out) Art each December 1. Its mission statement is as follows: "We are an inclusive and diverse community comprised of the young and the old, people living with chronic illness, college students, people living with mental illness, families, artists, gay, straight, a great mix of ethnicity and race, children and the occasional animal."

Welcome, one and all! (You too, Fido.)

Mighty Joe Rollino

♥ ♥ ♥ ♥

*A centenarian Coney Island strongman laughed at
the odds and never gave in as time marched on.*

New York has had more than its fair share of colorful characters
with unique stories, but few could outstrip the feats of The Great
Joe Rollino. A Coney Island strongman who once purportedly lifted
475 pounds with his teeth and 635 pounds with one finger, he still
took a daily five-mile stroll around his Brooklyn neighborhood—
until a car struck him at age 104.

Mighty Mite

Standing just five foot five and weighing between 125 and 150
pounds, Mighty Joe was, relative to his size, one of the most powerful men alive, not just in terms of muscle strength but also with
regard to individual body parts. Think about it: How come his
weightlifting teeth weren't shattered or ripped from his
gums, or the back with which he shifted
3,200 pounds didn't succumb to the slipped
disc or lumbago that any normal person
might suffer? No doubt about it, Joe was a tough
guy, and he enjoyed demonstrating and talking
about this virtually until he took his last breath.

Born on March 19, 1905, to Italian immigrants who presented him with 13 siblings,
Rollino spent even his earliest years building his body and flexing his muscles while
training with America's first great strong-
man, Warren Lincoln Travis. After touring the United States as a boxer
under the name of Kid Dundee, Rollino began showing off his strength
as a Coney Island performer. Squashing nails with his gnashers and
bending coins with his bare hands—you name it, The World's Strongest
Man (as he liked to call himself) could do it. He labored as a longshore-
man, served as a bodyguard to film star Greta Garbo, and got to know
Harry Houdini. While in the Pacific during World War II, he earned a

Silver Star, a Bronze Star, and three Purple Hearts (he took shrapnel in his legs and rescued several soldiers on the field of battle by grabbing and transporting each of them under one arm).

The Colder, the Better

Aside from working out, part of Joe's secret was a healthy lifestyle that included yogurt and wheat germ long before they were popular. Joe abstained from meat, booze, and cigarettes. What's more, he took frequent swims in the Atlantic Ocean, regardless of whether it was lukewarm or freezing. As far as he was concerned, the colder, the better. During one winter in the 1950s, when the police didn't have the necessary protective gear to jump into icy waters, Joe retrieved the bodies of two people who had drowned in Prospect Park. A couple of decades later, in January 1974, a six-degree day saw the then 68-year-old "Puggy" (as his acquaintances called him) join a half dozen other members of the appropriately named Iceberg Athletic Club for a swim in the frigid waters off Coney Island. Nothing was too daunting for Mr. Rollino.

A Marvel to the End

A longtime member of the not-for-profit, New York–based Association of Oldetime Barbell & Strongmen—which educates people about the hazards of drug use and the benefits of drug-free weightlifting and other sporting activities—Joe was handing out free advice to fellow "Iron Game" participants when celebrating his 103rd birthday at a Brooklyn restaurant. And he was still bending quarters with his teeth and regaling people with tales of his past achievements. "Fighters would hit me in the jaw and I'd just look at them," he told thesweetscience.com. "You couldn't knock me out." However, just before seven in the morning on January 11, 2010, "Old Man Joe" took one hit he couldn't shake off.

After buying newspapers at a local deli, 104-year-old Joe Rollino was struck by a Ford Windstar as he crossed Bay Ridge Parkway in Dyker Heights. He suffered a broken pelvis and severe head and chest injuries and died shortly after. His friend Charlie Laird told the *New York Daily News,* "Father Time didn't stand a chance against Joe Rollino. It took all the speed and might of a minivan, and I'm shocked that *that* was even able to take him down."

Bragging Rights

When it comes to skyscrapers, New York City is the nation's capital! Chicago may be the "city of the big shoulders," as poet Carl Sandburg once observed, but New York is the undisputed city of big buildings! In fact, the Big Apple has the most skyscrapers—defined as a building more than 650 feet tall—of any city in the world (although competition with Hong Kong is tight).

Until it was brought down by terrorists on September 11, 2001, the World Trade Center was the city's tallest building, reaching skyward a remarkable 1,368 feet. With its destruction, the 1,250-foot-tall Empire State Building reclaimed the title, which it had held from 1931, when it was completed, until the opening of the World Trade Center in 1972.

Currently, the second tallest building in New York City is the Bank of America Tower (1,200 feet), followed by the Chrysler Building and the New York Times Building, which tie for third at 1,046 feet each.

Though it doesn't meet the current definition of a skyscraper, the first tall building to be constructed in New York City was the World Building. Completed in 1890, it towered over the city at 309 feet. The World Building held the title of New York's Tallest Building until 1899 and was demolished in 1955 to make room for an expanded entrance to the Brooklyn Bridge.

With the success of the World Building, high-rises soon took New York City by storm, one superstructure after another vying for the title of tallest. Between 1960 and the present, roughly 70 buildings taller than 600 feet high were constructed in Manhattan and surrounding boroughs.

The tallest building in the world as of this book's publication is the Barj Khalifa, in Dubai, United Arab Emirates. Completed in 2010, it stands an unbelievable 2,717 feet tall. The next highest is the Taipei 101 Tower in Taipei, Taiwan, a monster at 1,667 feet.

New York City may no longer be the title holder of World's Tallest Building, but it still stands proud as the city that did it first and, in the minds of many architecture buffs, did it best.

Fast Facts

- Babe Ruth managed to get suspended five times in 1922, including a season-starter that lasted 22 games (for barnstorming). The others were for umpire-related misbehaviors, such as throwing a handful of dirt in the face of one of them.

- Why did early skyscrapers taper? It resulted from NYC's "wedding cake" zoning. Essentially, once a building's area tapered to 25 percent of its lot size, it could be as tall as the builders wished.

- Prohibition in the city: In 1919 New York had 16,000 places to swill demon rum. By 1929 (with Prohibition in force for ten years), there were twice as many spots to celebrate your victories and drown your sorrows.

- During the Revolutionary War, every Loyalist with sense got out of Manhattan. The city confiscated their real estate in 1779, and although a 1792 law allowed them to return, they didn't get their land back.

- Brooklyn native Mickey Rooney (born Joe Yule Jr. in 1920) was discovered when he was just one year old. Little Joe sneezed during his dad's vaudeville act. When a spotlight found him, he blew his mouth organ; everyone laughed, and the Mick was on his way.

- New Year's 1898 saw the consolidation of Richmond, Manhattan, Brooklyn, and Queens into today's five boroughs. The Bronx, of course, was split from Manhattan; Richmond became Staten Island in 1975.

- On May 10, 1849, a mob attempted to storm the Astor Place Opera to protest the Anglophile theater tastes of New York's elite. Unfortunately for the mob, said elite controlled the militia. Death toll: 22.

- During the 1934 NFL Championship, with the Polo Grounds turf frozen like a hockey rink, the New York Giants came out for the second half in borrowed sneakers. This must have given them the traction they needed, because they stomped the skittering Chicago Bears, 30–13.

The High Line, Naturally

♥ ♥ ♥ ♥

An abandoned elevated railroad track that once delivered
cattle to the city's meatpacking district is now one of
the most extraordinary public parks in America.

Where else but New York will you find native grasses, wildflowers, butterflies, trees, and a fountain 30 feet in the air? Not on top of a building, you understand, but on top of a former railroad bed.

This is the High Line, a one-of-a-kind public park that opened in June 2009 and was immediately embraced by New Yorkers. Its popularity continues to grow, as visitors stroll its lushly landscaped concrete paths and lounge on its benches, all the while relishing some of the city's most striking green space and best views. *New York Times* architecture critic Nicolai Ouroussoff called the High Line "one of the most thoughtful, sensitively designed public spaces built in New York in years." When Mayor Bloomberg dedicated the park he described it as "an extraordinary gift to our city's future."

The first phase of the three-phase park runs along the former CSX train tracks, from Gansevoort Street on the city's far west side up to 20th Street. A second section, which will extend the park to 30th Street, is scheduled to open in the autumn of 2010. A final section, which would take the park farther north to 34th Street, is under discussion.

Recycling the Railroad

The High Line has been on the public agenda since 1999, when two friends who lived in the area, writer Joshua David and painter Robert Hammond, began lobbying for fresh use of tracks that hadn't seen activity since 1980. Although some neighborhood property owners hoped to see the old rail line razed, David and Hammond and their group, Friends of the High Line, prevailed after countless public meetings and careful coordination among city, state, and federal officials, as well as widespread grass-roots support from the public.

More than 720 interdisciplinary teams from around the world submitted plans to "recycle" the High Line. The winning idea came

from Diller, Scofidio & Renfro and James Corner Field Operations. The firms' mantra: "Keep it Simple, Keep it Wild, Keep it Slow, and Keep it Quiet."

Friends of the High Line, which manages the park in an arrangement with the city's Parks Department, raised more than $44 million at the project's outset. Much of that money was contributed by Diane von Furstenberg and her husband, Barry Diller, and hedge fund billionaire Philip Falcone and his wife, Lisa Maria Falcone. The city kicked in another $112 million, the federal government $20 million, and the state $400,000.

Flora and Fauna

The unusual plantings—more than 100 native plants perk up the first half-mile section alone—were carefully chosen to reflect the park's beginnings. Railroad tracks peek out from flowerbeds and grasses. Gardens are deliberately a little wild and even scraggly, a nod to the isolated, deserted feel of the tracks after years of abandonment. The trees, flowers, and shrubs have a natural, unforced feel. Green spaces and flower plantings are punctuated by steel rails, massive metal support beams, and views of the Hudson River. Visitors gaze down on new and vintage buildings and lively street life.

Entrances to the park, architectural accomplishments themselves, are accessible at Gansevoort Street, 14th Street, 16th Street, 18th Street, and 20th Street. A new branch of the Whitney Museum, designed by the world-famous architect Renzo Piano, is planned for the Gansevoort entrance to the High Line.

This being New York, unexpected fun popped up soon after the High Line's opening, when an enterprising young woman whose apartment faces directly onto the park realized that the fire escape where she had been hanging her laundry to dry also offered an excellent performance venue. The Renegade Cabaret was born, to the delight of appreciative crowds that gather along the High Line.

The Mayor of Strawberry Fields

♥ ♥ ♥ ♥

A unique tribute to John Lennon is regularly embellished with peace-and-love adornments by a faithful park dweller.

In 1985, Yoko Ono, the widow of former Beatle John Lennon, inaugurated Strawberry Fields, a Central Park memorial to her late husband. Named after his composition "Strawberry Fields Forever," this triangular 2.5-acre site, designed by landscape architect Bruce Kelly, is located across from the Dakota building where Lennon lived and died. Centerpiece of the site is a circular, Italian-style mosaic with the word "Imagine," the title of another well-loved Lennon song.

Divine Guidance

The memorial serves not only as a place where people can pay their respects but also as the "residence" of Ayrton Ferreira dos Santos Jr. Better known as Gary, he is a homeless Beatlemaniac-cum-performance-artist who subsists on tips he earns for embellishing the mosaic with flowers and trinkets, while also treating tourists to a three-minute monologue. The subject of a documentary, *The Mayor of Strawberry Fields*, dos Santos enthusiastically trash dives for art materials to provide the world with "the peace sign it needs." Indeed, according to a 2009 *New York Times* interview, he benefits from a little guidance. "The Brother visited me in a dream," he claimed, referring to Lennon, "and said, 'Gary, keep doing what you're doing, every day.'"

What a Downer

City authorities don't necessarily concur. Police confiscated the marijuana-emblazoned guitar that dos Santos used as a donation box. And then park authorities left a sign, warning: "Any objects left on the mosaic will be confiscated and disposed of."

"Now, who do you think they're targeting?" dos Santos mused. "They put it right behind my bench."

What would John Lennon make of this? He'd probably shake his head with a rueful smile. To quote the Brother, it's really "nothing to get hung about."

King Kong's Perch: The Empire State Building

♥ ♥ ♥ ♥

What goes into a legend? How about 60,000 tons of steel, 200,000 cubic feet of Indiana limestone and granite, 10 million bricks, five lives—and a Great Depression price tag of almost $41 million.

The world-renowned Empire State Building is something of a miracle, having taken only one year and 45 days (7 million man hours) to build—still a world record. It went up at an average of four and a half stories a week during Depression years 1930–31, with a peak labor force of more than 3,000 working every day, including Sundays and holidays. The undisputed star of the New York skyline was inspired by the subtle configuration of an architect's pencil, although its design changed more than a dozen times during planning and construction.

Smile, You're in the Movies

Soaring 102 stories above the city, the Empire State Building has been struck by lightning (it happens about a hundred times a year), hit by a military plane (in 1945, due to dense fog), and climbed by a fictional giant ape. It remains one of the most romantic edifices ever built—with no small part played by the movies. The Empire State has been featured in dozens of films, most famously in 1933's *King Kong*, of course, and in its 2005 remake. Even pop artist Andy Warhol got into the act, filming a continuous, eight-hour, black-and-white view of the building at night for his experimental 1964 film, *Empire*.

The 86th-floor observatory, which soars more than 1,000 feet in the air, is where Cary Grant waited for Deborah Kerr in *An Affair to Remember* (1957), and where Tom Hanks and Meg Ryan finally met in 1993's *Sleepless in Seattle*.

While there's no official estimate of how many marriage proposals have been made at the observatory, every Valentine's Day 14 happy

couples win a contest sponsored by a wedding-themed Web site to be married within the building (which doesn't host any other weddings).

The Race for Height

With its enduring fame, the Empire State seems as if it's always been there. But in the late 18th century, the junction of 34th Street and Fifth Avenue was just a farm with a stream running through it. By the early 19th century, it was the site of the first Waldorf=Astoria Hotel (now located on Park Avenue). And by the time John Jakob Raskob, former VP of General Motors, decided to buy and build on the site, the land alone cost $16 million.

The Empire State was actually the result of a competition between Raskob and Walter Chrysler, founder of the car corporation, to build the tallest tower in Manhattan. Chrysler kept the projected height of his skyscraper a secret. Raskob had planned for 80 stories but added another five after learning that the Chrysler might go that high—which made the Empire State only four feet taller. Raskob was legitimately worried that Chrysler might pull a last-minute height grabber (he'd done so once before, topping 40 Wall Street by hiding his building's spire inside in sections, then assembling and hoisting it within a matter of minutes). When the Chrysler, with 77 stories at 1,046 feet, opened in May 1930, it was the highest in Manhattan and remained so for 11 months—until Raskob decided to erect a dirigible mooring mast, making the Empire State a record 1,250 feet tall. Thus, an egocentric rivalry between two moguls wound up enriching one city with two spectacular edifices.

The Empire State remained the tallest building in the city until the twin towers of the World Trade Center were completed in 1972 (the North Tower was taller than the South). Today, the Empire State is again the tallest 'scraper in Manhattan, and the third tallest in America (the other two, Willis Tower and Trump International Hotel and Tower, are in Chicago). The Empire State Building ranks 14th in the world, very impressive for a building that's nearly 80 years old.

In 2007 the American Institute of Architects asked 2,000 members to name their favorite building in the United States. The Empire State was the clear winner—suggesting that there's only one building that would tempt a giant ape to clamber up its side in the name of undying love.

Some Lesser-Known Museums

♥ ♥ ♥ ♥

*In cultural matters, New York residents and visitors
alike are spoiled for choice. Herewith, a truncated
list of frequently overlooked treasures.*

The Cloisters

Located in Fort Tryon Park, overlooking the
Hudson River at Manhattan's northern tip,
the Cloisters offers serene space for reflection. This branch of the Metropolitan, once
hailed as "the crowning achievement of
American museology," showcases 6,000
examples of medieval-period European
devotional art—illuminated manuscripts,
stained glass, ironwork, architecture, and
sculpture. Must-sees include the fabled
Unicorn Tapestries and historically accurate
gardens divided into categories (medicinal,
useful, and "magical"). There are also scheduled educational workshops for those aged 4 through 12, and concerts and lectures for
grown-ups.

The Museum of Biblical Art

Feeling the need for even more reverence? The Museum of Biblical
Art (1865 Broadway) features a diverse collection of works inspired
by the Good Book, presented in historical context. Interfaith dialogue is encouraged through films, lectures, concerts, family-oriented
programs, and exhibits such as "Tobi Kahn: Sacred Spaces for the
21st Century," designed by a Jewish artist. On permanent display: a
spectacular turn-of-the-century Tiffany stained-glass window.

The Jewish Museum

Thousands of items spanning four millennia are organized chronologi-
cally, fourth floor on down, by the Jewish Museum (1109 Fifth Ave-

nue). "Multiple facets of Jewish identity" are explored in this former family mansion, with exhibits that range from a 1647 Persian marriage contract to works by Marc Chagall and Man Ray (born Emmanuel Radnitzky, and a significant contributor to Dada and surrealism). Group shows of contemporary artists can often be found on the menu. Speaking of menus, you should also enjoy the nice kosher café!

The Rubin Museum of Art

Get your dharma on at the Rubin (150 West 17th Street) via 2,000 examples of Himalayan-related paintings, textiles, and sculptures. Twelfth-century artifacts mingle with present-day art through interactive displays, educational family programs, and special events, such as concerts by Laurie Anderson, Debbie Harry, and Elvis Costello, or talks with the likes of Lou Reed, Gloria Steinem, and Martin Scorsese. There's an authentically themed (i.e. mostly vegetarian) café, a uniquely stocked gift shop, and a theater whose stairs were once traversed by Carrie Bradshaw on *Sex and the City*.

The Museum of Sex

Speaking of Carrie and pals, they'd be good patrons (or a good topic) for the Museum of Sex (233 Fifth Avenue), where admittance is restricted to those 18 and over. It's appropriately located in an area that was known in the 19th century as the "Tenderloin," when the streets absolutely teemed with vice. Opened in 2002 and boasting many eminent consultants, the museum presents themed exhibits ("The Sex Lives of Animals," "Stags, Smokers, and Blue Movies") that are both fun and educational. The gift shop stocks amusing and/or pleasurable items, including seasonal tree "pornaments." Next time Grandma's in town, give it a whirl.

Fraunces Tavern® Museum

Fraunces Tavern® (54 Pearl Street) occupies what may be the oldest house in Manhattan still standing on its original foundation. Here, in 1783, General George Washington bade farewell to his troops. First constructed as a home in 1719 and sold in 1763 to a tavern-keeper, the building has a fully operational tavern (and restaurant) still on the premises. The focus here is on the colonial and Revolutionary

War eras, with period-accurate furnishings. The first U.S. president gets some love with his own portrait gallery.

Ellis Island Immigration Museum

The largest migration in modern history took place from 1892 to 1954, when millions of our ancestors entered the United States via Ellis Island. The museum, located in New York Harbor next to the Statue of Liberty (herself an émigré from France), was restored in 1990 to an approximation of its original appearance. Features include audio tours, a library, an oral-history recording studio, and exhibits such as "The Peopling of America." There's also the "Living Theater," a 30-minute fact-based dramatization featuring professional actors. One such production told the story of Hungarian immigrant Bela Lugosi, who found film immortality in America with the role of Dracula. Researchers help trace family roots for a modest fee, or do-it-yourself at the American Family Immigration History Center.

The Morgan Library and Museum

See how the other half lived when money actually *bought* something at the Morgan Library and Museum (219 Madison Avenue). Unimaginably wealthy financier J. Pierpont Morgan went on a spending spree from the 1890s through 1913, dropping $60 million ($900 million in today's currency) on his astonishing collection. Planned as a library next to the mansion, begun in 1902 and finished in 1906, the Morgan houses three original Gutenberg Bibles, letters from Mozart, rare books and manuscripts (Twain, Thoreau), as well as thousands of irreplaceable *objets de art,* including Egyptian artifacts, porcelains, bronzes, armor, paintings, and drawings. The library consistently presents interesting shows, including a sold-out 2006 event focused on "Bob Dylan's American Journey." Old Pierpont must have been rolling over—or maybe not.

The Paley Center for Media (formerly the Museum of Television & Radio)

Intriguing even to moody teenagers, the Paley Center (25 West 52nd Street) has nearly 150,000 programs and advertisements, covering more than 85 years of television and radio history. Individual video

consoles, rarely unoccupied, provide access to the vast database. Past exhibits have included "Perspectives: Seventy Years of Pop Idols and Audiences," *"The Johnny Cash Show* (1969–71)" and *"Soul Train:* The Hippest Trip in America." The center also hosts special events, such as preview movie screenings, followed by discussions with stars and directors; as well as presentations as diverse as interviews with writers for Conan O'Brien and Jon Stewart, and a screening of Lucie Arnaz's family videos.

A few more intriguing museums include:

- **National Museum of the American Indian** (One Bowling Green), free and refreshingly current ("Ramp It Up: Skateboard Culture in Native America" was a recent exhibit), represents other indigenous peoples as well, with art, films, and readings. This New York outpost of the Smithsonian Institution also periodically schedules events such as ceremonial dances and fee-based doll- and bag-making workshops.

- **The Forbes Galleries** (62 Fifth Avenue), located at magazine HQ, is a showcase of vintage toy boats and soldiers, 1920s–30s Monopoly boards, and costume and real jewelry. The *piece de resistance*? A dozen drop-dead gorgeous Fabergé eggs commissioned by 19th-century royals.

- **International Center of Photography** (1133 Sixth Avenue), includes, but is not limited to, Richard Avedon, Irving Penn, and similarly elegant sophisticates.

- **The Frick Collection** (1 East 70th Street), housed in an 1880s mansion built with aggressive extravagance, is a work of art unto itself. Features sculptures, furniture, porcelains, Limoges, and a world-class collection of French Impressionists.

- **Cooper-Hewitt National Design Museum** (91st Street and Fifth Avenue), a division of the Smithsonian, is all about design— from vintage textiles to 1950s Russel Wright dinnerware.

- **The Skyscraper Museum** (39 Battery Place, Manhattan), founded in 1996, is devoted to the study and preservation of high-rise buildings throughout the world. Its permanent exhibits include hand-carved miniature models of Downtown and Midtown Manhattan, and the history of the World Trade Center Complex.

NYC Timeline

(Continued from p. 165)

1900
The population of New York is 3.4 million, up from 1.5 million in 1890.

May 11, 1901
Industrialist Andrew Carnegie donates $5.2 million to the public libraries of New York.

April 22, 1903
The New York Highlanders, fore-runners of the New York Yankees, play their first game.

1904
New York Highlander pitcher Jack Chesbro sets the single-season wins record at 41, which still stands.

October 27, 1904
The first underground subway opens in New York, 35 years after the city's elevated line.

June 12, 1909
The Queensboro Bridge, of double-decker cantilever design, opens.

August 9, 1910
A fired dockworker shoots Mayor William A. Gaynor, who dies in 1913.

March 25, 1911
A sudden fire in the Triangle Shirtwaist Company kills 150 young Jewish and Italian seamstresses. The owners had locked the exits.

May 11, 1911
The Brooklyn Botanic Garden opens on what used to be an ash dump.

1912
New York theaters are desegregated.

February 2, 1913
Grand Central Terminal opens at midnight.

July 31, 1914
The New York Stock Exchange closes for six months due to World War I.

August 30, 1917
The 27th Division of the National Guard marches down Fifth Avenue, shipping out to war eight months later.

January 5, 1920
Babe Ruth is acquired by the Yankees.

September 16, 1920
A bomb goes off in front of a bank on Wall Street, killing 38 people; the crime is never solved.

October 5, 1921
The New York Yankees play in the World Series for the first time.

April 18, 1923
At the official opening of Yankee Stadium, John Philip Sousa plays "The Star-Spangled Banner."

October 29, 1929
The New York Stock Exchange crashes, setting into motion the Great Depression.

May 1, 1931
Lights in the Empire State Building are switched on for the first time, from Washington, D.C.

July 28, 1945
Following a freak crash of a wayward B-25 bomber into the 79th floor of the Empire State Building, elevator operator Betty Lou Oliver survives a 75-story fall inside her elevator car.

July 1, 1948
The first commercial flight lands at New York International Airport (later renamed John F. Kennedy International Airport).

(Continued on p. 266)

Gummo: Marx Brother #5

♥ ♥ ♥ ♥

Everyone has heard of the Marx Brothers. Many can name three;
buffs can name four. If you know all five, you're a true Marxist!

Milton "Gummo" Marx was born October 23, 1892, in Manhattan to
Sam and Minnie Marx, Jewish immigrants from France and Germany. The couple eventually raised five sons (from eldest to youngest): Leonard ("Chico"), Adolph ("Harpo"), Julius ("Groucho"),
Milton ("Gummo"), and Herbert ("Zeppo").

Milton began doing vaudeville around 1905 as the dummy in his
uncle's ventriloquism act. The brothers were all naturals at the performing arts, especially music. Milton had a fine singing voice and
vocalized with Julius onstage beginning in 1907. The brothers seem
to have coined their nicknames in 1914. Why "Gummo"? The obvious problem with asking Marx brothers to explain nicknames is
that any explanation could be a joke. Potential reasons, in order of
plausibility:

- Gummo liked to sneak up on people backstage, like a gumshoe
  (detective).

- He wore gum (rubber) boots to avoid wet feet as a boy because he
  was susceptible to illness.

- He would never stick to the stage (Gummo's usual wisecrack).

He Did It His Way

The United States entered World War I in 1917. Gummo was the only
Marx brother the Army wanted. Onstage, Zeppo stepped in while
Private Gummo defended his nation.

Gummo finished military service in 1919 and tried to start a
dressmaking business. It failed, but Gummo landed on his feet as a
theatrical agent and manager for his brothers and for numerous
others. He developed such an honest reputation that his clients
rarely wanted or needed a contract; Gummo's word was golden.

After a long and prosperous career, Gummo died in 1977—the
behind-the-scenes Marx Brother who was known to relatively few.

"Yes, Virginia"

♥ ♥ ♥ ♥

As the 19th century drew to a close, New York's Sun *penny
newspaper answered a query from a little girl, and in so doing,
created a holiday tradition that continues to the present day.*

Virginia O'Hanlon, an Upper West Side resident who had just celebrated her eighth birthday in 1897, was so delighted by her presents
that she began to wonder what she might receive at Christmas. "[As]
a child, I just existed from July to December, wondering what Santa
Claus would bring me," O'Hanlon later revealed. "I think I was a
brat." She worried whether Santa Claus even existed at all, because
school friends had been saying otherwise. Virginia's father ducked the
issue by telling her to ask the newspaper because "if you see it in the
Sun, it's so." Ah, those were less cynical times!

Beloved Reply

An unsigned September 21, 1897, *Sun* editorial (written by Francis
Pharcellus Church) was entitled "Is There a Santa Claus?" It touched
a nerve with the public. "Virginia," the piece begins, "your little
friends are wrong." And later: "Yes, Virginia, there is a Santa Claus.
He exists as certainly as love and generosity and devotion exist."

Readers asked for seasonal reprints of the editorial. By 1902, the
Sun grudgingly noted, "This year requests for its reproduction have
been so numerous that we yield." In 1924, the paper ran it as the
lead editorial in the Christmas Eve edition, and the paper began
routinely republishing the piece every Christmas season. Even after
the *Sun* folded in 1950, other newspapers kept the custom going.

Santa's Legacies

Virginia O'Hanlon, who grew up to become an educator, received
correspondence about the letter throughout her life. In 1998, PBS's
Antiques Roadshow authenticated and appraised Virginia's original
letter at $20,000–$30,000. Over a century later, the newspaperman's
impassioned reply to a small child's question remains one of the most
cherished Christmas messages ever published.

Macy's Thanksgiving Day Parade

♥ ♥ ♥ ♥

If you're like millions of Americans, you spend a good part of your Thanksgiving Day mornings with Mickey Mouse, Snoopy, and Santa Claus—while you wear your fuzzy slippers and eat Froot Loops.

It's one of the great national traditions, the annual Macy's Thanksgiving Day Parade that provides a showcase to those beloved giant balloon figures, plus a bevy of cheerleaders, marching bands, clowns, Broadway dancers, and a revolving selection of who's-hot-this-nanosecond pop stars. It's all direct from the streets of New York to Main Street. While some 3.5 million spectators crowd the 2.5-mile parade route each year, more than 50 million viewers join in the fun from the comfort of their living rooms.

That's Not a Turkey, That's a Lion!

Originally named the Macy's Christmas Parade in 1924, even though it took place on Thanksgiving Day, the event was renamed in 1927 and has been a fixture on the New York holiday scene ever since, except for three years during World War II when it was canceled in deference to rubber and helium demands made by the war effort.

The parade was originally the work of a small group of dedicated Macy's employees, many of whom were first-generation immigrants who wanted to celebrate their American Christmas with a festival reminiscent of those they knew in Europe. In the early parades they marched costumed as clowns, knights, and cowboys. Though they have been joined by thousands of other volunteers and professionals since, more than 300,000 Macy's employees have worked on the parade over the years.

Until 1939, the floats were pulled by horses along a 5.5-mile route from 145th Street to Macy's flagship store in Herald Square (West 34th Street). Central Park Zoo animals were part of the parade in those early days, although lions and tigers and bears were eliminated from the fun when they proved too scary for children.

Lighter than Air

In the late 1920s, balloons were released into the sky after the parade, bearing address labels that promised a $100 reward if the deflated balloon was returned to Macy's. In 1947, television audiences around the country watched the parade for the first time, the same year the event was featured in the now-classic film *Miracle on 34th Street.*

The first bigger-than-life Macy's balloon was Felix the Cat, the comic strip and animated cartoon star who joined the parade in 1927. Since then, the celebration has been joined by inflatable comic strip and movie characters the likes of Kermit the Frog, Mickey Mouse, Underdog, and, more recently, Rugrats and Sonic the Hedgehog. Of all the characters that have appeared over the years, Snoopy has had the largest number of balloon incarnations: six.

The balloons are inflated the day before the parade on 77th and 81st streets between Central Park West and Columbus Avenue, an event open for public viewing and considered by some to be more fun than the parade itself. The parade's traditional floats, which can measure over 40 feet, are constructed in a former Tootsie Roll factory in Hoboken, New Jersey, and are brought into New York the night before the parade, folded down so they fit through the Holland Tunnel. Twenty-four floats showed up in the 2009 parade.

Everybody Comes Back to Macy's

The parade route has changed several times since 1924, most recently in 2009 when it bypassed Broadway and followed Central Park West, Seventh Avenue, and Sixth Avenue. The six additional street corners along the new route worried some, because of past difficulties with unpredictable winds. Bystanders have been injured when balloons collided with streetlights, most recently in 2005. Because of safety concerns, each intersection is now monitored for winds as the parade progresses. Whether the new route or the old, the parade always ends in front of Macy's—where else?

Fast Facts

- In one sordid period in 1856 and '57, two rival New York police forces (the legislature's Metropolitan Police and Tammany's Municipal Police) literally fought each other more often than crime. The Metropolitan Police eventually became the NYPD.

- The short-lived (1974–75) World Football League's New York Stars played at forlorn Triborough Stadium under lights scavenged from Ebbets Field. Maybe the team's nickname was arrived at because the lights were so weak fans could see stars overhead.

- Manhattan's free African American community dates back to 1644, when slaveholders freed 11 slaves and gave them land to farm. After a slave revolt in 1716, the British revoked African American land rights.

- Fidel Castro stayed in Murray Hill's Shelburne Hotel when he was in town to address the United Nations in 1960. His huge entourage made such a mess cooking chickens that the hotel management demanded more money and eventually booted the whole lot of them out.

- Louis Armstrong, a longtime Queens resident, had one odd quirk: He liked to record almost any conversation that took place in his house, even his own personal reflections and ramblings.

- Parking meters arrived in New York on September 19, 1951, on one block in Harlem. Establishing a hallowed tradition, police hovered to write citations the instant meters expired.

- From about 1948 until 1972, Midtown had Moondog, aka "The Sixth Avenue Viking." His real name was Louis Hardin, and he was a blind musician who sold his poetry and music while wearing Viking drag. He passed away in 1999.

- New York native Vera Wang came close to making the 1968 U.S. Olympic team as a figure skater. Before she became one of the world's leading bridal designers, she was Vogue's senior fashion editor.

Quotables

"This is the town that never sleeps. That's why we don't live in Duluth. That plus I don't know where Duluth is. Lucky me."

—Woody Allen

"It'll be a great place if they ever finish it."

—O. Henry

"If you live in New York, even if you're Catholic, you're Jewish."

—Lenny Bruce

"Living in New York is like being at some terrible late-night party. You're tired, you've had a headache since you arrived, but you can't leave because then you'd miss the party."

—Simon Hoggart

"New York City is a great apartment hotel in which everyone lives and no one is at home."

—Glenway Wescott

"When it's 100 degrees in New York, it's 72 in Los Angeles. When it's 30 degrees in New York, in Los Angeles it's still 72. However, there are 6 million interesting people in New York, and only 72 in Los Angeles."

—Neil Simon

"Living in New York City gives people real incentives to want things that nobody else wants."

—Andy Warhol

"The wise people are in New York because the foolish went there first, that's the way the wise men make a living."

—Finley Peter Dunne

"There is something distinctive about living in New York; over eight million other people are doing it."

—Don Herold

"If you're not in New York, you're camping out."

—Thomas E. Dewey

Taste of New York

Shiny. Chewy. Crusty. A pal to cream cheese and smoked salmon alike. What's not to love about a bagel?

Possibly the archetypal New York food—many swear that New York City tap water makes the city's bagels the best in the world—these dense rolls with the hole in the middle have a long and fascinating history. And, as is the case with lots of edible goodies, that history is—wait for it— shrouded in mystery.

The English name is derived from the Yiddish *beygl,* "to bend." Some say it's from the German *beugel,* a round roll shaped like a stirrup, invented in Vienna in the mid-1600s in honor of the victorious general Jan Sobieski, an avid horse rider. Maria Balinska, author of the definitive *The Bagel: The Surprising History of a Modest Bread,* dates the bagel's beginning earlier, given its mention in the 1610 municipal law of Krakow, Poland. The law, the story goes, provided for a gift of bagels to women in childbirth—perhaps the first acknowledgment of the bagel's status as comfort food.

In any case, the bagel made its way to New York from Eastern Europe in the late 19th and early 20th century. It was so important to the immigrant diet that it spawned the formation of a tightly run International Bagel Bakers Union in 1907.

Until the 1960s, bagels were almost all made by hand. Then, Daniel Thompson invented a machine that could produce hundreds of bagels an hour. Murray Lender successfully used the first of these in a garage in Connecticut for his nascent commercial frozen bagel line. For better or worse, frozen bagels immediately went national. By 1993, Americans averaged one bagel every two weeks, and by 2009 the top ten purveyors of fresh and frozen bagels did better than $650 million in business.

The secret to bagel excellence lies in just the right combination of flour, water, yeast, salt, and malt. Once the dough is made, it rises, and then the bagels are "kettled"—boiled in water—and finally baked. The result, says Balinska, "should be that you feel like a stone has landed in your stomach—in the best possible way, of course."

Acting Up in School

♥ ♥ ♥ ♥

*Where else but Manhattan will you find a high school
that has inspired a television series, an off-Broadway
show, and two movies? "The Fame high school" is
everything you saw in the movies—and more.*

They come to La Guardia High School from all over the city, from
all kinds of homes, with dreams of becoming pop stars, ballet dancers, opera divas, painters, and instrumentalists. After they leave this
unique public school four years later, many of them become stars.

A Fine Pedigree

Jennifer Aniston, Adrien Brody, Bela Fleck, Ben Vereen, Steven
Bochco, NPR's Susan Stamberg, Eartha Kitt, Isaac Mizrahi, Wesley
Snipes, and Al Pacino are just a few of the scores of big names you'll
find on the La Guardia alumni rolls. And there's more talent waiting
in the wings.

Safe to say, no high school on earth has produced more notable
performers than Fiorello H. La Guardia High School of Music & Art
and Performing Arts, located on Amsterdam
Avenue across the street from Lincoln Center.

First, there's the name, a nod to one of
NYC's greatest mayors, Fiorello La Guardia.
La!, as its students call it, was originally two
public schools, the High School of Performing
Arts in the theater district, which taught 600
students, and a smaller, 300-student sister
school, High School of Music & Art in upper
Manhattan. Both schools were highly respected and graduated stellar talents over the
years, but they both struggled financially,
leading to the merger in 1961. The new
institution was named for the iconic La
Guardia in 1969, in honor of his founding of
Music & Art. In 1984 the new school moved to

its current, well-equipped home, which comes complete with a 1,150-seat concert hall, a 450-seat theater, and a small "black box" theater, plus dance and musical studios, a recording studio, and an art gallery—all of this in addition to the usual classrooms and labs.

La Guardia is one of nine specialized high schools in the city and the first high school in the country to offer a free, publicly funded professional education in the arts.

Grueling

La Guardia continues the grand tradition of Performing Arts and Music & Art, with a complete college prep academic curriculum, supplemented with three or four hours of daily work in a student's particular discipline. Do you doubt that many high school kids really want to work as hard as all that? In 2008, more than 9,000 students applied for a place in La Guardia's freshman class. Only 664 were accepted.

The application process is daunting, especially considering that all the applicants are young kids in eighth and ninth grade. The requirements are stiff. Students' academic records and artistic achievements are considered; visual artists must present a 10- to 20-piece portfolio of their work, then participate in a drawing class in which they sketch a live model, create a still life from memory, and draw on an assigned subject. Dancers take part in ballet and modern dance classes, and if called back, take more classes and do a solo performance. Musicians perform a solo piece and then must pass tests that gauge rhythm, tonal memory, and sight-reading. Students interested in the backstage world may audition for the technical theater program.

A Complete Education

Get through all of that and you're in—in for some serious sweat, that is. There are no snap courses at La Guardia. The academic curriculum is the same as that followed by students in high schools around the city and includes a heavy schedule of social studies, English, math, foreign languages, science, and physical ed.

The instruction is superb. The full-time dance instructors have performed with the country's most prestigious dance companies.

Master classes for musicians are likely to be taught by members of the New York Philharmonic or the City Opera.

Many of the 2,600 students take honors and advanced-placement classes, and the school boasts a graduation rate of 97 percent.

Even with all this going on, La Guardia students enjoy a full array of extracurricular activities and clubs to fill their spare time (as hard as it is to believe they have any), from yearbook, Key Club, and the literary magazine to the anime club, knitting for charity, Embracing the Inner Child, and the Enigmatology and Film Club. Many students participate in a full calendar of theater, opera, and concerts. Especially gifted incoming ninth-graders may be chosen to participate in the DaVinci Scholars, a four-year enrichment program for math and science wizards. And if you think French horn players don't like sports, listen up. La Guardia students compete very successfully in the citywide public school league. The school offers 10 boys' sports and 13 sports for girls, as well as sports for all, such as bowling and fencing.

Student life? Well, famous people stop by from time to time to chat, and during Spirit Week the cafeteria has an open mic. But this isn't the movies, so there's no dancing on the tables, and everyone sweats the theatrical and musical production auditions. Just as they do everywhere, seniors get measured for caps and gowns.

Just an Ordinary High School?

A glance at the student handbook leaves the impression that La Guardia is like any other American high school. Students are reminded that they are not to bring cell phones to school or loiter in front of the building after class. Bring a note from home after an illness. Get a bathroom pass. But then you come across the section that instructs kids on appropriate audience etiquette and another on blackout days, when students are excused from classes for rehearsals.

The annual picture of the La! senior class is shot at Bethesda Fountain in the middle of Central Park, and graduation exercises take place in Avery Fisher Hall at Lincoln Center. The school provides a unique education that lets kids take full advantage of all that New York has to offer. It's an education, and then some!

Sandy Koufax: Brooklyn's Best

♥ ♥ ♥ ♥

Sandy was a Jewish son of Brooklyn who became a Dodger. How bittersweet that he didn't show Hall of Fame form until he was playing in Los Angeles!

Born Sanford Braun in Brooklyn on December 30, 1935, young Sandy changed his last name at age nine when his mother remarried. The family soon moved from Borough Park to Long Island but returned to Brooklyn during Sandy's later teens.

Sandy excelled in basketball at Lafayette High. He walked onto the University of Cincinnati's hoop squad, earning a partial scholarship. Sandy also tried out for baseball and proved a terror on the mound—not always in a good way. A blazing lefthander, he struck out 51 players in 32 innings, which means shock and awe . . . but he walked 30, which means he was wilder than a bag of bobcats.

Artless Dodger

Sandy left Cincy after his freshman year and accepted an offer from the Brooklyn Dodgers that included bonus money. In an unfortunate twist, the bonus probably shortened his career. Why? Well, at the time, baseball rules required "bonus babies" to spend two years on a major league roster—no minor league—and that could stunt their development. Sandy Koufax never got the gradual grooming one would see today in the minor leagues.

Instead, Sandy Koufax went home to Brooklyn and made his big league debut on June 24, 1955. A wild, inconsistent spot starter and reliever, he won nine games and lost ten in the borough. Had he retired rather than gone to Los Angeles, only dedicated Dodger nuts would remember him today. On the bright side, Sandy did get a 1955 World Series championship ring—without throwing a pitch.

On to L.A.

As every loyal Brooklynite knows, in 1957 Walter O'Malley "stole" the Dodgers and lured the Giants away to California with him, leaving the city a National League–free (and Sandy Koufax–free)

zone. Once on the West Coast, Sandy gradually improved, working into the starting rotation. However, through 1960, only once did he lead the league in a pitching category: In 1958 he sailed a league-high 17 wild pitches. After the '60 season, he seriously considered quitting baseball.

But as every baseball fan knows, Sandy didn't ditch baseball. From 1961 to '66, he became a nightmare for National League hitters, winning 129 games and losing just 47. He led the league in strikeouts four times, wins and shutouts three times, and earned run average five times. He won four World Series games, three Cy Young Awards, and copious other performance awards. He threw four no-hitters, one of which was the rarest of the rare: a perfect game. Koufax accomplished most of this while in pain from worsening arthritis, using an abused left arm that had come to the major leagues far too early.

But the pain aside, Sandy's dominance while in California was one of the weirdest and most complete career turnarounds in the history of sports, making Koufax a lock for the Hall of Fame. What changed between Brooklyn and L.A.?

It started with advice during 1961 spring training from catcher (and fellow Jewish New Yorker) Norm Sherry, who counseled Koufax to work on being subtle rather than overpowering. Sandy improved his curveball, stopped trying to blow the fastball past everyone, and concentrated on motion, timing, and control. In simple terms, Koufax became a pitcher rather than a thrower.

Shalom

After one last sparkling season in 1966 (27–9, 1.73 ERA), Sandy Koufax retired at age 30. It was that or risk losing the use of his left arm, so bad was the arthritis. He was inducted into the Hall of Fame at 36, an age when most stars are just starting to fade. Today, he roves the country, offering guidance to young big league players and prospects, a lifetime student of the physics of pitching. He's one of the most admired figures in sports.

Koufax did get one opportunity for a comeback. In 2007, when a baseball league finally started in Israel, the septuagenarian Koufax was the final player drafted. Sandy declined to suit up again, but it's no stretch to suppose that the opportunity warmed his soul.

97 Orchard Street: A Storied Past

♥ ♥ ♥ ♥

It seems as if every other New Yorker has a story about his or her family's New World beginnings in the tenement houses of Manhattan's Lower East Side, but nowhere in the city can you find these stories more lovingly told than at the Tenement Museum, one of New York's jewels.

After searching for years for a storefront space from which to lead tours of the Lower East Side, Ruth Abram and Anita Jacobson stumbled across a treasure trove at 97 Orchard Street. It was a tenement building, built in 1863, that had been shuttered with the departure of the last tenant in 1935. For more than 50 years it was untouched, the tiny apartments growing more and more dusty and derelict, but still full of the detritus of the lives that had been lived there.

Abram and Jacobson recognized that this was a rare find and the perfect place for a museum documenting the lives of immigrants and their place in New York and the nation's history.

Not the Lap of Luxury

Tenements were modest five- or six-story buildings built in what was once farmland to house the city's growing population. They were also home to hundreds of thousands of immigrants in the 19th and early 20th centuries. Behind unassuming walls, the newcomers struggled to raise families, work, and build better lives.

At a typical tenement address, 20 or more families crowded into cramped, largely airless apartments that had no indoor plumbing, no lighting, and only rudimentary heat. So enormous was the largely Irish and European immigration in the 19th century that by 1864 a survey found that nearly 500,000 people, half the city's population at the time, lived in tenements. That worked out to some 240,000 people to the square mile, most likely the densest population on earth at the time. In 1843 the tenements were described by a reform organization as "defective in size, arrangement, supplies of water, warmth and ventilation, also the yards, sinks and sewage are in bad conditions."

The house at 97 Orchard Street, a typical tenement, was home to an estimated 7,000 people over the course of its life, most of them Irish, Italian, German, and Eastern European.

Restoration

For several years researchers painstakingly explored the old build-ing, as well as official records, restoring the ramshackle apartments and finding whatever information was available about their inhabit-ants. Finally, in 1992, the first restored apartment was opened to the public, and then, over the next few years five additional apartments. More than 1,500 former residents of the building were identified, and many of their families contributed a wealth of information and artifacts to the museum.

The museum offers unusual tours—the only way you may see the inside of the museum—that give visitors a sobering, close-up view of how hardworking men and women survived and even prospered in a difficult environment that must be seen to be appreciated.

How They Lived

The rooms are dark and the stairways claustrophobic. The many layers of wallpaper are faded. Visions of entire families living in three rooms, negotiating five flights of stairs to use the outdoor privy, or teenagers hand-sewing ladies' garments by candlelight are haunt-ing. But visitors leave inspired by what is undoubtedly one of New York's most unusual experiences, and one that's not to be missed if you want to understand the city's soul.

The museum offers walking tours of the area and boasts one of the city's most delightful gift and bookshops. It also hosts an amazing array of panel discussions, programs, and readings throughout the year, exploring everything from new books about New York history to Irish music to the history of the bagel. The museum proper is located steps away from 97, at 103 Orchard Street.

Cold and Clammy

♥ ♥ ♥ ♥

Gangster "Crazy" Joe Gallo went about his underworld business with style and panache. If there was limelight to be sampled, chances are Gallo would be standing directly beneath it. Unfortunately for the crime boss, such flamboyance would trigger his early demise.

Wise Guy of Note

In some ways, Joe Gallo was a gangster ahead of his time. He certainly viewed himself that way. Here was a dutiful, workaday mobster who, for all of his limitations, saw opportunity in areas of criminal activity where others saw only strife. Before long, Gallo pioneered alliances with non-Mafia gangs that proved profitable all around. These unlikely but shrewd couplings of rival groups were masterful strokes.

But there was another side to Gallo that wasn't nearly as good for business: his public side. Much like Benjamin "Bugsy" Siegel before him, Gallo had a sense of flair, a taste for the good life, and plenty of celebrity friends.

Gallo and his boys were well-known for their keen sense of style. The wise guys looked like they had come straight from central casting in their black suits, narrow black ties, and darker-than-pitch sunglasses. Tabloids often ran covers of the boys done up in such "gangster chic." The public seemed to love it. The mob, not so much.

Gallo simply couldn't resist being the center of attention. And he liked to talk. In an enterprise that conducts its business well beneath the radar, this was *not* the preferred path.

Wild Child

Born on April 7, 1929, in the tough Red Hook section of Brooklyn, Gallo quickly rose from street criminal to key enforcer in the Profaci

Crime Family. With help from brothers Albert and Larry—as well as mobsters Frank Illiano, Nicholas Bianco, and Vic Amuso—no tactic seemed too ruthless or too bloody. In 1957, after allegedly rubbing out gangster Albert Anastasia in a barber chair at New York's Park Sheraton Hotel, Gallo (perhaps not unreasonably) asked mob boss Joseph Profaci for a bigger slice of the pie. The don's refusal sparked a turf war between the Gallo gang and the Profacis. The bloody feud continued into the 1960s, ultimately working to the favor of the Profacis.

Can't Win for Trying

After Joe Profaci died of cancer in 1962, power was transferred to his underboss, Joseph Magliocco, then later to Joseph Colombo. Due to Gallo's inability to achieve the exalted seat—as well as his ten-year incarceration for extortion—the mobster's leadership skills were placed in question. It wasn't that the Gallo boys didn't try. They had even gone so far as kidnapping Magliocco (during the Profaci-Gallo wars) in hopes that a human bargaining chip would bring them better profits. It didn't. In the long run nothing seemed to work out for the gang. The huge cash tributes that Profaci demanded of the Gallos prior to the kidnapping were suspended—but only for a brief period. After Magliocco was returned, the fees were reinstated. In the bloody dream of big-time money, Gallo and his crew had been effectively squeezed out of the action.

The Gang That Couldn't Shoot Straight

The gang's big ideas and general ineptitude caught the eye of *New York Post* columnist Jimmy Breslin, who lampooned them in his bestselling 1969 novel, *The Gang That Couldn't Shoot Straight.* A movie would follow with the buffoonish lead role (loosely based on Gallo's life) given to actor Jerry Orbach.

Things got interesting after the movie's release when Gallo, fresh out of prison, approached Orbach to set history straight. Oddly, the two men took to each other and became friends. Orbach was astonished by Gallo's grasp of art and literature and introduced him to his circle of friends. Soon, Gallo was hobnobbing with Hollywood figures and members of the literary set. Everybody, it seemed,

wanted to meet this real-life *Mafioso* with the cultural dexterity to quote from such figures as Camus and Sartre. After rotting for ten long years behind bars and suffering countless indignities as Profaci's underpaid soldier, could Gallo's star finally be on the rise?

Stars in His Eyes

Although suspected in the recent assassination of boss Joe Colombo, Gallo announced that he was "turning legit" in 1972. The purportedly reformed mobster planned to write a book about his life and perhaps even try his hand at acting. This might explain why Gallo found himself in the company of Jerry Orbach, comedian David Steinberg, and columnist Earl Wilson at New York's Copacabana one night before his 43rd birthday. It may also explain why the mob no longer wanted Gallo around. In the eyes of syndicate members, they didn't come much riskier than a starstruck, publicity-mad mobster who invited the scrutiny of federal agents bent on destroying La Cosa Nostra. In fact, the only thing that might trump such an actionable offense would be a gangster who had taken the oath of omertà, only to go straight and announce plans to write a tell-all book.

Bad Clams

During the wee hours of April 7, 1972, the unlikely group disbanded. Gallo, his bodyguard Pete Diapoulas, and four women made their way to Umberto's Clam House on Mulberry Street. While mobsters regarded this popular Little Italy location as Mafia holy ground, a hit was nevertheless in the making. As Gallo and his bodyguard pondered menu choices with their backs to the door, one or two gunmen barged in. Hearing the danger, Gallo and Diapoulas instinctively rose and made a run for it. Despite their maneuvers, both men were hit. Diapoulas took a bullet to his hip (he would later recover) and Gallo caught no less than five slugs. The mortally wounded mobster wobbled out the front door, making it as far as his Cadillac before collapsing in a lifeless heap. While it wasn't quite the Hollywood ending that the mobster had hoped for, it was a Hollywood ending of sorts. The death of "Crazy" Joe Gallo had been every bit as flamboyant as his existence. To live in the limelight, to die in the limelight—maybe it was all somehow equal.

John Lennon Sees a UFO

♥ ♥ ♥ ♥

Lucy in the sky with warp drive.

In May 1974, former Beatle John Lennon and his assistant/mistress May Pang returned to New York City after almost a year's stay in Los Angeles, a period to which Lennon would later refer as his "Lost Weekend." The pair moved into Penthouse Tower B at 434 East 52nd Street. As Lennon watched television on a hot summer night, he noticed flashing lights reflected in the glass of an open door that led onto a patio. At first dismissing it as a neon sign, Lennon suddenly realized that since the apartment was on the roof, the glass *couldn't* be reflecting light from the street. So—sans clothing—he ventured onto the terrace to investigate. What he witnessed has never been satisfactorily explained.

Speechless

As Pang recollected, Lennon excitedly called for her to come outside. Pang did so. "I looked up and stopped mid-sentence," she said later. "I couldn't even speak because I saw this thing up there . . . it was silvery, and it was flying very slowly. There was a white light shining around the rim and a red light on the top . . . [it] was silent. We started to watch it drift down, tilt slightly, and it was flying below rooftops. It was the most amazing sight." She quickly ran back into the apartment, grabbed her camera, and returned to the patio, clicking away.

Lennon friend and rock photography legend Bob Gruen picked up the story: "In those days, you didn't have answering machines, but a service [staffed by people], and I had received a call from 'Dr. Winston.'" (Lennon's original middle name was Winston, and he often used the alias "Dr. Winston O'Boogie.") When Gruen returned the call, Lennon explained his incredible sighting and insisted that the photographer come round to pick up and develop the film personally. "He was serious," Gruen said. "He wouldn't call me in the middle of the night to joke around." Gruen noted that although Lennon had been known to partake in mind-altering substances in the past, during this period he was totally straight. So was Pang, a nondrinker who never took drugs and whom Gruen characterized as "a clear-headed young woman."

The film in Pang's camera was a unique type supplied by Gruen, "four times as fast as the highest speed then [commercially] available." Gruen had been using this specialty film, usually employed for military reconnaissance, in low-light situations such as recording studios. The same roll already had photos of Lennon and former bandmate Ringo Starr, taken by Pang in Las Vegas during a recording session.

Gruen asked Lennon if he'd reported his sighting to the authorities. "Yeah, like I'm going to call the police and say I'm John Lennon and I've seen a flying saucer," the musician scoffed. Gruen picked up the couple's phone and contacted the police, *The Daily News,* and the *New York Times.* The photographer claims that the cops and the *News* admitted that they'd heard similar reports, while the *Times* just hung up on him.

It Would Have Been the Ultimate Trip

Gruen's most amusing recollection of Lennon, who had been hollering "UFO!" and "Take me with you!" was that none of his NYC neighbors either saw or heard the naked, ex-Beatle screaming from his penthouse terrace. And disappointingly, no one who might have piloted the craft responded to Lennon's pleas.

Gruen took the exposed film home to process, "sandwiching" it between two rolls of his own. Gruen's negatives came out perfectly, but the film Pang shot was "like a clear plastic strip," Gruen says. "We were all baffled . . . that it was completely blank."

Lennon remained convinced of what he'd seen. In several shots from a subsequent photo session with Gruen that produced the iconic shot of the musician wearing a New York City T-shirt (a gift from the photographer), John points to where he'd spotted the craft. And on his *Walls and Bridges* album, Lennon wrote in the liner notes: "On the 23rd Aug. 1974 at 9 o'clock I saw a U.F.O.—J.L."

Who's to say he and May Pang didn't? Certainly not Gruen, who still declares—more than 35 years after the fact—"I believed them."

And so the mystery remains.

Fast Facts

- Although the first Jewish settlers arrived in New Amsterdam in 1654, the city's first synagogue wasn't established until 1730.

- There was talk about mooring zeppelins at the spire of the Empire State Building when the skyscraper opened in 1931. For numerous scientific reasons, it was unfeasible—starting with high winds that could be counted on to blow the tethered gasbags around—that is, if they could tether themselves at all.

- Former mayor Ed Koch plans to be buried in Trinity Cemetery, even though he's Jewish. If he wants to be buried belowground in Manhattan, Trinity is his only option: It's the only city cemetery accepting new burials.

- Tammany Hall drew a distinction between "honest graft" and "dishonest graft." Inside investment info that led to monster profits counted as honest graft. Extorting crooks rather than arresting them was dishonest, and thus frowned upon.

- The odd frown and distinctively slurred speech of Hell's Kitchen native Sylvester Stallone are no act—they're real. Little Sly sustained nerve damage from clumsily wielded forceps during his 1946 birth.

- Some of old Manhattan's original topography was visible in the Polo Grounds. The outfield sloped downward, so that a center-fielder on the warning track was barely visible from the dugouts.

- Travel biographer Paul Theroux on surviving the NYC subway: "You have to look as if you're the one with the meat cleaver."

- When the Ku Klux Klan–glorifying silent film Birth of a Nation unspooled at the Liberty Theater in 1915, many patrons took offense. They hissed and booed its numerous race-baiting scenes.

- It's hardly imaginable today, but on September 22, 1966, the Yankees' fortunes had fallen so far that only 413 spectators were in the stands. Broadcaster Red Barber remarked on the tiny crowd over the air—and the Yanks canned him.

9/11 by the Numbers

♥ ♥ ♥ ♥

Years after the devastating events of September 11, 2001, statistics still paint a chilling picture of what happened in New York that day.

Length of time the North Tower burned after American Flight 11 hit: 102 minutes

Length of time the South Tower burned after United Airlines Flight 175 hit: 56 minutes

Time it took the South Tower to crumble: 10 seconds

Seismic magnitude of the North Tower collapse: 2.3

Number of people who survived the collapse in a North Tower stairwell: 16

Number of tenant companies in the Towers: 283

Number of hijackers in the two planes that attacked the WTC: 10

Number of people in the WTC that day: 16,400–18,800

Children attending public schools in District 2, in the shadow of the WTC: 2,300

Number of people killed in the buildings and on the planes: 2,973

Number of people who jumped to their deaths from the Towers: 200 (est.)

Number of NYC emergency personnel killed at the WTC site: 403

Countries that lost citizens in the WTC attack: 90

Number of U.S. states that lost residents: 25

Youngest and oldest victims: 2 and 85 years old

Estimated heat of fires in the Towers: 2,000 degrees Fahrenheit

Tons of debris removed from the site: 1.5 million

Worldwide insurance payments related to the disaster: $40.2 billion

Number of meals served onsite by Salvation Army during recovery and cleanup: 3,231,681

Local Legends

The 1960s sparked some of the wildest urban legends ever to come out of the Big Apple. Two, in particular, continue to make the rounds and are still believed by many: that the crime rate plummeted nationwide the night The Beatles appeared on *The Ed Sullivan Show* in 1964, and that the city's birthrate skyrocketed nine months after the Great Blackout of 1965.

The Beatles Sweep America: It's true that The Beatles were already wildly popular when they made their first trip to the United States in 1964 and that their February 9 appearance on *The Ed Sullivan Show* drew 73 million viewers, the largest audience the show had ever seen. But the claim that the crime rate dropped during their appearance, first made by an editor at the *Washington Post* and later picked up by others, is more fancy than fact. In truth, the comment wasn't even a compliment but a put-down of the band's fans, which were perceived by many at the time to consist primarily of lazy, criminally inclined teenagers. Only in the repeated retelling was the statement transformed into a positive reflection of The Beatles' general popularity. Regardless, an examination of police records for that evening from New York—or any town—will show that crime did, indeed, continue apace.

Getting Busy During the Blackout: And the "skyrocketing" birthrate that supposedly followed the Great Blackout of November 9, 1965? Also unfounded, say researchers. The 12-hour blackout, which affected more than 30 million people throughout eight American states and Ontario, Canada, was huge news at the time. And it's certainly likely that a lot of couples,  lacking electricity and thus in need of something to pass the time, jumped into bed for an amorous romp. However, despite reports by the *New York Times* and other outlets, a review of hospital birth records nine months after the blackout show no statistically significant spike in births, compared to the same period in the previous five years, anywhere in the affected area.

Leo "The Lip"

♥ ♥ ♥ ♥

*New York fit Leo Durocher, and Leo fit New York. He ran
the Dodgers for eight seasons and the Giants for seven.
He won three National League pennants and one World
Series, leaving a profane trail of heckling, beanballs, brawls,
ejections, suspensions, and scrappy baseball in his wake.*

Born in 1905 to parents of French extraction, Leo
Durocher came from Massachusetts. He did three
things well in life: think, shoot pool, and play shortstop. His first major league tour began with the
Yankees in 1925, where he suited the Roaring
Twenties perfectly: a slightly built but tough
player who hated losing with a passion. At
ease with the people, he was a spiffy
dresser and an inveterate nightclubber.

Babe Ruth called the mouthy Leo
"fresh as paint," but he soon did so with a
smile. Durocher was too light a hitter to play daily, but his outstanding
glove work and baseball smarts helped him carve his niche. Leo also
honed his skills as a bench jockey. In one celebrated episode, Durocher
called legendary El Cheapo and brawler Ty Cobb a "pennypincher,"
then broke for the clubhouse while Ruth restrained the fuming Cobb.

Leo spent freely. He bounced numerous checks and . . . spoke his
mind. During an argument one fine day in 1930, Durocher offered
Yankee GM Ed Barrow an obscene (and anatomically improbable)
suggestion. Barrow was too conservative to stoop to Leo's level.
Instead, he traded "The Lip" to the lowly Reds. Leo wouldn't wear a
New York team's uniform again until 1938.

A Decade in Brooklyn

When Durocher returned, his playing career was in its twilight. After
becoming player-manager of the Brooklyn Dodgers in 1938, Leo
transformed the team's past "Daffiness Boys" culture of mediocrity
into a smart, rugged, aggressive brand of ball. His Dodgers were

usually contenders and were always fun to watch. They represented Brooklyn's heart and soul. When the team lost, the borough lost.

While many often cite Durocher (justly) as a powerful force for the end of baseball's racist color line, often forgotten today is that Commissioner Happy Chandler had suspended Leo from baseball during Jackie Robinson's first season (1947) for "incidents detrimental to baseball"—a hazy way to say that Durocher happily socialized with gamblers. By that measure, numerous baseball people deserved similar vacations; the flamboyant Leo was just more obvious about it. He also had media enemies, and his "incidents" (marital scraps, more whiffs of gambling, scuffles) got prominent coverage.

One can only imagine how the combative Leo must have felt as he watched his team win the NL pennant in 1947 only to lose the Series to the Yanks in seven. In 1948, the team played poorly. Leo had worn out his welcome with Dodger management.

Switching Sides

How often do hateful crosstown rivals agree that the manager of one should switch to the other team in midyear? It happened in 1948, as Dodger GM Branch Rickey finagled a deal for Durocher to manage the New York Giants. This was serious. A National League fan in New York could not serve two causes. You were a Dodger fan or a Giant fan, Brooklyn or Manhattan.

Leo, the former arch-foe, naturally had to prove himself to Giants fans. As for Bums fans, Leo's betrayal was the worst until Walter O'Malley stole their team and took it to the West Coast. As things played out, Durocher won over the die-hards when his Giants took the pennant from the Dodgers in the dramatic 1951 "Miracle of Coogan's Bluff" playoff. A young Willie Mays was a rising star whose confidence Durocher built day and night. Leo punctuated his Giants success by beating the 1954 Cleveland Indians (winners of a record 111 regular-season games) four straight in the World Series.

Leo lasted only one more year with the Giants, wrapping up with a disappointing 1955 campaign, when the team put together an 80–74 record. Two years later, both New York NL teams went west. An era in New York was over, and Durocher, as much as anyone, emblematized that era for most of its final two decades. Durocher passed away in 1991. He was inducted into the Baseball Hall of Fame three years later.

Growing Up Capone

♥ ♥ ♥ ♥

He's the racket guy everyone's heard of, and most people associate him with Chicago. But Al Capone was a native Brooklynite.

Alphonse Gabriel Capone entered the world January 17, 1899, in Brooklyn. Papa Capone came from a town just south of Naples, while Mama hailed from a smaller town farther south, near Salerno. Alphonse was the fourth child (and fourth son) for Gabriele and Teresina Capone; three more boys and two girls (one survived infancy) would follow. Gabriele was a barber, while Teresina made dresses. They initially lived near the Navy Yard and then moved to Park Slope.

Fourteen-year-old Alphonse was a promising student, but he was naturally foul tempered. One day, after his sixth-grade teacher hit him, he swiftly retaliated against her with a punch. Not surprisingly, such behavior was frowned upon. The principal whaled the daylights out of Alphonse, who had had enough and quit school.

Street Education

Because Alphonse was drawn to the action, he began hanging out near the John Torrio Association. Torrio's Five Points Gang had begun in Manhattan's notorious neighborhood of that name and expanded into Brooklyn. Now, Torrio was a prominent local racketeer and pimp, and he'd occasionally hire Alphonse to carry out errands. Torrio came to trust Alphonse immensely over time, and he and Frankie Yale, another notorious Brooklyn thug and loan shark, mentored young Alphonse in crime. Another early Brooklyn associate was Salvatore Lucania, who, after a slight name change, became world famous as "Lucky" Luciano.

In 1918 Alphonse got his girlfriend pregnant. They married and moved to Chicago, where Torrio advised his protégé that fortunes were to be made—and thus ended both the youth and the New York days of Al Capone. His subsequent rise—and fall—in the Chicago underworld was brutal and startling and, well, that's another story!

Central Park's Carousel

♥　♥　♥　♥

*For most New Yorkers, the city is all about moving—
quickly—from one place to another. But some residents,
especially kids, would much rather go in circles.*

Ask local grownups about Manhattan landmarks, and you'll hear
about the Statue of Liberty, the Empire State Building, and the
clock at Grand Central Station. Ask a New York kid about the most
famous place in the city, and you're likely to hear about the carousel
in Central Park, one of New York's iconic and best-loved sites, and
one of the largest merry-go-rounds in the country. Some
250,000 children and grownups head to the park annually to whirl
around on painted horses while a calliope grinds out classic merry-
go-round music to the delight of all.

Going 'Round Merrily

The current carousel, one of six in parks around the city, is actually
the fourth in Central Park. The very first, built in 1871, sat about 50
yards from the current site, midpark at 64th Street. The first Central
Park carousel was "powered" by a blind mule and a horse, which
pulled the carousel from a recessed circular track. Around 1912 a
new carousel was electrified, but in 1924 it burned down and was
replaced. The third carousel, too, burned down in 1950, leaving city
officials to search mightily for a replacement. A 1908 carousel that
had done long duty in Coney Island until the early 1940s was
retrieved from storage, and expert carousel woodcarvers fabricated
new horses. This renovation was financed with funds donated by the
Michael Friedsam Foundation.

Today the Friedsam Memorial Carousel is open to the public
year-round. A three-and-a-half-minute ride costs two dollars, but what
a ride it is. This carousel's 57 horses are unusually large: three-quarters
the size of real horses, and the carousel itself spins around at 12 miles
an hour—twice as fast as your ordinary merry-go-round. What, you
were expecting a *slow* merry-go-round? Hey, this is New York.

NYC on TV!

♥ ♥ ♥ ♥

New York helped birth the medium of television and has been the backdrop for many of its most beloved shows. As a result, viewers often feel they know the city intimately even if they've never visited.

New York City has served as a very visible setting for every kind of series imaginable (even if all of them weren't necessarily shot on location). A few of these include:

I Cover Times Square (ABC, 1950–51). Johnny Warren (Harold Huber) was a hard-nosed Broadway columnist based (or so it's said) on equally hard-nosed real-life entertainment writer Walter Winchell. Warren's beat: the seedy underside of New York showbiz.

I Love Lucy (CBS, 1951–57). Lucille Ball and Desi Arnaz became one of television's best-loved comedic couples as a result of this New York–set series, which ran for the better part of a decade before finding even greater success in syndication.

The Honeymooners (CBS, 1955–56). Grouchy but lovable Brooklynite Ralph Kramden (Jackie Gleason) is perhaps the most famous New York City bus driver in history.

Car 54, Where Are You? (NBC, 1961–63). Goofball cops Gunther Toody (Joe E. Ross) and Francis Muldoon (Fred Gwynne) patrolled the Bronx. Hilarity ensued.

N.Y.P.D. (ABC, 1967–69). This realistic cop show was unique for filming on location throughout the Big Apple.

Fame (NBC and Syndicated, 1982–87). Based on the movie of the same name, *Fame* followed students and instructors at New York's famous School for the Performing Arts.

Night Court (NBC, 1984–92). For nine seasons, Judge Harry T. Stone (Harry Anderson) administered comedic justice to the wacky miscreants of Manhattan's night court. Crime was never funnier.

Law & Order (NBC, 1990–2010). One of TV's longest-running series, *Law & Order* (and several spin-offs) focused on the cops who caught the city's bad guys and the district attorneys who tried them.

Washington Square Is for Everybody

♥ ♥ ♥ ♥

Just south of Eighth Street at the foot of Fifth Avenue lies "the beating heart of Greenwich Village," better known as Washington Square Park. Its main claim to fame might be as the public gathering place that hosted the 1950s and '60s folk music revival. But Washington Square Park has a much longer and more fascinating history.

In the early 1600s, the now-covered Minetta Brook—once a favorite trout stream—cut through the area that is now Washington Square Park, dividing Manhattan Island from the north to the East River. New Amsterdam then had a population of around 200. The Dutch—having driven Native Americans off this land—wanted to turn the duck marsh into viable farmland and also protect it from reclamation by the natives. So in 1644, in return for acting as a buffer against Indian attacks, as well as surrendering an annual share of their crop yield, 11 African slaves were given ownership of a two-mile strip of land that included the park area. They also received their freedom (but not that of their descendants). For the following two decades, this area was known as "The Land of the Blacks."

Caution: Dead Underground

The area continued as farmland until 1797, when the city's Common Council acquired it as a potter's field (a burial ground for the unknown or poor), which is what it remained until 1825 or '26. To this day, most park visitors don't realize that they are walking over 20,000 bodies interred underfoot.

However, the legend that the park was a public execution ground is uncertain. The only recorded hanging took place in 1820, when Rose Butler was put to death for arson—and even the two eyewitness accounts to that event differ over exactly where it happened. A 300-year-old English elm (the oldest known living tree in Manhattan) at the northwest corner of the park is still referred to as the "Hanging Tree."

Fashionable Living

In 1826, the square briefly became the Washington Military Parade Ground, where volunteer militia trained; the following year, it was dedicated as a public park. Between 1829 and 1833, a row of Greek-Revival red-brick townhouses that still stand were built on the north side of the square. The wealthy inhabitants would eventually serve as inspiration for novelists such as Henry James and Edith Wharton. Interestingly, though, land south of the park—just a few blocks away—was home to poor immigrants who were jammed into miserable tenements known as "rookeries."

In 1889, a plaster-and-wood arch was erected to commemorate the centennial of George Washington's inauguration; it proved so popular that a permanent marble structure, designed by renowned architect Stanford White after Paris's *Arc de Triomphe*, was put up in 1892. Interestingly enough, excavations uncovered human remains, coffins, and at least one headstone.

Battleground I

Beginning in 1935, New York Parks commissioner Robert Moses fought to route traffic either through or around the park according to plans that Moses never bothered to run past the locals. His schemes were finally defeated in 1963 after a long battle led by residents such as urbanologist Jane Jacobs and former First Lady Eleanor Roosevelt, when Fifth Avenue was cut short at Washington Square Arch and the park became a pedestrian-only zone. It now offers playgrounds, a much-loved chess and scrabble playing area at the southwest corner, commemorative statuary, and two popular dog runs (for little and larger canines).

The first fountain, in the center of the park (but not aligned with the entrance under the arch), was completed in 1852. A redesign in 2009 brought it in line with the arch—despite fervent protest by Village residents, who are almost always in conflict with nearby New York University, which owns much of the area.

Battleground II

Artists have always been part of the Village, but the park's open space particularly lends itself to musicians, who have gathered there

on Sundays since at least 1947. As the late Mary Travers, of Peter, Paul & Mary, who grew up in the Village, once reminisced: "It was writers, sculptors, painters, whatever, listening to Woody Guthrie, Pete Seeger, the Weavers. People sang in Washington Square Park on Sundays, and you really did not have to have a lot of talent."

Even those with plenty of talent were drawn to the park. During the brief period in 1958 when Buddy Holly lived with his bride Maria Elena two blocks north, he came to the park incognito in sunglasses almost every morning to strum his Gibson guitar. His widow remembers that Buddy would "just sit there, and all these other young musicians—a lot of folksingers—used to come and talk with him. . . . He'd advise them, 'Look at anything you see here in the park and then write something about that—that's how you compose.'"

But the city soon began to require permits for public performances, and by the early '60s a crackdown had begun on music in the park. On April 9, 1961, Folklore Music Center founder Izzy Young led a few thousand supporters in a march through the park that ended with ten people being arrested; one local newspaper reported the clash as a "beatnik riot." But the ban on music was soon lifted, and Bob Dylan and other aspiring folksingers began calling the park their own. By the time the '60s were in full swing, the park had become de rigueur as a hippie hangout.

A Dada-esque Declaration

During the '70s and '80s, the park fell into disrepair, attracting drug dealers and other disreputable types. The situation led the local citizenry to complain—and stay away. Concerted efforts by neighbors and law enforcement eventually managed to turn the tide, and the park has once more become a comfortable gathering place for students and professors; musicians and artists; lovers and dog-lovers; parents and children, and tourists and locals alike.

One final interesting footnote: On the snowy night of January 23, 1917, Surrealist/Dada artist Marcel Duchamp and several friends got into the interior stairway of the marble arch and climbed the spiral staircase to the roof. From that lofty perch, a local poet playfully announced the Village's secession from the United States, designating the land below as the "Free and Independent Republic of Washington Square." What foresight those irreverent pranksters had!

Noteworthy Folks from the Bronx

♥ ♥ ♥ ♥

*Let's have a cheer for some of the Bronx's
favorite sons and daughters.*

- **Bella Savitsky Abzug** (1920–98): U.S. representative and lifelong women's rights activist; Bronx icon.

- **June Allyson** (1917–2006): Bronx native; Broadway and film star.

- **Anne Bancroft** (1931–2005): Born Anna Italiano and raised in Throggs Neck; had successful acting career spanning half a century, and a long marriage to Mel Brooks.

- **Ellen Barkin** (1954–): Native Emmy-winning actress with a very successful feature-film career, as well.

- **James Caan** (1939–): A native, though he grew up in Queens; actor, best known for *Brian's Song* (1971), *The Godfather* (1972), *Rollerball* (1975), *Misery* (1990), and TV's *Las Vegas* (2003–7).

- **Samuel Clemens** (1835–1910): Better known by his pen name Mark Twain; humorist and satirist who called the borough home for a while and whose leased estate there is now a public garden.

- **Claudette Colvin** (1939–): Civil rights activist who resides there; refused to go to the back of a bus in Montgomery, Alabama, and was jailed for nine months before Rosa Parks did the same thing.

- **Tony Curtis** (1925–): Native, raised in Hunts Point; versatile actor with enormous filmography—real name is Bernie Schwartz.

- **Art Donovan** (1925–): NFL Hall of Fame defensive tackle, Bronx native, and popular commentator on the game.

- **Louis Farrakhan** (1933–): Native; leader of Nation of Islam.

- **Jules Feiffer** (1929–): Cartoonist, Pulitzer Prize winner, longtime staple in the *Village Voice;* Bronx native.

- **John Gotti Jr.** (1940–2002): Bronx native, Gambino crime family's "Teflon Don"; ironically, he died in prison.

- **Grandmaster Flash** (1958–): Grew up in the Bronx as Joseph Sadler; pioneering hip-hop M.C.

- **Hank Greenberg** (1911–86): Famed Tiger slugger, baseball Hall of Famer, and a Bronx native.

- **David Halberstam** (1934–2007): Acclaimed journalist and historian; born and spent early years in the Bronx.

- **Stanley Kubrick** (1928–99): Visionary author and filmmaker (*Dr. Strangelove, Lolita, A Clockwork Orange, 2001: A Space Odyssey, Full Metal Jacket,* many others) grew up in the borough.

- **Jennifer Lopez** (1969–): Born and raised in the South Bronx, "J-Lo" is a famed singer, dancer, and actress.

- **Jerry Orbach** (1935–2004): A Bronx native, best known as Detective Lennie Briscoe, sardonic *Law & Order* TV cop, but he was an immense success in Broadway musicals as well.

- **Edgar Allan Poe** (1809–49): Legendary mystery and suspense author who spent his last years in Fordham; his cottage still stands.

- **Rabbi Chaim Potok** (1929–2002): Bronx native, prolific novelist on Jewish-themed subjects; best-known work: *The Chosen* (1967).

- **General Colin Powell** (1937–): Grew up in Hunts Point, of Jamaican ancestry; after a long Army career leading to four stars on his shoulders, he served as U.S. secretary of state (2001–5).

- **William Safire** (1929–2009): Bronx High School of Science alum, speechwriter for Richard Nixon, and political columnist.

- **Sonia Sotomayor** (1954–): Bronx native and associate justice of the U.S. Supreme Court.

- **Eliot Spitzer** (1959–): Native Bronxite, scourge of white-collar crooks, and state governor until a messy prostitution scandal led to his resignation.

- **Luther Vandross** (1951–2005): Spent teen years in the borough; won eight Grammys for his R&B/soul singing and songwriting.

- **Herman Wouk** (1915–): Acclaimed novelist who grew up in the Bronx is especially famous for *The Caine Mutiny, The Winds of War,* and *War and Remembrance.*

NYC Timeline

(Continued from p. 233)

1950
The city's population tops 7.8 million.

1952
The United Nations Secretariat Building is completed. Considered international territory, it is not subject to U.S. law.

August 24, 1967
Yippie activist Abbie Hoffman and friends toss dollar bills from the New York Stock Exchange gallery.

December 28, 1967
Muriel "Mickie" Siebert becomes the first female member to own a seat on the New York Stock Exchange.

June 28, 1969
The Stonewall riots break out following a police raid on a gay bar.

February 12, 1970
Joseph L. Searles III becomes the first African-American member of the New York Stock Exchange.

June 1970
Penn Central Railroad goes bust in the biggest bankruptcy in history.

December 23, 1970
The topping out ceremony of 1 World Trade Center (North Tower) is held.

1972
Yankees owner CBS sells team to George Steinbrenner for $10 million.

August 7, 1974
Philippe Petit spends 45 minutes walking a high wire between the Twin Towers. He's arrested—as punishment, he must put on a children's show.

October 1975
The city narrowly avoids bankruptcy thanks to the Municipal Assistance Corporation, headed by Felix Rohatyn.

July 29, 1976
David Berkowitz kills his first victim, terrorizing the city for a year as "Son of Sam."

July 13–14, 1977
Lightning strikes set off a blackout.

December 8, 1980
John Lennon is shot and killed outside his home at the Dakota by a deranged fan.

February 26, 1993
Muslim terrorists set off an explosion in the underground garage of the North Tower of the World Trade Center.

September 11, 2001
Two commercial airliners are crashed into the Twin Towers by Muslim hijacker-terrorists, killing 2,973.

March 30, 2003
Smoking is banned in all NYC restaurants and bars.

April 26, 2006
Governor George Pataki declares construction begun on the Freedom Tower project at Ground Zero.

August 8, 2007
Brooklyn is hit by a rare tornado that whips winds to 135 mph.

December 2007
City reports less than 500 homicides (494) for the first time since 1963.

March 12, 2009
Ponzi schemer Bernie Madoff, who bilked investors out of billions, pleads guilty in a Manhattan court.

July 13, 2010
George Steinbrenner, long-term owner of the Yankees, dies of a heart attack at age 80. During his tenure, the Yanks won seven World Series.

Fast Facts

- *If placed end to end, the webbing lines enclosing the Spider-Man balloon in Macy's Thanksgiving Day Parade would extend for half a mile.*

- *On April 11, 1912, baseball's New York Giants opened against the Trolley Dodgers in Washington Park. With tickets oversold by 7,000, angry fans stormed the stadium and took over the ballfield. The game went on anyway.*

- *When did Tammany Hall really die? Arguably in 1962, when Tammany Enemy No. 1 Edward Costikyan became head of New York County's Democratic Party. Few mourned the entity that was so synonymous with bad government.*

- *When Philippe Petit walked a tightrope between the towers of the World Trade Center in 1974, how did he get the cable across? Simple: with accomplices and a huge 5-foot crossbow.*

- *If you visited the Union Square Greenmarket between the early 1990s and 2009, you saw and heard Joe Ades, the Potato Peeler Pitchman. That's all he did: sell $5 potato peelers.*

- *New York native Sarah Michelle Gellar (born in 1977) was spotted by a talent scout in a local restaurant when she was only four years old. She did her first movie at age six, becoming a working professional long before gaining fame as Buffy the Vampire Slayer.*

- *Known as the Harlem Hellfighters, the all-black 369th Infantry Regiment (National Guard) compiled a very proud service record in World War I. Hellfighter Henry Johnson was the first American to earn the prestigious French Croix de Guerre with star and gold palm.*

- *On the Lower East Side, you can visit a Troll Museum with a boggling variety of troll-doll memorabilia. The curator wears elf ears. Appointments are required.*

- *On September 29, 1957, Sandy Koufax became the last player to throw a pitch for the Brooklyn Dodgers.*

Quotables

"Everybody ought to have a lower East Side in their life."

—Irving Berlin

"New York is large, glamorous, easy-going, kindly and incurious, but above all it is a crucible—because it is large enough to be incurious."

—Ford Madox Ford

"The city is an addiction."

—Timothy Leary

"The only real advantage of New York is that all its inhabitants ascend to heaven right after their deaths, having served their full term in hell right on Manhattan Island."

—*Barnard Bulletin*

"New York is not a city to return to in defeat."

—Moss Hart

"It's a fickle town, a tough town. They getcha, boy. They don't let you escape with minor scratches and bruises. They put scars on you here."

—Reggie Jackson

"The faces in New York remind me of people who played a game and lost."

—Murray Kempton

"New York City is a great monument to the power of money and greed… a race for rent."

—Frank Lloyd Wright

"Robinson Crusoe, the self-sufficient man, could not have lived in New York City."

—Walter Lippman

"It isn't like the rest of the country—it is like a nation itself—more tolerant than the rest in a curious way. Littleness gets swallowed up here. All the viciousness that makes other cities vicious is sucked up and absorbed in New York."

—John Steinbeck

The Garibaldi-Meucci Museum

♥ ♥ ♥ ♥

Next time you take the Staten Island ferry, visit the home in which two great men made Italian and American history. One of the fellows helped unify his country; the other probably invented the telephone. After they joined forces to make candlesticks, some intriguing things happened.

During the first half of the 19th century, when the Italian peninsula was divided into separate states that were either ruled or "influenced" by other European nations, Giuseppe Garibaldi and Antonio Meucci involved themselves in the movement to unify Italy. Because their radical activities landed each of them in hot water in 1833–34, Garibaldi fled to South America (after receiving a death sentence from a Genoese court), and Meucci spent three months behind bars before departing with his wife for Cuba.

While working on the island as a theatrical technician, Meucci invented a system of communication between the stage and control room based on the pipe-telephones that were used aboard ships. In Havana, he began developing what he called a "talking telegraph," and in 1850, when his association with Garibaldi had made him *persona non grata* in Cuba, Meucci continued his research in the United States. Garibaldi, you see, had not only been stirring things up in Uruguay by taking a leading role in that country's civil war, but he'd also returned to Italy to lead an uprising there. When this failed, he once again went into exile.

A New Home

So it was that, in July 1850, Garibaldi arrived in the United States and moved into the Staten Island home of the Meuccis, who had relocated there just over three months earlier. Having made good money in Cuba, Meucci opened a candle factory, and Garibaldi worked there on and off during the next couple of years before bidding New York *arrivederci* and making his way back to Italy, where he would eventually spearhead unification.

Pick Up the Phone!

Meucci, meanwhile, allegedly constructed his first electromagnetic communications device in 1856, but he was evidently a better inventor than a businessperson. His candle factory went bankrupt, and by 1861 he was forced to auction off his Staten Island cottage. (Fortunately for Meucci, the buyer allowed him to continue living there, rent free, while continuing his research.) Nevertheless, his phone device won only a provisional patent that he didn't renew upon expiration in 1874. Meucci's oversight prompted major litigation when Alexander Graham Bell patented his own telephonic invention in 1876.

The protracted court proceedings effectively ended with Meucci's death on October 18, 1889, and Bell emerged as the recognized inventor of the electromagnetic telephone. Meucci was credited merely with creating a mouthpiece that transmitted sound vibrations to an earpiece connected by a wire. It wasn't until 2002 that the U.S. House of Representatives passed a resolution recognizing that "if Meucci had been able to pay the $10 fee to maintain the provisional patent after 1874, no patent could have been issued to Bell." Ten days later, the Canadian government unanimously passed a motion stating that Bell invented the telephone, and so the waters remain muddied. Yet, what no one disputes is the historical importance of the house in which Meucci once hosted Garibaldi.

A First Son of Italy

Following Garibaldi's death in 1884, a marble plaque was placed over the entrance to the Meucci home, commemorating the Italian unifier's stay on Staten Island. Then, when Meucci himself died five years later, his house was turned over to New York's Italian community so that it could be preserved as a permanent Garibaldi memorial. In 1907, the house was relocated to its current address on Tompkins Avenue; in 1919, the National Order Sons of Italy Foundation assumed control to take care of the building's ongoing maintenance. In 1923, a bust of Meucci was erected in front of his own house; in 1956 the home was opened to the public as the Garibaldi-Meucci Museum; and in 1980 it was listed on the National Register of Historic Places.

You Can Thank New York

Next time you're enjoying time off for Labor Day, relishing cold beer and grilled bratwurst in the backyard, you can thank Peter J. McGuire of New York. Or maybe Matthew Maguire (no relation).

In the 1880s, Peter J. McGuire, one of the cofounders of the American Federation of Labor, is said to have developed the idea of a holiday for American workers in homage to those "from whom rude nature have delved and carved all the grandeur we behold." On the other hand, Matthew Maguire, a machinist and secretary of the Central Labor Union, is also credited with that honor.

In any case, the CLU and the Knights of Labor decided to go ahead with the holiday in New York City, and the first Labor Day was observed on September 5, 1882, with a grand parade and festival in Union Square. By 1885, as the labor movement continued to gain ground and organized labor lobbied vigorously in state legislatures, Labor Day was celebrated in cities around the country. The first Monday of September was agreed upon as the official date, roughly halfway between the Fourth of July and Thanksgiving.

Prompted by widespread labor unrest, and perhaps the fact that 1894 was an election year, President Grover Cleveland was eager to appease the labor movement. On June 28, 1894, Congress unanimously named the first Monday in September a legal holiday. That didn't stop labor unrest—the 1894 Pullman strike was still going strong—but it was a step forward.

Today, Labor Day is still marked with speeches and celebrations, though with fewer of the large parades of the past. But many still regard it, as AFL leader Samuel Gompers did in 1898, as "the day for which the toilers in past centuries looked forward, when their rights and their wrongs would be discussed . . . that the workers of our day may not only lay down their tools of labor for a holiday, but upon which they may touch shoulders in marching phalanx and feel the stronger for it."

A Few Facts About the Statue of Liberty

♥ ♥ ♥ ♥

- The statue's real name is "Liberty Enlightening the World."

- Lady Liberty was sculpted by Frédéric Auguste Bartholdi; Alexandre Gustave Eiffel was the structural engineer.

- The statue was completed in Paris in June 1884, given to the American people on July 4, 1884, and reassembled and dedicated in the United States on October 28, 1886.

- The model for the face of the statue is reputed to be the sculptor's mother, Charlotte Bartholdi.

- There are 25 windows and 7 spikes in Lady Liberty's crown. The spikes are said to symbolize the seven seas.

- The inscription on the statue's tablet reads: July 4, 1776 (in Roman numerals).

- More than four million people visit the Statue of Liberty each year.

- Lady Liberty is 152 feet 2 inches tall from base to torch and 305 feet 1 inch tall from the ground to the tip of her torch.

- The statue's hand is 16 feet 5 inches long, and her index finger is 8 feet long. Her fingernails are 13 inches long by 10 inches wide and weigh approximately 3.5 pounds each.

- Lady Liberty's eyes are each 2 feet 6 inches across, she has a 35-foot waistline, and she weighs about 450,000 pounds (225 tons).

- Lady Liberty's sandals are 25 feet long, making her shoe size 879.

- There are 192 steps from the ground to the top of the pedestal and 354 steps from the pedestal to the crown.

- The Statue of Liberty functioned as an actual lighthouse from 1886 to 1902 and could be seen 24 miles away.

- Until September 11, 2001, the statue was open to the public. Visitors were able to climb the winding staircase inside the statue to the top of her crown for a spectacular view of New York Harbor.

New York's Precision Beauties!

♥ ♥ ♥ ♥

No trip to New York City would be complete without a visit to Radio City Music Hall to see the Rockettes. With tradition built on more than eight decades of acclaimed performances, the dancers actually make a precisely synchronized chorus line look easy.

When it comes to precision choreography, no one rocks like the Rockettes. One of the best-known dance troupes in the world, the gorgeous, long-legged hoofers have been entertaining audiences for more than 85 years and are just as amazing to watch today as when they first hit the stage.

That was in 1925, when the dancing "Missouri Rockets," assembled by Russell Markert, made their debut in St. Louis. The gals put on a stunning show of eye-high kicks and tap routines that wowed audiences and eventually caught the eye of producer S. L. "Roxy" Rothafel. He changed their name to the Roxyettes and, in 1932, brought them to New York's famed Radio City Music Hall, where they took the city by storm.

A Double Bill

Beginning in 1933, Radio City offered a new movie and an extravagant Rockettes stage show every week. Until his retirement in 1971, Markert choreographed the show, which made precision dancing its hallmark. Markert also added to the number of beauties in the line, which today totals 36—all of whom perform with amazing exactness.

Over the years, the Rockettes have danced in a variety of venues outside of Radio City. They entertained troops as part of USO tours during World War II, wowed audiences during Super Bowl halftime shows, and performed on the steps of the Lincoln Memorial during George W. Bush's presidential inauguration in 2001.

Since the troupe's debut, more than 3,000 women have carried on the Rockette tradition. It's not an easy gig to land, either: Dancers must be between five foot six and five foot ten and a half and skilled in tap, jazz, and modern dance. Those who make the cut can proudly call themselves members of the highest-kicking sorority in the world.

Index

♥ ♥ ♥ ♥

Languages, 161
Larsen, Don, 33
Last Exit to Brooklyn, 54–56
Law & Order, 260
Lazarus, Emma, 73
Leisler, Jacob, 75
Lenape villages, 178
Lennon, John, 73, 226, 251–52, 266
Les Misérables, 124
Levenson, Larry, 138
Libraries, 202, 231, 233
Lincoln Center for the Performing Arts, 39
Lindsay, John, 27
Lion King, The, 125
Little Africa, 41
Little Denmark, 110
Little Eva, 136
Little Fugitive, 10
Little Italy, 37–38
Lord & Taylor, 68
Lorillard, Pierre, IV, 210
Lost Weekend, The, 13
Lower East Side
　Germans, 202
　synagogues, 145
　Tenement Museum, 246–47
　Troll Museum, 267
Lucchese Family, 212

M

Macy's, 69, 236–37
Macy's Thanksgiving Day Parade, 159, 236–37, 267
Mad Bomber, 28–29
Madison Square Garden, 99–101, 109
Mafia, 37–38
Maguire, Matthew, 271
Manhattan
　Alphabet City, 193
　Blockhouse #1, 151
　Bowery, 218–19
　census statistics, 182–83
　Chinatown, 80–81, 90, 176
　11th Avenue, 105–6
　famous residents, 64–65, 67, 176, 180–81, 192, 202, 234, 235, 253
　Five Points, 23, 102, 177
　42nd Street, 70–71, 87–88
　geology, 24, 41
　Greenwich Village, 72–74, 107–8, 202, 261–63

Harlem, 24, 107, 128–29, 186, 192, 202
Little Africa, 41
Little Italy, 37–38
Lower East Side, 145, 202, 246–47, 267
Manhattan Detention Center Complex, 165
movies filmed in, 154
SoHo, 193
TriBeCa, 193
Wall Street, 57, 179
See also Central Park.
Manhattan, 158
Manhattan Detention Center Complex, 165
Mantle, Mickey, 106, 120
Marathons, 145
Maris, Roger, 33, 106
Maritime Industry Museum, 151
Marshall, Garry, 201
Marx Brothers, 167, 234
Masonic "Wall of Fame," 47
Mathewson, Christy, 34–35
Matos, John, 209
Mattingly, Don, 120
Mau Maus, 212
Max's Kansas City, 142–43
Mayor of Strawberry Fields, The, 226
Mayors, 25–27
　assassination, 233
　burial, 253
　defense of city, 160
　first, 42
　Walker, 214–15
Mays, Willie, 35, 120, 257
McClellan, George Binton, 25–26
McEnroe, John, 120
McGraw, John "Muggsy," 134
McGuire, Peter J., 271
Merchant's House Museum, The, 62–63
Mermaid Parade, 30
Messier, Mark, 120
Metesky, George, 28–29
Metropolitan Museum of Art (the Met), 49–51, 165, 229
Metropolitan Transit Authority, 89
Meucci, Antonio, 269–70
Midnight Cowboy, 158
Military bases, 151, 160, 177
Millay, Edna St. Vincent, 72
Miller, Hubert, 87–88

Contributing Writers

♥ ♥ ♥ ♥

Jeff Bahr has contributed to a half-score of Armchair Readers™. Flanked by his gifted researcher, Howard, Jeff took a hoggish bite out of the Big Apple and has proved beyond doubt the validity of the Peter Principle. Hey, New York is nothing if not diverse.

Richard Buskin is an English-accented, Chicago-based, *New York Times* bestselling author who loves to explore the Big Apple and visit friends there who insist it is the "Center of the Universe." Having written more than 15 books on subjects ranging from Marilyn Monroe, The Beatles, and Phyllis Diller to record production, mountaineering, and serving in Congress, he has also contributed to newspapers and magazines around the world, including *Playboy, Paris Match,* and the *New York Post.*

Mary Fons-Misetic was born in Iowa, lives in Chicago, and spends a whole lot of time in New York. She found her wedding gown in the East Village, loves the restaurants in Chelsea, and has a bazillion friends in Brooklyn. Go Yankees!

Dave Gerardi is a New York–based writer whose work has appeared in *Newsweek, ESPN The Magazine,* and dozens of other publications. He also continues to work on his MaximumAwesome .com humor site. After watching hipsters, frat boys, and other idiots ruin his favorite New York bars, he built his own in his home.

Amanda Green lives and writes in New York City. Her work has appeared in *New York Press, The Guardian,* the *New York Times* City Room blog, and the Web site, Mr. Beller's Neighborhood. She also blogs about her misadventures in the city at noisiestpassenger .com. Amanda breaks into song on the rare occasion that she's alone on the subway.

Bruce Herman is a sports writer, editor, and consultant based in Blacksburg, Virginia. Editorial consultant to The Topps Company since 1991, he is the author of *Hall of Fame Players: Cooperstown, St. Louis Cardinals: Yesterday & Today,* and *New York Mets: Yesterday & Today.* Bruce grew up in Jim Thorpe, Pennsylvania, rebelliously rooting for the Mets in remonstration of all the obnoxious Phillies fans in his life.

Laura Hill's first New York apartment had a kitchen that was so small she once got wedged between the stove and a wall while trying to make an omelet. Having survived two muggings, countless mornings on the 104 bus, and being blown over on Riverside Drive one winter, she now lives and writes near Nashville, Tennessee. She visits New York often and still passionately loves The City.

J. K. Kelley has a BA in history from the University of Washington in Seattle. He has contributed to numerous Armchair Readers™, and he hopes someday to boo the Yankees at Yankee Stadium and live to tell about it. He resides in the sagebrush of eastern Washington with his wife, Deb; his parrot, Alex; his Labrador Retriever, Fabius; and his Miniature Schnauzer, Leonidas.

Rhonda Markowitz is inordinately proud of having been born in Manhattan as a second-generation New Yorker. A writer, television producer, and former entertainment publicist, she has for decades called Greenwich Village home; and, despite an enduring infatuation with London, she can see no reason to live anyplace else.

Winter D. Prosapio is a syndicated writer, award-winning humor columnist, and travel writer who has a few trivia books under her belt. A long-time admirer of the Big Apple, she crashed at many a New Yorker's pad in her day. Winter's work has appeared in essay collections, national publications, and on her mom's refrigerator. You can find out more at winterdprosapio.com.

Suzanne Reisman lives in Manhattan with her husband and 13-pound rabbit, but in honor of her Chicago-area roots, she insists on referring to soda as "pop." She is the author of *Off the Beaten (Subway) Track: New York City's Best Unusual Attractions.* Her writings about the city, public policy, and feminism have appeared in print and online. Suzanne has an MPA from Columbia University and is working on her MFA in creative nonfiction at The New School.

Donald Vaughan is a freelance writer based in Raleigh, North Carolina. His work has appeared in an eclectic array of publications, including *Military Officer Magazine, Nursing Spectrum, Filmfax, Mad Magazine,* and the *Weekly World News.* Whenever he visits New York, Don makes a pilgrimage to the top of the Empire State Building in honor of the original King Kong.

Hope you enjoyed this Armchair Reader™

You'll find the rest of the crop quite exciting.
Please look for these titles wherever books are sold.

Visit us at *www.armchairreader.com*
to learn all about our other great books from
West Side Publishing, or just to let us know
what your thoughts are about our books.
We love to hear from all our readers.

WEST SIDE PUBLISHING